THE FATHERS
OF THE CHURCH

A NEW TRANSLATION

VOLUME 40

THE FATHERS OF THE CHURCH

A NEW TRANSLATION

EDITORIAL BOARD

HERMIGILD DRESSLER, O.F.M.
Quincy College
Editorial Director

ROBERT P. RUSSELL, O.S.A.
Villanova University

THOMAS P. HALTON
The Catholic University of America

WILLIAM R. TONGUE
The Catholic University of America

SISTER M. JOSEPHINE BRENNAN, I.H.M.
Marywood College

FORMER EDITORIAL DIRECTORS

LUDWIG SCHOPP, ROY J. DEFERRARI, BERNARD M. PEEBLES

TERTULLIAN

DISCIPLINARY, MORAL AND ASCETICAL WORKS

Translated by
RUDOLPH ARBESMANN, O.S.A.
SISTER EMILY JOSEPH DALY, C.S.J.
EDWIN A. QUAIN, S.J.

THE CATHOLIC UNIVERSITY OF AMERICA PRESS
in association with
CONSORTIUM BOOKS
Washington, D.C.

NIHIL OBSTAT:

JOHN A. GOODWINE
Censor Librorum

IMPRIMATUR:

✠ FRANCIS CARDINAL SPELLMAN
Archbishop of New York

June 29, 1959

The *nihil obstat* and *imprimatur* are official declarations that a book or pamphlet is free of doctrinal or moral error. No implication is contained therein that those who have granted the *nihil obstat* and *imprimatur* agree with the content, opinions, or statements expressed.

Library of Congress Catalog Card No. 77-081352
ISBN 8132-0040-7
ISBN-13: 978-0-8132-1566-2 (pbk)

Copyright © 1959 by
THE CATHOLIC UNIVERSITY OF AMERICA PRESS, INC.
All rights reserved
Reprinted 1977
First paperback reprint 2008

CONTENTS

FOREWORD 7

TO THE MARTYRS
Introduction 13
Text 17

SPECTACLES
Introduction 33
Text 47

THE APPAREL OF WOMEN
Introduction 111
Book I 117
Book II 129

PRAYER
Introduction 153
Text 157

PATIENCE
Introduction 191
Text 193

THE CHAPLET
    Introduction 225
    Text 231

FLIGHT IN TIME OF PERSECUTION
    Introduction 271
    Text 275

INDEX 311

FOREWORD

This volume contains seven of Tertullian's works which deal with disciplinary, moral, and ascetical questions.[1] The first five (*To the Martyrs, Spectacles, The Apparel of Women, Prayer,* and *Patience*) belong to the author's Catholic period; the two remaining (*The Chaplet; Flight in Time of Persecution*) were written after he had broken with the Church and given his intellectual adhesion to Montanism.

Considering Tertullian's moral writings as a whole, we cannot help admiring the sincerity, earnestness, and zeal with which he sets forth the ideals of Christian life. The imitation of God and Christ is, as it were, the *leitmotif* of his moral teachings. All that man is and possesses is a free gift of God's grace; having lost his supernatural union with God through the fall of the first parents, he was restored to God's friendship and love by the Redemption. The thought

---

[1] Volume 10 of this series contains a selection of Tertullian's apologetical works. Since its publication in 1950, the task of the translator has been made easier by the appearance of the critical edition of Tertullian's *opera omnia* in the *Corpus Christianorum,* Series Latina, vols. 1-2 (Turnhout, Belgium, 1954). Special mention must also be made of the second volume of J. Quasten's *Patrology* (Westminster, Md. 1953) which, in its section on Tertullian (pp. 246-340), contains a comprehensive and detailed bibliography on this African writer and his works.

of God's infinite mercy and of the Redemption must impel the Christian to bear witness to God and Christ in the world, without himself being of the world. No compromise, therefore, is allowed with idolatry. For, this would mean forsaking God and Christ again, and giving allegiance to God's rival, the perverter of man and all things created by God, Satan. The trials of life must be borne with patience whose origin is found in God, the Creator Himself and Christ being the prototypes of this virtue. Even martyrdom is a gift of God, a noble contest whose crown is eternal life, a storm that separates the chaff from the wheat. The Christian should be spurred on by the exceeding joy awaiting him in the life to come. Being of predominantly practical disposition, Tertullian is not content with stating general principles. He is always eager to give minute rules not only for the Christian's behavior in daily life, especially in his contacts with the pagan world, but also for such minute liturgical details as the tone, the gestures, and the attitudes to be observed in prayer.

In view of Tertullian's uncompromising attitude toward everything that, in his opinion, was related to idolatry, it is hardly surprising that his treatise, *Spectacles,* contains an out-and-out indictment of the performances given in the circus, theater, stadium and amphitheater, such entertainments being absolutely incompatible with the faith and moral discipline of Christianity. Equally strong language is found in his two books on *The Apparel of Women.* There is a certain serenity in the treatises, *Prayer* and *Patience,* and a gentle and tender charity in the address *To the Martyrs.* But, at times, even there the harshness of his asceticism pierces through, rejecting what seems to him a compromise or even a toleration.

After his contact with Montanism, this harshness increases steadily and brings him into conflict with the authorities of the Church. Exasperated by this opposition, he stubbornly clings to his own private judgment, pushing his principles to the extreme and trying to convince by the pressure of invective rather than by the attraction of an ideal. In the treatise, *The Chaplet,* he declares unlawful not only military service, but also the acceptance of any public office. In the treatise, *Flight in the Time of Persecution,* he brands as disguised apostasy every attempt to elude persecution. Bishops who, in time of persecution, govern their dioceses from a place of safety are to him not shepherds of their flocks, but hirelings who flee when the wolf comes and attacks the sheep. The Catholic brethren who place themselves beyond the reach of the persecutors he calls moral cowards who are afraid of losing the comforts of life. To be sure, Montanism did not bring about a radical change in Tertullian's moral teaching, because his asceticism was marked with a certain rigor and inflexibility from the beginning. Since his contact with Montanism, however, this rigor increased in strength until the ideal of austere virtue which he wanted to impose on the faithful as a whole became more Stoic than Christian.

We may well wonder how a man of so rare intelligence as Tertullian, a man, in addition, who had defended so vigorously the concept of tradition and stressed so much the apostolic succession of the Catholic hierarchy, could turn his back upon the Church and be led astray by an Oriental sect whose frenzied excesses could hardly attract him. Once he saw himself rebuffed in his demands for a severer and more rigid asceticism, he discovered in the Montanist tenets some ideas that appealed to him. In the feverish expectation of the imminent end of the world and in preparation for it, Montanus and his associates, the prophetesses Maximilla and Prisca (or Priscilla), had demanded the most severe asceticism. Second marriages were forbidden, and virginity strongly recommended; longer and stricter fasts were made obligatory, and only dry foods permitted; flight from persecution was disapproved, and the joyful acceptance of martyrdom advocated; reconciliation was denied to all those who had committed capital sins. Here, then, Tertullian found a moral code that satisfied his own desires for a more perfect and purer life. He could give his adhesion all the more easily as it was divine authority, the 'Paraclete' who, as Montanus claimed, spoke through him and his prophetesses.

The memory of a brilliant man who had served the Church so well and then became her bitter enemy is always sorrowful. The ideal Tertullian sought outside the Church proved to be a mirage. He died a disillusioned and embittered man.

Roy J. Deferrari

TO THE MARTYRS

Translated by
RUDOLPH ARBESMANN, O.S.A., Ph.D.
Fordham University

INTRODUCTION

THE REIGN OF the African Septimius Severus (193-211) was not a time of peace for the Church in his native land where popular hatred intermittently led to sudden and violent outbursts against the Christians. The crises which persecution brought on for the Church called forth the remarkable pieces of apologetical literature which Tertullian, a recent convert to the faith, wrote in defense of his harassed brethren. From 197 he threw himself vigorously into the Christian cause, protesting against the lack of legal fairness in the treatment of Christians, who were simply condemned as such without previous examination of their morals and beliefs, and exhorting confessors in prison to face death courageously. To the year 197 belong his two books *To the Heathen* (*Ad nationes*) and his masterpiece, the *Apology*. A number of scholars are of the opinion that the short address *To the Martyrs* (*Ad martyras*) dates from the same year. They interpret Tertullian's phrase 'our present days' in the closing paragraph of the small work (Ch. 6.2) as the time of liquidation and purge following the slaughter of the army of Clodius Albinus, Serverus' last and most powerful rival to the throne, in the battle of Lyons on February 19, 197. Other scholars, finding the reference too vague, prefer to assign the treatise to the year 202. They think that Tertullian's addressees are the group of catechumens whose martyrdom at Carthage in that year is so touchingly recounted in the *Passion of Saints Perpetua and Felicitas*.

However this may be, the exhortation *To the Martyrs*, distinguished by simplicity of style and great warmth of feeling, belongs to Tertullian's earliest works. It is gentle in persuasion and quiet in tone. The unrestrained fire of the author's later writings seems under control. He is a man sympathetic with human frailty; he shows understanding of suffering; he exhibits no harshness. With the exception, perhaps, of his condemnation of the world (2.1-3), he holds no extreme view. He warmly approves of the solicitude of 'Lady Mother the Church' and individual brethren who provide for the bodily sustenance of the confessors who are kept in prison and will soon die for the faith (1.1; 2.7). He also seems to recommend the intercession of these confessors in behalf of penitent apostates (1.6). These views are quite different from those manifested in some of his Montanist writings in which he strongly condemns both practices (see Ch. 1 nn. 3,8).

In the opening sentence of his address, Tertullian says that he hopes to speak words which will sustain the spirit of the confessors while they suffer imprisonment. Throughout, even to the conclusion, he seeks to strengthen and encourage them in the face of trials and hardships, which, if bravely borne, will remove fear of martyrdom and inspire courage for the great act to come. The first three chapters are enlivened by graphic pictures, some of them likening the present sufferings of the confessors to the privations endured by athletes during their rigid training preceding a contest and to the hardships soldiers have to undergo in the field. In the three remaining chapters Tertullian produces a long array of examples, showing that men and women did not shrink from the most painful sufferings and even sacrificed their lives for the sake of inordinate ambition and vanity, or died by accident and fate, while the confessors suffer in the cause of God.

The text of the treatise was handed down in a group of rather late manuscripts, all belonging to the fifteenth century. The first printed edition by Beatus Rhenanus appeared at Basel in 1521. The present translation is based on the critical text of E. Dekkers in *Corpus Christianorum*, Series Latina 1 (Turnholti 1954) 1-8.

SELECT BIBLIOGRAPHY

Texts:

T. H. Bindley, *Quinti Septimi Florentis Tertulliani De praescriptione haereticorum, Ad martyras, Ad Scapulam*, edited with introduction and notes (Oxford 1893).

E. Dekkers, *Corpus Christianorum*, Series Latina 1 (Turnholti 1954) 1-8.

Translations:

S. Thelwall, in *The Ante-Nicene Fathers* (American reprint of the Edinburgh edition) 3: *Latin Christianity. Its Founder, Tertullian* (New York 1903) 693-696.

K. A. H. Kellner, in *Tertullians private und katechetische Schriften* (Bibliothek der Kirchenväter. Tertullians ausgewählte Schriften 1; Kempten and Munich 1912) 215-223.

Secondary Sources:

O. Bardenhewer, *Geschichte der altkirchlichen Literatur* 2 (2nd ed., Freiburg i. B. 1914) 415.

J. Quasten, *Patrology* 2 (Westminister, Md. 1953) 290-292.

G. D. Schlegel, 'The *Ad Martyras* of Tertullian and the Circumstances of Its Composition,' *Downside Review* 63 (1945) 125-128.

TO THE MARTYRS

Chapter 1

BLESSED MARTYRS ELECT,[1] along with the nourishment for the body which our Lady Mother the Church[2] from her breast, as well as individual brethren from their private resources, furnish you in prison,[3] accept also from me some offering that will contribute to the sustenance of the spirit. For it is not good that the flesh

---

1 'Blessed' (*benedicti*) was an appellation given especially to catechumens and neophytes. The addressees are headed for martyrdom, hence Tertullian calls them 'martyrs elect' (*martyres designati*); the more common title for those awaiting martyrdom was 'confessors.'

2 The notion of the Church as a mother occurs here for the first time in early Latin Christian literature. Two earlier instances of 'Mother' as a direct appellative for the Church are found in Greek Christian literature, namely, in a letter written in 177 or the year following by the Christian communities of Lyons and Vienne to their brethren in Asia Minor and Phrygia (Eusebius, *Hist. eccl.* 5.1.1-2.8). Cf. J. Plumpe, *Mater Ecclesia. An Inquiry into the Concept of the Church as Mother in Early Christianity* (Washington, D. C. 1943) 35-62.

3 In his Montanist period Tertullian bitterly denounced the custom of sending food to brethren awaiting martyrdom in prison, on the ground that this practice only weakened their preparedness for the final conflict. Cf. *De ieiunio* 12.2-3.

be feasted while the spirit goes hungry. Indeed, if care is bestowed on that which is weak, there is all the more reason not to neglect that which is still weaker.[4] (2) Not that I am specially entitled to exhort you. Yet, even the most accomplished gladiators are spurred on not only by their trainers and managers but also from afar by people inexperienced in this art and by all who choose, without the slightest need for it, with the result that hints issuing from the crowd have often proved profitable for them.

(3) In the first place, then, O blessed, 'do not grieve the Holy Spirit'[5] who has entered prison with you. For, if He had not accompanied you there in your present trial, you would not be there today. See to it, therefore, that He remain with you there and so lead you out of that place to the Lord.[6] (4) Indeed, the prison is the Devil's house, too, where he keeps his household. But you have come to the prison for the very purpose of trampling upon him[7] right in his own house. For you have engaged him in battle already outside the prison and trampled him underfoot. (5) Let him, therefore, not say: 'Now that they are in my domain, I will tempt them with base hatreds, with defections or dissensions among themselves.' Let him flee from your presence, and let him, coiled and numb, like a snake that is driven out by charms or smoke, hide away in the depths

---

4 Cf. Matt. 26.41; Mark 14.38.
5 Eph. 4.30.
6 In early Christian literature death is often referred to as a going to the Lord *(migratio ad Dominum)*. Cf. A. C. Rush, *Death and Burial in Christian Antiquity* (Washington, D.C. 1941) 54-71.
7 Cf. *Passio SS. Perpetuae et Felicitatis* 4, where Perpetua describes her first vision. In her ascent to heaven on a golden ladder on the sides of which there were fixed all kinds of instruments of torture, she saw a dragon crouching under the first step and frightening those who ascended, but, invoking the Lord Jesus Christ, she 'trampled upon the dragon's head' and went up.

of his den. Do not allow him the good fortune in his own kingdom of setting you against one another, but let him find you fortified by the arms of peace among yourselves, because peace among yourselves means war with him. (6) Some, not able to find this peace in the Church, are accustomed to seek it from the martyrs in prison. For this reason, too, then, you ought to possess, cherish and preserve it among yourselves that you may perhaps be able to bestow it upon others also.[8]

Chapter 2

(1) Other attachments, equally burdensome to the spirit, may have accompanied you to the prison gate; so far your relatives, too, may have escorted you. From that very moment on you have been separated from the very world. How much more, then, from its spirit and its ways and doings? Nor let this separation from the world trouble you. For, if we reflect that it is the very world that is more truly a prison, we shall realize that you have left a prison rather than entered one. (2) The world holds the greater dark-

---

8 During persecution a number of Christians had denied the faith in the face of torture. To be sure, many had done so only to save their property, life, and freedom, and at heart had wished to remain Christians. But readmission to the communion of the Church was not so easy, since the then existing penitential discipline demanded a life-long penance for apostasy. The universal respect accorded to the martyrs, however, induced some bishops to recognize letters of recommendation (*libelli pacis*), written by confessors on the eve of martyrdom in behalf of penitent apostates, as availing to shorten the length of canonical penance. In the above passage Tertullian refers to such a speedier restoration to the communion of the Church through the intercession of the martyrs. There is no doubt that the exaggerated honors paid to martyrdom occasionally led to abuses. However this may be, in his Montanist period Tertullian strongly condemns these letters of martyrs recommending lapsed brethren to the bishop's consideration (cf. *De pudicitia* 22).

ness, blinding men's hearts. The world puts on the heavier chains, fettering the very souls of men. The world breathes forth the fouler impurities—human lusts. (3) Finally, the world contains the larger number of criminals, namely, the entire human race. In fact, it awaits sentence not from the proconsul but from God. (4) Wherefore, O blessed, consider yourselves as having been transferred from prison to what we may call a place of safety. Darkness is there, but you are light;[1] fetters are there, but you are free before God. It breathes forth a foul smell, but you are an odor of sweetness.[2] There the judge is expected at every moment, but you are going to pass sentence upon the judges themselves.[3] (5) There sadness may come upon the man who sighs for the pleasures of the world. The Christian, however, even when he is outside the prison, has renounced the world, and, when in prison, even prison itself. It does not matter what part of the world you are in, you who are apart from the world. (6) And if you have missed some of the enjoyments of life, remember that it is the way of business to suffer some losses in order to make larger profits.

I say nothing yet about the reward to which God invites the martyrs. Meanwhile, let us compare the life in the world with that in prison to see if the spirit does not gain more in prison than the flesh loses there. (7) In fact, owing to the solicitude of the Church and the charity of the brethren, the flesh does not miss there what it ought to have, while, in addition, the spirit obtains what is always beneficial to the faith:[4] you do not look at strange gods; you do not

---

1 Cf. Matt. 5.14; Eph. 5.8; 1 Thess. 5.5.
2 Cf. Ezech. 20.41; Eph. 5.2.
3 Cf. Wisd. 3.8; 1 Cor. 6.2.
4 In the following Tertullian enumerates those features of pagan life which, because of their idolatrous or immoral character, the Christians found especially revolting. Cf. a similar account in his *Apology* 35.

chance upon their images; you do not, even by mere physical contact, participate in heathen holidays; you are not plagued by the foul fumes of the sacrificial banquets, not tormented by the noise of the spectacles, nor by the atrocity or frenzy or shamelessness of those taking part in the celebrations; your eyes do not fall on houses of lewdness; you are free from inducements to sin, from temptations, from unholy reminiscences, free, indeed, even from persecution.

(8) The prison now offers to the Christian what the desert once gave to the Prophets.[5] Our Lord Himself quite often spent time in solitude to pray there more freely,[6] to be there away from the world. In fact, it was in a secluded place that He manifested His glory to His disciples.[7] Let us drop the name 'prison' and call it a place of seclusion. (9) Though the body is confined, though the flesh is detained, there is nothing that is not open to the spirit. In spirit wander about, in spirit take a walk, setting before yourselves not shady promenades and long porticoes but that path which leads to God. As often as you walk that path, you will not be in prison. (10) The leg does not feel the fetter when the spirit is in heaven. The spirit carries about the whole man and brings him wherever he wishes. And where your heart is, there will your treasure be also.[8] There, then, let our heart be where we would have our treasure.

---

5 Cf. 3 Kings 19.4.
6 Cf. Mark 1.35.
7 Cf. Matt. 17.1,2; Mark 9.1,2; Luke 9.28,29; 2 Peter 1.16,17.
8 Cf. Matt. 6. 21

Chapter 3

(1) Granted now, O blessed, that even to Christians the prison is unpleasant—yet, we were called to the service in the army of the living God in the very moment when we gave response to the words of the sacramental oath.[1] No soldier goes out to war encumbered with luxuries, nor does he march to the line of battle from the sleeping chamber, but from light and cramped tents where every kind of austerity, discomfort, and inconvenience is experienced. (2) Even in time of peace soldiers are toughened to warfare by toils and hardships: by marching in arms, by practising swift maneuvers in the field, by digging a trench, by joining closely together to form a tortoise-shield.[2] Everything is set in sweating toil, lest bodies and minds be frightened at having to pass from shade to sunshine, from sunshine to icy cold, from the tunic to the breastplate, from hushed silence to the warcry, from rest to the din of battle.[3]

---

1 In military language, the term *sacramentum* was used to denote the military oath of allegiance. It is in this sense that Tertullian employs the word here, referring to the baptismal vows of the Christian.

2 In military language, the term 'tortoise-shield' (*testudo*) denoted a shelter used in attacking ramparts or walls. The soldiers interlocked their shields over their heads, thus forming a protective cover like the shell of a tortoise.

3 A reminiscence of this passage is found in St. Jerome's letter to Heliodorus (*Ep.* 14.2.1-2). Jerome reproaches Heliodorus for having gone back from the perfect way of the ascetic life: 'What are you, dainty soldier, doing in your father's house? Where are your ramparts and trenches? When have you spent a winter in the camp? . . . Do you intend to march straight from the sleeping chamber to the line of battle, from the shade into the heat of the sun? A body used to a tunic cannot endure a heavy breastplate, a head that has worn a cap refuses a helmet, a hand made tender by disuse is galled by the hard handle of a sword.'

(3) In like manner, O blessed, consider whatever is hard in your present situation as an exercise of your powers of mind and body. You are about to enter a noble contest[4] in which the living God acts the part of superintendent and the Holy Spirit is your trainer, a contest whose crown is eternity, whose prize is angelic nature, citizenship in heaven and glory for ever and ever. (4) And so your Master, Jesus Christ, who has anointed you with His Spirit[5] and has brought you to this training ground, has resolved, before the day of the contest, to take you from a softer way of life to a harsher treatment that your strength may be increased. For athletes, too, are set apart for more rigid training that they may apply themselves to the building up of their physical strength. They are kept from lavish living, from more tempting dishes, from more pleasurable drinks. They are urged on, they are subjected to torturing toils, they are worn out: the more strenuously they have exerted themselves, the greater is their hope of victory. (5) And they do this, says the Apostle, to win a perishable crown. We who are about to win an eternal one[6] recognize in the prison our training ground, that we may be led forth to the actual contest before the seat of the presiding judge well practised in all hardships, because strength is built up by austerity, but destroyed by softness.

---

4 Cf. 1 Tim. 6.12.
5 Cf. 1 John 2.20. This anointing of the Christian with the Holy Spirit Tertullian compares to the use of oil to anoint the bodies of athletes in the palaestra.
6 Cf. 1 Cor. 9.25.

Chapter 4

(1) We know from our Lord's teaching that, while the spirit is willing, the flesh is weak.[1] Let us, however, not derive delusive gratification from the Lord's acknowledgment of the weakness of the flesh. For it was on purpose that He first declared the spirit willing: He wanted to show which of the two ought to be subject to the other, that is to say, that the flesh should be submissive to the spirit, the weaker to the stronger, so that the former may draw strength from the latter. (2) Let the spirit converse with the flesh on their common salvation, no longer thinking about the hardships of prison but, rather, about the struggle of the actual contest. The flesh will perhaps fear the heavy sword and the lofty cross and the wild beasts mad with rage and the most terrible punishment of all—death by fire—and, finally, all the executioner's cunning during the torture. (3) But let the spirit present to both itself and the flesh the other side of the picture: granted, these sufferings are grievous, yet many have borne them patiently, nay, have even sought them on their own accord for the sake of fame and glory; and this is true not only of men but also of women so that you, too, O blessed women, may be worthy of your sex.

(4) It would lead me too far were I to enumerate each one of those who, led by the impulse of their own mind, put an end to their lives by the sword. Among women there is the well-known instance of Lucretia. A victim of violence, she stabbed herself in the presence of her kinsfolk to gain glory for her chastity.[2] Mucius burnt his right

---

1 Cf. Matt. 26.41; Mark 14.38.
2 Lucretia, the Roman model of womanly conduct, killed herself after

hand on the altar that his fair fame might include this deed.³ (5) Nor did the philosophers act less courageously: Heraclitus, for instance, who put an end to his life by smearing himself with cow dung;⁴ Empedocles, too, who leaped down into the fires of Mt. Etna;⁵ and Peregrinus who not long ago threw himself upon a funeral pile.⁶ Why, even women have despised the flames: Dido did so in order not to be forced to marry after the departure of the

   having been violated by Sextus Tarquinius, the son of King L. Tarquinius Superbus. According to Roman tradition, this misdeed brought about the overthrow of the monarchy in Rome. Cf. Livy 1.58-59; Cicero, *De re publica* 2.25.46; Valerius Maximus, *Facta et dicta memorabilia* 6.1.1.
3 According to Roman tradition, C. Mucius Scaevola, a Roman youth, was caught in the attempt to assassinate Porsenna, the Etruscan king of Clusium, who had made war upon Rome in order to restore the monarchy of the Tarquinian family. Threatened with torture, he burned off his right hand over a brazier to show his courage, and hence received the surname Scaevola, i.e., Left-handed. Cf. Livy 2.12; Valerius Maximus, *Facta et dicta memor.* 3.3.1. Tertullian cites this example also in his *Apology* 50.5.
4 Very little is known about the life of Heraclitus of Ephesus (*c.* 500 B.C.). Of his death we have the unsupported story, told by Diogenes Laertius in his *Lives of the Philosophers* (9.1.3), which runs as follows. Attacked by dropsy and challenging the physicians he had consulted first, Heraclitus covered himself with cow dung, hoping that the warmth thus produced would cause the excess of water in his body to evaporate. The experiment, however, ended fatally.
5 A popular story in antiquity, but likewise unworthy of credence, related that Empedocles of Acragas (*c.* 500-430 B.C.), committed suicide by leaping into the fiery mouth of Mt. Etna so that he might die without leaving a trace behind him, and thereby confirm his divinity. Cf. Diogenes Laertius 8.2.69. Tertullian cites this example also in his *Apology* 50.5.
6 Finding his popularity waning, Peregrinus Proteus, a wandering Cynic philosopher, decided to immolate himself on a funeral pile at the celebration of the Olympic Games in A.D. 165 to set an example of contempt of death. In his *On the Death of Peregrinus*, Lucian of Samosata, the second-century Greek sophist and satirist, tells us the story, asserting that he was an eye-witness of the event.

man she had loved most dearly;⁷ the wife of Hasdrubal, too, with Carthage in flames, cast herself along with her children into the fire that was destroying her native city, that she might not see her husband a suppliant at Scipio's feet.⁸ (6) Regulus, a Roman general, was taken prisoner by the Carthaginians, but refused to be the only Roman exchanged for a large number of Carthaginian captives. He preferred to be returned to the enemy, and, crammed into a kind of chest, suffered as many crucifixions as nails were driven in from the outside in all directions to pierce him.⁹ A woman voluntarily sought out wild beasts, namely, vipers, serpents more horrible than either bull or bear,

---

7   This refers to the well-known legend of Dido, the mythical foundress of Carthage, and Aeneas. After various adventures during his wanderings, Aeneas and his men were driven by a storm upon the coast of Africa, near the site of Carthage. There they were hospitably received by Dido, whom Venus caused to fall violently in love with Aeneas. When, after a stay of a few months, Aeneas was ordered by Jupiter to leave, Dido in despair at his departure killed herself. Cf. Virgil, *Aeneid* 4.504ff. The example is also cited by Tertullian in his *Apology* 50.5 and *Ad nationes* 1.18.3.

8   In the Third Punic War (149-146 B.C.) Carthage had stood a siege of four years, when at last the Roman legions forced their way over the walls of the unhappy city. Fighting in the streets continued for several days, until Hasdrubal, the Carthaginian commander, with a few surviving defenders at last surrendered to the Roman general, Scipio the Younger. But Hasdrubal's wife, upbraiding her husband for his cowardice, slew her two boys and cast herself with them from the top of a burning temple into the ruins. Cf. Florus, *Epitome* 1.31 (2.15) .17; Valerius Maximus, *Facta et dicta memor.* 3.2 ext. 8. Tertullian cites this example also in his *Ad nationes* 1.18.3.

9   M. Atilius Regulus, a Roman consul, was taken prisoner during the First Punic War (264-241 B.C.). According to tradition, he was sent to Rome on parole to negotiate a peace, but urged the Senate to refuse the proposals of the Carthaginians; on his return to Carthage he was tortured to death. Cf. Cicero, *De officiis* 3.26.99; Horace, *Odes* 3.5; Valerius Maximus, *Facta et dicta memor.* 1.1.14; Aulus Gellius, *Noctes Atticae* 7 (6) .4. Tertullian cites this example also in his *Apology* **50.6** and *Ad nationes* **1.18.3.**

which Cleopatra let loose upon herself as not to fall into the hands of the enemy.¹⁰

(7) You may object: 'But the fear of death is not so great as the fear of torture.' Did the Athenian courtesan yield on that account to the executioner? For, being privy to a conspiracy, she was subjected to torture by the tyrant. But she did not betray her fellow conspirators, and at last bit off her own tongue and spat it into the tyrant's face to let him know that torments, however prolonged, could achieve nothing against her.¹¹ (8) Everybody knows that to this day the most important festival of the Lacedaemonians is the διαμαστίγωσις, that is, The Whipping. In this sacred rite all the noble youth are scourged with whips before the altar, while their parents and kinsfolk stand by and exhort them to perseverance. For they regard it as a mark of greater distinction and glory if the soul rather than the body has submitted to the stripes.¹²

(9) Therefore, if earthly glory accruing from strength

---

10 After their defeat by Octavian at Actium in 31 B.C., Cleopatra and Mark Antony escaped to Egypt. When Octavian landed there, Antony committed suicide. Cleopatra tried in vain to entice Octavian by her charms and, according to the common tradition, put an end to her life by applying an asp to her bosom. Cf. Florus, *Epitome* 2.21 (4.11) .11; Horace, *Odes* 1.37.25-28. The example is also found in Tertullian's *Ad nationes* 1.18.3.

11 The story of the Athenian courtesan is told by Pliny, *Naturalis Historia* 7.23.87 and Pausanias, *Descriptio Graeciae* 1.23.1-2. The courtesan's name was Leaena, and Harmodius and Aristogiton were the conspirators. Tertullian cites this example of female fortitude also in his *Apology* 50.8 and in *Ad nationes* 1.18.4.

12 This test of endurance in pain, which formed an element in the rigorous training of the Spartan youth, took place at the festival of Artemis Orthia. The original meaning of the ceremony is obscure. Some scholars have thought to recognize in this practice the blow with the sacred bough, whereby its power is communicated to man. Tertullian mentions this example of endurance in pain also in his *Apology* 50.9 and in *Ad nationes* 1.18.11.

of body and soul is valued so highly that one despises sword, fire, piercing with nails, wild beasts and tortures for the reward of human praise, then I may say the sufferings you endure are but trifling in comparison with the heavenly glory and divine reward. If the bead made of glass is rated so highly, how much must the true pearl be worth? Who, therefore, does not most gladly spend as much for the true as others spend for the false?

Chapter 5

(1) I omit here an account of the motive of glory. For inordinate ambition among men as well as a certain morbidity of mind have already set at naught all the cruel and torturing contests mentioned above. How many of the leisure class are urged by an excessive love of arms to become gladiators? Surely it is from vanity that they descend to the wild beasts in the very arena, and think themselves more handsome because of the bites and scars. Some have even hired themselves out to tests by fire, with the result that they ran a certain distance in a burning tunic. Others have pranced up and down amid the bullwhips of the animal-baiters, unflinchingly exposing their shoulders.[1] (2) All this, O blessed, the Lord tolerates in the world for good reason, that is, for the sake of encouraging us in the present moment and of confounding us on that final day, if we have recoiled from suffering for the truth unto salvation what others have pursued out of vanity unto perdition.

---

1 Tertullian mentions these degrading practices also in *Ad nationes* 1.18.8-11.

Chapter 6

(1) Let us, however, no longer talk about those examples of perseverance proceeding from inordinate ambition. Let us, rather, turn to a simple contemplation of man's ordinary lot so that, if we ever have to undergo such trials with fortitude, we may also learn from those misfortunes which sometimes even befall unwilling victims. For how often have people been burned to death in conflagrations! How often have wild beasts devoured men either in the forests or in the heart of cities after escaping from their cages! How many have been slain by the sword of robbers! How many have even suffered the death of the cross at the hands of enemies, after having been tortured first and, indeed, treated with every kind of insult! (2) Furthermore, many a man is able to suffer in the cause of a mere human being what he hesitates to suffer in the cause of God. To this fact, indeed, our present days may bear witness. How many prominent persons have met with death in the cause of a man, though such a fate seemed most unlikely in view of their birth and their rank, their physical condition and their age! Death came to them either from him, if they had opposed him, or from his enemies, if they had sided with him.[1]

---

1 This may refer to the destruction of the army of Clodius Albinus, the most powerful rival of Septimius Severus for the throne of the Caesars, near Lyons, in A.D. 197 and to the still more terrible massacre of Albinus' partisans throughout the empire. At Rome the victor wreaked vengeance especially upon a number of senators who had sided with his opponents.

SPECTACLES

Translated by
RUDOLPH ARBESMANN, O.S.A., Ph.D.
Fordham University

INTRODUCTION

IN THE TIME of the emperors the Roman world knew and enjoyed especially four kinds of public amusement: the chariot-races of the circus; the gladiatorial combats and hunting spectacles of the amphitheater; the performance of farces, such as mimes and pantomimes, in the theater; and the athletic contests of the stadium. The omnipotent rulers saw in these amusements the best means for purchasing popular favor, keeping the masses contented, and making them forget their own insignificance. Each emperor tried to outdo his predecessor in the frequency and splendor of his spectacles, so that, under some emperors, almost one half of the days of the year were given to public exhibitions. The Roman poet Juvenal (*Sat.* 10.81) summed up the desires of the people in the often-quoted words *panem et circenses* ('bread and races'). Still worse, every art was employed on such occasions to intoxicate the senses of the spectators and quiet their moral scruples. Thus it is not surprising to find a number of passages in the works of pagan authors, cautioning against the degrading influences of the spectacles. Yet the adverse judgment of these writers was not primarily evoked by those very features which, because of their moral perversity, justly deserved condemnation: the wholesale destruction of life, human and animal, in the arena for the amusement of spectators, or the crude coarseness and frivolous obscenity of the mimes and pantomimes which had long displaced the tragedies and comedies of old. Their criticisms are rather philosophical commonplaces, emphasizing some evil effects of the spectacles on men. Dio Chrysostom, for instance, disapproves of the undignified behavior of the spectators in the circus, theater, and stadium (*Orat.* 32.41-43); Libanius takes exception to the races in the circus because they keep men from studying rhetoric (*Orat.* 35.13), or he finds fault with people going to the theater because this pastime leads to idleness (*Orat.* 41.7). Only the philosopher Seneca, speaking of the crude slaughter in the amphitheater (*Ep.* 7.2ff.), finds words of condemnation which, to some extent at least, express our own thought and feeling concerning these inhuman delights. Unlike the pagan authors, the Christian writers, beginning with the early Greek apologists, are uncompromising in their attitude toward the spectacles. They do not content themselves with merely censuring the brutalizing effects of the circus, theater, athletic contests, and gladiatorial encounters on the minds and souls of the spectators. They rather attack the very nature of these amusements and find them incompatible with the idea of God as Creator of the world and with man's right and dignity. Accordingly, they assert that it is the stern duty of all men to absent themselves from such pastimes. Weaning the Roman world from its long-cherished amusements was a long and painful process. Legislation, both ecclesiastical and imperial, had to be added to the untiring efforts of Christian writers and preachers to stamp out the last vestiges of the pagan spectacles. Even so, it lasted centuries, until the race courses, theaters, amphitheaters, and gymnasia, whose walls had begun to crumble and fall into decay, were finally abandoned.

In view of Tertullian's fiery, irascible and intolerant disposition, it is hardly surprising that none of the early Christian authors has attacked the pagan spectacles so relentlessly and violently as this aggressive and headstrong African writer. He missed no opportunity to demonstrate and expose their deceitful character. Hence, longer or shorter passages condemning one or the other kind of these amusements can be found in several places of his works (*Apology* 6.3; 15.1-6; 38.4; 42.7; *De cultu feminarum* 1.8.4-5; *Scorpiace* 6.2-5; *De corona* 6.3; *De pudicitia* 7.15). Moreover, he considered the question whether a Christian was allowed to attend the performances in the circus, theater, amphitheater, and stadium so important that he wrote a special treatise on this subject, entitled *De spectaculis*. In Tertullian's day some Christians evidently held rather broad views concerning the lawfulness of frequenting the pagan spectacles. Catechumens, still only slightly familiar with the demands of Christian life, or too ready to elude them, seem to have thought these amusements permissible, as long as they were, at least formally, still pagans. But a number of baptized Christians, too, apparently found it difficult to give up entertainments they had greatly enjoyed in their former life.

It was, then, for very practical pastoral reasons that Tertullian addressed this treatise to both catechumens and baptized Christians, reminding them of their most solemn responsibility as to faith and morals, and telling them categorically that participation in pagan spectacles under whatever form was incompatible with the tenets of Christianity and, therefore, forbidden under any circumstances.

His argumentation can briefly be summed up as follows. Since the spectacles are idolatrous in their very origin and spirit, a Christian cannot take part in them without making himself guilty of idol worship and without injury to his own faith (Ch. 4-13). Moreover, frequenting these amusements necessarily undermines moral discipline, since they rouse the most violent passions (Ch. 14-27). Of the arguments produced by Tertullian to prove the unlawfulness of frequenting the spectacles, those based on the charge of idolatry are of special interest. To be sure, Tertullian is not the first Christian author to point out the idolatrous character of the spectacles, since the idea appears a few years earlier in St. Irenaeus' work *Adversus haereses* 1.1.12 (ed. W. W. Harvey [2 vols., Cambridge 1857] 1.55-56). There the bishop of Lyons upbraids the Valentinian Gnostics for 'being the first to assemble at every festival amusement of the heathen, taking place in honor of the idols, some of them going even so far as not to keep away from that bloody spectacle, hateful both to God and men, in which men fight with wild beasts or engage each other in single combat.' While, then, Tertullian cannot be credited with introducing the idea of idolatry into the literary feud against the spectacles, he has developed the arguments based on it in great detail. As a matter of fact, the charge of idolatry is the main theme of the antiquarian part of the treatise (Ch. 5-13), whose purpose is to prove the idolatrous character of the various kinds of spectacles from their origin, names, founders and equipment, from the deities to whom they are dedicated, the superstitions observed in them, the places where they are held, and the arts displayed in them.

Tertullian's out-and-out indictment of the spectacles comes hardly as a surprise. In the question of conformity and non-conformity to worldly pleasures, this 'first great Puritan of the West,' as some have called him, refuses any compromise. Whatever savors of paganism is hateful to him, because it belongs to 'the pomp of the Devil' which the Christian has solemnly renounced in baptism (Ch. 24). He cannot tolerate anything which has even the slightest appearance of guilt in matters of faith and moral discipline. He believes that there exists a clear line of demarcation between the world and Christ (26.4). Though he acknowledges that there are some features worthy of praise in dramatic art, he is quick to point out that, because of the idolatrous and immoral character of the theater, these features are but 'drippings of honey from a poisoned cake' (27.5). In his eagerness to define rigidly every single thing by authority, he forbids participation in the pagan spectacles in the name of holy Scripture (Ch. 3), giving a most fanciful interpretation of Ps. 1.1: 'Happy is the man who has not gone to the gathering of the ungodly, nor stood in the way of the sinners, nor sat in the chair of pestilence.' It is only fair to point out that Tertullian was not the only Christian author to refer to this scriptural passage, while attacking the pagan spectacles. We also find it quoted by his contemporary Clement of Alexandria in his *Paedagogus* 3.11.76.3, and similarly in his *Stromata* 2.15.68.1. In the latter passage Clement states that he had heard this interpretation from a learned man, most probably a member of the catechetical school of Alexandria. From there, in some way unknown to us, this interpretation must have found its way to Tertullian, and later (about 400) into the *Apostolic Constitutions* 2.61.1-2. It also occurs in St. John Chrysostom, *De poenitentia, hom.* 6.1. While, however, Clement merely alludes to the scriptural passage (see below, Ch. 3 n. 2), Tertullian devotes an entire chapter to its interpretation, straining and twisting its meaning to make the sacred text speak on his behalf, and maintaining that the rules of the Gospel must be referred to, as suitable to all the experiences of those who embrace it. It is especially the last chapter (30) in which we can well discern the real character of Tertullian. It contains an impressive and truly poetical description of the Last Judgment, and the thoughtful reader cannot fail to be struck by the intense earnestness and absolute sincerity of the writer. But is also reveals his greatest weakness, which is a regrettable lack of moderation. He is not able to curb the passionate fire of his nature, the hatred of everything pagan that burns in his soul and makes him gloat over the punishment of the wicked. Carried away by his cause, he marshals all the resources of his brilliant mind and vast erudition: his profound knowledge of the past and its literature, his superb mastery of the Latin language, his rhetorical and dialectical skill, his extraordinary gift of wit and sarcasm.

De spectaculis is one of Tertullian's most interesting and original works. It not only throws revealing light on his peculiar character as a writer and his attitude as regards pagan society and certain forms of the civilization of his day, but also holds a unique position in ancient literature inasmuch as it is the only comprehensive treatise on the subject which has come down to us. Suetonius' *Historia ludicra,* listed as *Spectacles and Games among the Romans* in the rather long catalogue of Suetonian works preserved in *Suidas,* is lost. So are the writings of Varro in this field (especially the section of his *Antiquities of Things Human and Divine* which deals with the subject) and similar works by the grammarian Sinnius Capito and King

Juba II of Mauretania. Mention must also be made of a small tract, likewise entitled *De spectaculis,* which, on insufficient grounds, has been claimed for St. Cyprian and is now generally assigned to Novatian. It is, however, considerably briefer than the treatise of Tertullian and, with regard to contents, sinks into insignificance in comparison with the wealth of information offered by Tertullian. In addition, its author has made ample use of Tertullian's work. This being the situation, the latter's treatise gains in importance. As a matter of fact, without it our literary sources on the subject would amount only to a number of passages found here and there in the works of ancient authors, leaving us with lamentable blanks in our knowledge about the various kinds of spectacles in antiquity. We mention especially Tertullian's rather minute description of the circus (Ch. 8), which supplements our other main source of information, namely, archaeological material.

Tertullian's familiarity with the past and its literature has been mentioned before. In the antiquarian part of *De spectaculis* he quotes the following ancient authors: Timaeus, Varro, Piso, Tranquillus Suetonius (Ch. 5); Hermateles (Ch. 8); Stesichorus and Virgil, though the latter not by name (Ch. 9). There is, however, no need for supposing that Tertullian had a first-hand knowledge of all these authors. Timaeus, for instance, was hardly his direct source for the information on the origin of the Etruscans. As a matter of fact, he himself points to the secondary source he used in this case, namely, one of the 'many authors who have published treatises on the subject' (5.2.) The same holds true concerning the Roman annalist L. Calpurnius Piso and Stesichorus, a Greek lyric poet of the sixth century B. C. Finally, in quoting Hermateles, Tertullian apparently made a slip, since a writer by this name seems to be unknown. Considering the method ancient writers followed in using and quoting sources, it is best to assume that Tertullian used mainly one of the works that had been written on *spectacula,* and in which he found the quotations from ancient authors on the subject. Varro and Suetonius suggest themselves as such main authorities. Of the two Suetonius is the more probable, because Tertullian mentions some things which did not yet exist at Varro's time: for instance, the obelisk in the Circus Maximus (Ch. 8), placed there by Augustus in 10 B. C.; the four 'factions' of the circus (Ch. 9), of which the Greens and the Blues arose only at the beginning of the Empire; the *agones* (Ch. 11), which were likewise introduced into Rome under the emperors. Moreover, Tertullian refers those of his readers who want to have more particulars on the spectacles to Suetonius explicitly (5.8). All this, of course, does not exclude the possibility that, on a number of questions, he also consulted Varro, one of Suetonius' main sources, and added some more material from his own considerable knowledge of ancient literature. Nor were the works of the Greek apologists strangers to him, though, in borrowing a number of thoughts from them, he never lost his rugged independence and originality. Thus, in the treatise *De spectaculis,* he developed the arguments based on the charge of idolatry at great length, while his Greek predecessors censured the spectacles almost exclusively on moral grounds. Finally, mention must be made of the great number of texts from Scripture which he quotes, interprets, and paraphrases with remarkable skill, having only one thought in his eager and stubborn mind, namely, to convince.

The composition of the treatise shows a careful arrangement of the material. Several times Tertullian himself calls attention to the plan of his work (for instance, 4.4; 8.1; 9.1; 10.1; 10.13; 12.1; 12.5; 13.1; 14.1). The arrangement of the material in his antiquarian part according to origin, names, places, etc., may possibly go back to his main source, Suetonius. How Tertullian followed a well-contrived plan we may see from the following outline of the treatise.

Introduction.
1. Statement of subject: It is impossible for a Christian to attend the spectacles.

Part I (2-4):
2. Refutation of the objection that everything used in the spectacles comes from God and hence is good.
3. A condemnation of the spectacles can also be found in holy Scripture.
4. The Christian is bound by his baptismal vows to shun the spectacles because of their idolatrous character.

Part II (5-13):
5. The idolatrous character of the spectacles is evident from their very origin.
6. Likewise, from their names.
7. The same is true concerning all the equipment used in them.
8. Also, the place where they are performed (the circus) is defiled by idolatry.
9. In like manner, the arts displayed in the circus.
10. The theater is likewise related to idol worship (origin, name, equipment, place, arts displayed are dealt with in

one chapter; the same applies to the discussion of the *agones* and the amphitheater).

11. Likewise, the *agones* and
12. The amphitheater.
13. Recapitulation of the arguments based on the charge of idolatry.
14. Leading to Part III, Tertullian proposes to discuss the spectacles from another point of view, namely, 'lust of pleasure.'

Part III (15-27):
15. The spectacles are incompatible with true Christian spirit.
16. Frenzy and similar passions rule supreme in the circus.
17. The performances in the theater are noted for immorality and obscenity.
18. The gymnastic contests in the stadium are objectionable because of their moral worthlessness.
19. The various gladiatorial encounters in the amphitheater are detestable because of their inhuman cruelty and brutality.
20. Rejection of the objection that the sun and God Himself look on at the spectacles without being defiled.
21. At the shows the spectator does things which he loathes in ordinary life.
22. The wicked nature of the spectacles is also proved by the social and legal infamy attached to the profession of charioteer, actor, athlete and gladiator.
23. The conduct of the performers at the spectacles displeases God.
24. The pagans know the true Christian by his absence from the spectacles.

25. The behavior of the spectators at the shows is inconsistent with the Christian way of life.

26. At times, God inflicts sudden punishment on Christians for attending the spectacles.

27. Also, the apparently innocuous features of the spectacles are but enticements of the Devil.

Conclusion (28-30).

28. The pagans may enjoy themselves in this world, the Christian looks forward to the life to come.

29. Moreover, also in this life the Christian can find many exquisite pleasures given by God which amply compensate him for foregoing the pleasures of the world.

30. Lastly, for the Christian there are still greater spectacles to come: the second coming of the Lord to establish the kingdom of the just, and, finally, the greatest spectacles of all: the conflagration of the created world and the Last Judgment.

Tertullian himself refers to his *De spectaculis* in three of his later writings: *De cultu feminarum* 1.8.4, *De idololatria* 13.1, and *De corona* 6.3. While the third of these works definitely belongs to the Montanistic period of his life (written probably about 211), the first, showing no trace of Montanism, must have been composed during the first years of his literary activity and is thought to have appeared between 197 and 201. Accordingly, the treatise *De spectaculis* belongs to the period between 197 and 200. Tertullian, who wrote with equal facility in Latin and Greek, mentions (*De corona* 6.3) that he also published the treatise in Greek. Nothing more is known of this edition.

The text of the treatise came down in a single manuscript of the ninth century, the Codex Parisinus Latinus 1622, called Agobardinus after its owner, Agobard, Bishop of Lyons, who died in 840. The manuscript is generally reliable, though in some parts difficult to read and marred by a number of lacunae and mistakes made by the scribe in the process of copying. Hence, some recently discovered fragments and the two older editions are especially important for the reconstruction of the text: the edition by Martinus Mesnartius (Paris 1545) who, besides the Agobardinus, used another tradition and gave divergent readings in the margin; and the edition by Jacobus Pamelius (Antwerp 1579), who made use of the now lost Codex of Joannes Clemens Anglus. Mention must also be made of Isidore of Seville, who, in some parts of his *Origines* (especially Book 18 entitled *De bello et ludis*), sometimes incorporates verbatim passages from the antiquarian part of Tertullian's treatise. The text followed in the present translation is that of E. Dekkers in *Corpus Christianorum,* Series Latina 1 (Turnholti 1954) 225-253. The editions by A. Reifferscheid and G. Wissowa (CSEL 20.1-29) and A. Boulanger (Paris 1933) were consulted throughout. The English version by T. R. Glover in the Loeb Classical Library, and the German version by K. A. H. Kellner in the Bibliothek der Kirchenväter, have proved helpful. Some parts of the introduction and a number of footnotes are especially indebted to J. Büchner's excellent commentary on the treatise.

SPECTACLES

SELECT BIBLIOGRAPHY

Texts:

A. Reifferscheid and G. Wissowa, CSEL 20 (1890) 1-29.
A. Boulanger, *Tertullien. De spectaculis* (Paris 1933).
E. Dekkers, *Corpus Christianorum*, Series Latina 1 (Turnholti 1954) 225-253.
J. Marra, *Q. Septimii Tertulliani De spectaculis, De Fuga in persecutione, De pallio* (Corpus Scriptorum Latinorum Paravianum; Turin 1954).

Translations:

S. Thelwall, in *The Ante-Nicene Fathers* (American reprint of the Edinburgh edition) 3: *Latin Christianity. Its Founder, Tertullian* (New York 1903) 79-91.
K. A. H. Kellner, in *Tertullians private und katechetische Schriften* (Bibliothek der Kirchenväter. Tertullians ausgewählte Schriften 1; Kempten and Munich 1912) 101-136.
T. R. Glover, *Tertullian. De spectaculis*, in Loeb Classical Library (London and New York 1931) 229-301.

Secondary Sources:

O. Bardenhewer, *Geschichte der altkirchlichen Literatur* 2 (2nd ed., Freiburg i.B. 1914) 416.
M. Bieber, *The History of the Greek and Roman Theater* (Princeton 1939).
J. Büchner, *Quint. Sept. Flor. Tertullian de spectaculis. Kommentar* (Würzburg 1935).
E. K. Chambers, *The Mediaeval Stage* 1 (Oxford 1903) 1-22.
R. M. Chase, 'De spectaculis,' *Classical Journal* 23 (1927) 107-120.
W. W. Fowler, *The Roman Festivals of the Period of the Republic* (London 1916).
L. Friedländer, *Roman Life and Manners under the Early Empire* (Engl. trans. of 7th German edition by J. H. Freese and L. A. Magnus, 4 vols.; London 1908-1913) 2.1-130.

J. Köhne, *Die Schrift Tertullians* 'Ueber die Schauspiele' *in kultur- und religionsgeschichtlicher Beleuchtung* (Breslau 1929).

P. de Labriolle, *History and Literature of Christianity from Tertullian to Boethius,* trans. H. Wilson (New York 1925) 50-105.

G. I. Lieftinck, 'Un fragment de *de spectaculis* de Tertullien provenant d'un manuscrit du neuvième siècle,' *Vigiliae Christianae* 5 (1951) 193-203.

E. Löfstedt, *Zur Sprache Tertullians* (Lund and Leipzig 1920).

J. Marquardt, *Römische Staatsverwaltung* 3 (2nd ed. by G. Wissowa, Leipzig 1885) 482-566.

J. Morgan, *The Importance of Tertullian in the Development of Christian Dogma* (London 1928).

J. Quasten, *Patrology* 2 (Westminister, Md. 1953) 292-294.

M. Schanz, C. Hosius and G. Krüger, *Geschichte der römischen Literatur, Handbuch der Altertumswissenschaft* VIII 3 (3rd ed., Munich 1922) 283,284.

H. F. Soveri, *De ludorum memoria, praecipue Tertullianea* (Diss., Helsingfors 1912).

J. H. Waszink, 'Varro, Livy and Tertullian on the History of Roman Dramatic Art,' *Vigilae Christianae* 2 (1948) 224-242.

SPECTACLES

Chapter 1

LEARN, O YOU SERVANTS of God who are just now entering upon His service, and you who have already solemnly sworn allegiance to Him recall[1] what principle of faith, what reason inherent in truth, what rule in our way of life[2] forbid, along with the other errors of the world, also the pleasures of the spectacles, lest by ignorance or self-deception anyone fall into sin.[3] (2) For so strong is the appeal of pleasure that it can bring about a prolongation of ignorance with a resulting facility for

---

1 Tertullian addresses not only the general body of the faithful, but also the catechumens. While the catechumens are still going through a special course of preparation in order to learn the real meaning of Christianity and its doctrines, those already initiated in the Christian faith have only to recall their baptismal vows and the obligations they have taken upon themselves.

2 This figure of climax gives at the same time a general outline of the contents of the treatise. (1) The spectacles are forbidden not only by the Christian faith in particular, but, generally, by every religious faith that acknowledges God as the Creator of the world (Ch. 2). (2) They are also forbidden by a reason that follows from the truth revealed by God and found in holy Scripture (Ch. 3, where Tertullian attempts to prove that the spectacles are condemned by the Bible). (3) They are, finally, forbidden by the Christian way of life, and it is to arguments based on Christian faith and morals that Tertullian devotes almost the entire remaining part of his treatise (Ch. 4-27).

3 The introductory sentence shows strong rhetorical influence. There are not only balance of phrase and figure of climax, but also antithesis: by going to the spectacles, the catechumens fall into sins through ignorance, the baptized Christians through self-deception. The same is true of the following sentence, which gives an additional explanation of the preceding thought.

sin, or a perversion of conscience leading to self-deception.
(3) In addition, some may perhaps be allured to either
error by the opinions of the heathens who commonly use
the following arguments against us in this matter: such
comforting and merely external pleasures of the eyes and
ears are not opposed to religion which is founded in man's
mind and conscience; neither is God offended by a man's
enjoying himself, nor is taking delight in such enjoyment
in its proper time and place a sin as long as the fear of
God and God's honor remain unimpaired. (4) But this
is precisely what we intend to prove: that these things
are not compatible with true religion and true obedience
to the true God. (5) There are some who think that the
Christians, a sort of people ever ready to die,[4] are trained
in that stubbornness of theirs that they more easily despise
life, once its ties have been cut, as it were, and lose their
craving for that which, as far as they themselves are concerned, they have already made empty of everything desirable; and thus it is considered a rule laid down by human
design and forethought rather than by divine command.
(6) It would, indeed, be loathsome for people continuing
in the enjoyment of such delightful pleasures to die for
God.[5] On the other hand, if what they say were true,

---

[4] In those days everyone knew that, by embracing the Christian faith, he became a sort of outlaw, exposing himself to the danger of the heaviest penalties—usually, death. This readiness of the Christians to die for their faith is a commonplace with the Christian apologists; see, for instance, Tertullian, *Apology* 41.5: 'Nevertheless we in no way suffer harm; in the first place, because nothing is of importance to us in the world, except to leave it as quickly as possible . . .

[5] A cutting remark against the enthusiastic devotees of the spectacles who shun, of course, the lofty ideal of the early Christians, i.e., the steadfast confession of faith and hence martyrdom, because they do not want to part from such alluring pleasures of the world.

stubbornness in a rule of life so strict as ours might well submit to a plan so apt.⁶

Chapter 2

(1) Moreover, there is no one of our adversaries who will not offer this excuse, too: that all things have been created by God and handed over to man—just as we Christians teach—and that they are undoubtedly good, as coming from a good Creator; and among them we must count all the various components that make up the spectacles, the horse, for instance, and the lion, the strength of body and the sweetness of voice.¹ Accordingly, they say that a thing which exists by God's creation cannot be considered either foreign or opposed to God, nor must a thing which is not opposed to God, because it is not foreign to Him, be considered opposed to God's worshipers. (2) Obviously, they continue, the very structures of the places—the squared stones, unhewn stones, marble slabs and columns²—also are all the handiwork of God who gave them to furnish the earth; indeed, the performances themselves take place under God's heaven.

---

6 For epigrammatic effect, Tertullian uses the rhetorical figure of oxymoron, a witty saying which is pointedly paradoxical (*stubbornness . . . might well submit*).

---

1 Tertullian mentions one example for each of the four kinds of spectacles in Roman antiquity: the horse for the circus with its horse-races; the lion for the amphitheater where, besides gladiatorial games, hunts of wild beasts (*venationes*) took place; the strength of body for the stadium with its athletic games; and the sweetness of voice for the theater where the effect depended especially on the actor's voice.

2 The squared and unhewn stones represent the raw material for the structure, while the marble slabs and columns are used for the facing of the walls and the adornment of the building respectively.

How clever in adducing proofs does human ignorance think itself, especially when it is afraid of losing some of these delights and enjoyments of the world! (3) Accordingly, you will find more people turned away from our religion by the danger to their pleasures than by the danger to their lives. For of death even a fool is not particularly afraid, feeling that it is a debt he owes to nature; but pleasure, inasmuch as it is born with man, even a sage does not despise, since both fool and sage have no other gratification in life but pleasure. (4) No one denies—because everyone knows what nature of its own accord tells us—that God is the Creator of the universe, and that this universe is good and has been made over to man by its Creator. (5) But because they have no real knowledge of God—knowing Him only by natural law and not by right of friendship, knowing Him only from afar and not from intimate association—it is inevitable that they prove ignorant of His commands regarding the use of His creation. Likewise, must they be unaware of the rival power[3] that by its hostile actions seeks to pervert to wrong uses the things of divine creation. For with such defective knowledge of God one cannot know either His will or His adversary. (6) We must, then, consider not only by whom all things were created, but also by whom they were perverted. For in this way it will become clear for what use they were created, once it is evident for what use they were not. (7) The state of corruption differs vastly from that of innocence, because there is an enormous difference between the Creator and the perverter.

Why, every form of evil-doing—misdeeds which also the

---

[3] The rival power is Satan, as Tertullian explains especially in the concluding section of this chapter.

heathens forbid and punish as such—comes from things created by God. (8) You see murder committed by iron dagger, poison, or magic incantation:[4] but iron, poisonous herbs, demons are all equally creatures of God. Yet, did the Creator design those creatures of His for man's destruction? Certainly not. He forbids man-slaying by the one summary commandment: 'Thou shalt not kill.'[5] (9) In like manner, gold, brass, silver, ivory, wood, and any other material used in the manufacture of idols—who has brought them into the world if not God, the Maker of the world? Yet, has He done this that they may be made into objects of worship set up in opposition to Himself? Certainly not. For the most grievous sin in His eyes is idolatry. What is there that offends God and is not His own? But, when it offends God, it has ceased to be His; and when it has ceased to be His, it offends Him. (10) Man himself, the perpetrator of every kind of villainy, is not only the work of God, but also His likeness[6]—yet, both in body and spirit he has fallen away from his Creator. For we did not receive the eyes for gratifying carnal appetite, the tongue for speaking evil, the ears for listening to slander, the gullet for indulging in the sin of gluttony, the belly to be the gullet's partner, the organs of sex for immodest excesses, the hands

---

4 The idea that a person could be killed by the magic power of imprecations was very common in Graeco-Roman antiquity. This passage leaves no doubt that Tertullian, too, was convinced that a person could be destroyed by magic. As it is clear from the immediately following sentence, he thought that this could be accomplished with the help of demons (Tertullian says *angeli*, but it is clear from the context that these 'angels' are evil spirits, demons). It must be borne in mind that early Christianity found itself in an environment in which demonism was widespread. Thus it is hardly surprising that some of the earliest ecclesiastical writers, among them Tertullian, were not very happy in their treatment of this topic.
5 Exod. 20.13; Matt. 5.21.
6 Cf. Gen. 1.27.

for committing acts of violence, and the feet to lead a roving life; nor was the spirit implanted in the body that it might become a workshop for contriving acts of treachery and fraud and injustice. I think not. (11) For if God, who demands innocence of us, hates all wickedness, even if it be only in thought, then it is certain beyond all doubt that it was never His intention in creation that whatever He created should lead to acts He condemns, even if those acts are done through the medium of His handiwork. The whole reason for condemnation is, rather, the misuse of God's creation by God's creatures.

(12) We, therefore, in coming to know the Lord, have also looked upon His rival, and in learning the Creator, we have likewise detected the perverter; we ought, then, to feel neither surprise nor doubt. For man himself, God's handiwork and image, the lord of the whole universe, was hurled down in the very beginning from his state of innocence by the power of that angel, perverter of God's creation and His rival; at the same time, that same perverter corrupted along with man the whole material world, man's possession, created like man for innocence, and turned it against the Creator. And in his anger that God had given it to man and not to him he intended to make man in this very possession guilty before God as well as establish his own power in it.

Chapter 3

(1) Armed with this knowledge against heathen opinion, let us now turn, instead, to the same excuses put forward by people in our own ranks. For there are some brethren

who, being either too naive or overparticular in their faith, demand a testimony from holy Scripture, when faced with giving up the spectacles, and declare the matter an open question, because such a renunciation is neither specifically nor in so many words enjoined upon the servants of God.

(2) Now, to be sure, nowhere do we find it laid down with the same precision as 'Thou shalt not kill,' 'Thou shalt not worship an idol,' 'Thou shalt not commit adultery,' 'Thou shalt not commit fraud'[1]—nowhere do we find it thus clearly declared: 'Thou shalt not go to the circus,' 'Thou shalt not go to the theater,' 'Thou shalt not watch a contest or show of gladiators.' (3) But we do find that to this special case there can be applied that first verse of David, where he says: 'Happy is the man who has not gone to the gathering of the ungodly, nor stood in the ways of sinners, nor sat in the chair of pestilence.'[2] (4) For, even though

---

1 Exod. 20.13; 4; 14; 15.
2 Ps. 1.1. The train of thought of this chapter is characteristic of Tertullian and of a number of early Christian apologists. They are under the influence of the sophistic methods of argumentation, taught in the schools of rhetoric of the day: everything is capable of proof, if one is clever enough to twist the meaning of words. Since some Christians, who are 'either too naive or overparticular in their faith,' look for evidence in holy Scripture concerning the question of the spectacles, Tertullian sets out to provide them with such a proof. Though he cannot find a scriptural passage which explicitly forbids going to the spectacles, he thinks that Psalm 1.1 is applicable to the case, and does not shrink from straining and distorting the meaning of the text. He is not the only apologist who finds a relationship between Ps. 1.1 and the spectacles. Thus we read in Clement of Alexandria, *Paedagogus* 3.11.76.3: 'As for the theater, the Educator certainly does not lead us there; one could—not unreasonably—call the stadium and theater "seats of pestilence".' While Clement mentions the scriptural passage only by way of allusion, Tertullian comments on it at full length with special emphasis on the structural features of the buildings in which the spectacles take place, devoting the entire chapter to the interpretation of the passage in order to drive home his point.

David seems to have praised that well-known just man, because he took no part in the gathering and meeting of the Jews deliberating on the killing of the Lord,³ divine Scripture admits always a broader interpretation wherever a passage, after its actual sense has been exhausted, serves to strengthen discipline. So, in this case, too, the verse of David is not inapplicable to the prohibition of spectacles. (5) For, if then he called a mere handful of Jews 'a gathering of the ungodly,' how much more such a vast crowd of heathen people? Are the heathens less ungodly, less sinners, less the enemies of Christ that the Jews were then?

(6) Moreover, the other details also fit in well. For at the spectacles there is both sitting 'in the chair' [*in cathedra*] and standing 'in the way' [*in via*]. For 'ways' [*viae*] they term both the gangways that run round the girding walls and the aisles that slope down the incline and divide the seats of the populace;⁴ in like manner is the very place for

---

3 Tertullian means Joseph of Arimathea; cf. Luke 23.50-51.
4 The semicircular space set apart for the audience in a Roman theater was usually divided into three ranks, the lowest of which was reserved for the magistrates and other persons of distinction, while the middle and uppermost were assigned to the great masses of citizens and the lowest classes of the population respectively. The ranks were separated from each other by a wall which ran completely around the auditorium, like a belt, and was hence called *balteus* (Tertullian) or *praecinctio* (Vitruvius, *De architectura* 5.3.4). Along this dividing wall ran a curved level gangway, called *cardo* (Tertullian) or *iter* (Vitruvius, *ibid*.). Such a dividing wall with its gangway is preserved, for instance, in the theater of Timgad, in North Africa (see M. Bieber, *The History of the Greek and Roman Theater* [Princeton 1939], p. 363, Fig. 471). Each rank was again divided into wedge-shaped blocks or sections by aisles which ran transversely to the direction of the seats. Tertullian's description obviously presupposes a theater building in which only the upper ranks, i.e., those for the common people, were divided by aisles into wedge-shaped sections, while the seats of honor formed an unbroken semi-circle. This structural feature appears in theaters which have been excavated in Tertullian's native land, for instance in Timgad

chairs in the curving gallery called 'chair' [*cathedra*].⁵ (7) And so, to take the converse of the verse of David, 'he is unhappy who has gone to any gathering whatsoever of the ungodly, stood in any way at all of sinners, and sat in any chair of pestilence.'⁶

Let us take, then, the general application, even when, besides the general, a special interpretation is conceded. For some things that are said with special intent have also a general meaning. (8) When God reminds the Israelites of discipline and upbraids them, His words apply undoubtedly

---

and Dugga (see Bieber, *op. cit.* pp. 362-364, Figs. 470, 471, 473, and 474). Though both the gangways along the girding walls of the several ranks and the aisles within the latter served primarily as approaches to the tiers (Tertullian calls both *viae*—'ways'), they could also be used as a standingplace by those who were unable to secure seats. The circus and amphitheater had a similar layout, with the exception that the seats of the spectators did not form a semicircle, but encompassed the central arena.

5 The *cathedra* was a comfortable chair, equipped with a sloping back and intended especially for women. Since women used such chairs also at the spectacles, the name was accordingly transferred to the seats reserved for women in the theater and amphitheater, as we learn from Calpurnius, *Bucolica* 7.23-27, who adds that these seats were located at the top of the building, i.e., in the 'curving gallery' of Tertullian. The assignment of separate space to women in the theater and amphitheater seems to have been carried through at the order of Augustus (see J. Marquardt, *Römische Staatsverwaltung* 3 [2nd ed. by G. Wissowa, Leipzig 1885] 534-535). There was no such separation, however, in the circus (*ibid.* 507). Tertullian finds, therefore, three points of relationship between the spectacles and the scriptural passage he cited: 'the vast crowd of heathen people' at the spectacles and 'the gathering of the ungodly' in the psalm; the *viae*—'ways'—in the theater buildings and 'the ways of sinners' mentioned by the Psalmist; finally, there is also a special space for the spectators, called *cathedra*—'chair,' that agrees with 'the chair of pestilence' in Scripture.

6 After Tertullian has shown that there exists a relationship between the scriptural passage and the spectacles, he tries to prove that such an interpretation of the verse is quite justified. For this purpose he changes the originally affirmative sentence into a negative clause, inserts quite imperceptibly a few indefinite pronouns, and thus has a

to all men; and when He threatens destruction to Egypt and Ethiopia, He certainly cautions every sinful nation against judgment to come. Thus, if we reason from a special case to the general type that every sinful nation is an Egypt and Ethiopa, in the same manner we reason from the general class to a special case that every spectacle is a gathering of the ungodly.

Chapter 4

(1) Lest anyone think that I am avoiding the point in question, I shall now appeal to the prime and principal authority of our 'seal'[1] itself. When we step into the water and profess the Christian faith in the terms prescribed by its law, we bear public witness that we have renounced the Devil and his pomp and his angels. (2) What, however, shall we call the chief and foremost manifestation by which the Devil and his pomp and his angels are recognized, if not idolatry? From this source, in a few words—because I will not dwell any longer on this subject—comes every unclean and evil spirit. (3) So, if it shall be proved true

---

generally applicable and valid proposition. His whole method of argumentation shows how strongly he is influenced by the schools of rhetoric of his day. The same is true concerning the remaining part of the chapter, which abounds in pointed antitheses, all based on the idea that scriptural passages admit, besides the particular, a general interpretation. Thus, Israel upbraided by the Lord for its unbelief and Ethiopia threatened with punishments for its sins are the representatives of all rebellious and sinful nations.

1 The 'seal' (*signaculum*) is often simply the sign of the cross, which the Christian draws with the hand on his forehead, but here it means the sacrament of baptism, at which the candidate renounces publicly, before the whole Christian congregation, 'the Devil and his pomp and his angels', i.e., paganism, its worship, and lax morality.

that the entire apparatus of the spectacles originates from idolatry, we will have reached a decision in advance that our profession of faith in baptism refers also to the spectacles, since they belong to the Devil and his pomp and his angels because of the idolatry involved.

(4) We shall, therefore, set forth the origins of the various spectacles, explaining in what nurseries they grew up; next in order, the titles of some of them, that is, the names by which they are called; then their equipment and the superstitions observed in them; thereafter the places and the presiding spirits to whom they are dedicated; and finally the arts employed in them and the authors to whom they are ascribed. If, among these, we find anything that is not related to an idol, we shall declare it to be free from the stain of idolatry and, as a result, to have no connection with our renunciation.

Chapter 5

(1) Concerning the origins of the spectacles, which are somewhat obscure and, therefore, unknown among most of our people, we had to make a rather thorough investigation, our authority being none other than the works of pagan literature.

(2) There are many authors who have published treatises on the subject. They give the following report on the origin of the games.[1] The Lydians migrated from Asia and settled in Etruria, according to the account of Timaeus, under the

---
1 *Ludi* (Games) is a general term which includes the scenic exhibitions in the theater (*ludi scaenici*) as well as the races in the circus (*ludi circenses*), the gladiatorial displays in the amphitheater (*munera*), and the athletic and musical contests (*agones*).

leadership of Tyrrhenus, who, in the struggle for the kingship, had succumbed to his brother.² In Etruria, then, they also introduced, along with their other superstitious customs, the spectacles in the name of religion.

From that place, in turn, the Romans invited the performers, borrowing also the name, so that the 'performers' [*ludii*] were so called from the 'Lydians' [*Lydii*].³ (3) And though Varro derives *ludii* from *ludus*,⁴ that is, from *lusus*

---

2 The origin of the Etruscans has been a matter of dispute since ancient times. Many modern scholars share the opinion of Herodotus (c. 484-425 B.C.) that they came over the sea from Asia Minor. In his history of the Persian Wars (1.94), this Greek historian tells us that, leaving their original homes in Lydia under the leadership of Tyrrhenus, they finally settled in Etruria, Italy (north of the Tiber River, in what is now called Tuscany), laid aside their former name of Lydians, and called themselves after the name of their leader, Tyrrhenians. The Western or Latin name for this people is Etruscans. A number of later ancient authors agree with Herodotus. Though Tertullian gives one of them, Timaeus (c. 345-250 B.C.), as his authority, the latter is hardly his direct source; he probably took his information from one of the works on *spectacula*, mentioned at the beginning of the chapter, whose authors in turn had quoted Timaeus. The account that Tyrrhenus left his native land, after having been defeated by his brother in the struggle for the ancestral throne, is found only in Tertullian. The coming of the Etruscans to Italy is in all probability connected with the invasion of southeastern Europe and Asia Minor by powerful invaders of Indo-European stock in the later part of the second millennium B.C. The entire area remained full of unrest and disturbed for a long time. Many earlier inhabitants were driven out from their old abodes, among them the later Etruscans who, in their search for a new home, finally settled in Italy.
3 In a well-known chapter of his history (7.2), Livy describes how in 364 B.C. Etruscan actors came to Rome. Concerning the etymology *ludii* from *Lydii*, see A. Walde and J. B. Hofmann, *Lateinisches etymologisches Wörterbuch* (3rd ed., Heidelberg 1938-1956), s. v. *ludius*. The powerful influence of Etruscan on Roman civilization appears not only in the fields of politics and economic life, but is especially noticeable in the realm of religion, in which the games, being originally religious ceremonies, played an important role.
4 Concerning this etymology, see Walde and Hofmann, *loc. cit.* and s.v. *ludus*.

['the play'], as they used to call also the Luperci *ludii,* because, as *ludendo* ['in play'] indicates, they ran to and fro, this play of the youths belongs in his view to festal days, temples, and religious ceremonies.⁵ (4) But it is, after all, not the name that matters; the real issue is idolatry. For, since the games also went under the general name of Liberalia, they clearly proclaimed the honor of Father Liber.⁶ They were first held in honor of Liber by the country folk because of the blessing which they say he bestowed upon

---

5 The ceremony which Tertullian has in mind belonged to the Roman Lupercalia, originally a festival of shepherds, held on February 15. Youthful runners, chosen from the priesthood of the Luperci, ran about the bounds of the old Palatine city, striking at all the women who came near them, with strips cut from the hides of the sacrificial goats. It was a form of simple and old-fashioned fertility magic combined with the ritual beating of the bounds and with purificatory rites. The ritual performance of the Luperci was in a way akin to that of the Salii, the dancing priests of Mars, who went through the city in the month of March, dancing solemnly in measured time. Virgil (Aeneid 8.663), for instance, mentions in the same breath 'the dancing Salii and the naked Luperci.' Moreover, quoting the first book of Varro's work *De vita populi Romani,* Nonius (*De compendiosa doctrina,* p. 851 Lindsay) informs us that boys who acted as leaders in the dances at the games were called *ludii.* Thus we may understand that the Luperci also were termed *ludii.*
6 Liber, an old Italic deity of vegetation, is often identified with the Greek god Dionysus. Similarity in character and ritual no doubt facilitated such an identification. Moreover, ancient Latin authors sometimes use the term *Liberalia* to denote the Greek Dionysia, the Attic festivals in honor of Dionysus (thus Tertullian himself; see below, 10.7). Here, however, where the author discusses the very beginnings of the games in Rome, he means the old festivals celebrated by the country folk in honor of the native deity Liber. This is quite clear from the context. In the immediately following sentence Tertullian speaks of the old vintage festivals, and proceeds to give an account of the institution of the Consualia and Ecurria, both festivals which point to Rome as their place of origin. The first games, and at that early period the only ones which were held in Rome, were just those rural festivals in honor of Liber. Hence it can easily be understood that in those early times the games were called by the common name *Liberalia.*

them by making known to them the delicious taste of wine.

(5) Then came the games called Consualia, which originally were celebrated in honor of Neptune, because he is also called Consus.[7] After that, Romulus consecrated the Ecurria, derived from *equi* [horses], to Mars,[8] though they claim the Consualia as well for Romulus on the ground that he consecrated them to Consus, the god, as they will have it, of counsel, to wit, of that very counsel by which he arrived at the scheme of carrying off the Sabine girls to be wives for his soldiers.[9] (6) A noble counsel, indeed, even now considered just and lawful among the Romans themselves, not to say in the eyes of a god! For, also, this tends to stain their origin, lest you think something good that had its origin in evil, in shamelessness, violence and hatred, in a founder who was a fratricide and the son of Mars.[10]

---

7 The Consualia were celebrated twice a year (August 21 and December 15) in honor of the god Consus. The name of this deity is connected with the verb *condere*, to store. He is the god of the storebin or other receptacles for the garnered grain. The horse races held on his festivals and the occurrence of horses in the cult of Poseidon, the Greek equivalent of Neptune, may have led to his identification with Neptune.

8 Two festivals of horse-racing (Ecurria or Equirria) were held in honor of Mars, the first on February 27, the second on March 14. The races were appropriately run in the Field of Mars (Campus Martius). Why there should be two festivals of horse-racing at such short intervals is not known. They may, perhaps, be explained as preparation for the campaigning season, with performance of rites to benefit the horses.

9 Another tradition ascribed the institution of the Consualia to Romulus and, by a false etymology which explained the god Consus as *deus consiliorum*, the god of counsel, connected the festival with the famous story of the rape of the Sabine women, told by a number of ancient authors, for instance, Livy (1.9). According to this tradition, Consus gave Romulus the counsel to carry off the women, when the Sabines attended the games held in honor of the same god.

10 According to one story, Rhea Silvia (otherwise known as Ilia), a Vestal Virgin, met Mars while fetching water for the sacred rites, and became by him the mother of the twins Romulus and Remus. In the struggle for the kingship Romulus slew his brother for contemptuously leaping over the rising wall of Rome.

SPECTACLES   61

(7) Even now, at the first goal posts in the Circus, there is an underground altar dedicated to that Consus with an inscription that reads as follows: CONSUS MIGHTY IN COUNSEL, MARS IN WAR, THE LARES AT THE CROSSROAD.[11] Sacrifice in offered on this altar on the seventh day of July by the priests of the state,[12] and on the twenty-first of August by the Flamen of Quirinus[13] and the Vestal Virgins.

(8) On a later date, the same Romulus instituted games in honor of Jupiter Feretrius at the Tarpeian Rock, which, according to the tradition handed down by Piso, were called Tarpeian and Capitoline Games.[14] After him, Numa Pompilius initiated games in honor of Mars and Robigo—for they

---

11 That Consus, the deity who presided over the storing of the harvest, had an altar underground, may be due to the fact that corn was often stored underground. The inscription is known through Tertullian only. The Latin text as we have it now reads: *'Consus consilio Mars duello Lares + coillo potentes.'* A. von Blumenthal ('Die Inschrift des Consusaltares im Circus Maximus,' *Archiv für Religionswissenschaft* 33 [1936] 384-385) takes *coillo* as a synonym of *compito* (the crossroad), since the Lares were especially worshiped at crossroads. *Consilio* he considers a misreading of *consivio*, an old neuter, meaning 'the gathering of the harvest,' so that the first part of the inscription would read: 'Consus mighty at the gathering of the harvest.' The altar being underground, the inscription was no doubt hard to read. An error could, therefore, easily creep in when the text was copied by Varro or some other Roman antiquarian. However this may be, from the context in which the inscription occurs in Tertullian, it is clear that he himself found the reading *consilio*, 'counsel,' in his source—in all probability Suetonius, whom he mentions at the end of the chapter.
12 The priesthood of the pontiffs who were in charge of the worship of the native Roman gods.
13 The special priest of Quirinus, a very ancient deity, probably the god of the Sabine settlement on the Quirinal Hill. When this settlement was united with the Latin settlement on the Palatine to form the city of Rome, Quirinus became a Roman god. The ancients looked on him as a war god.
14 The Tarpeian Rock is a part of the Capitoline Hill; hence, 'on the Tarpeian Rock' is here synonymous with 'on the Capitoline Hill.' This agrees with the tradition handed down by Varro (*De lingua latina* 5.41), according to which the Capitol was formerly called the Tarpeian

invented also a goddess of *robigo* [mildew].¹⁵ Later still came Tullus Hostilius, then Ancus Martius and, in their order, the other founders of games.

As to the idols in whose honor they instituted these games, information is found in Tranquillus Suetonius or in his sources.¹⁶ But this will suffice to prove the guilty origin of the games in idolatry.

Hill. Thus 'Tarpeian' is equivalent to 'Capitoline.' 'The Tarpeian citadel' (Virgil, *Aen.* 8.652) is the Capitoline citadel. The Capitoline Jupiter is called 'the Tarpeian Thunderer' by Ovid (*Ex Ponto* 2.2.44) and 'the Tarpeian Father' by Propertius (*Eleg.* 4[5].1.7). Similarly, the Capitoline Games could also be called the Tarpeian Games. The origin of these games is obscure. According to Livy (5.50.4 and 52.11), for instance, they were instituted only after the withdrawal of the Gauls from Rome (c. 387 B.C.). However this may be, they were connected rather with the cult of Jupiter Capitolinus than with that of Jupiter Feretrius. Feretrius was another surname of Jupiter, in whose honor Romulus erected a small temple on the Capitol after defeating the people of Caenina and capturing their city (Livy 1.10). The direct source of Tertullian is, of course, not the Roman annalist L. Calpurnius Piso (consul in 133 B.C.), but a later work, dealing with spectacles (*spectacula*), in which he found whatever earlier authors had said on the subject.

15 Robigus, or Robigo (there was some difference of opinion as to the sex of the deity), was a Roman god or goddess to whom prayers were offered during a solemn procession on April 25 to protect the crops against mildew (*robigo*) from which he or she took his or her name. In the early days of Rome when the population lived on corn grown in the immediate neighborhood of the city, the Robigalia were a festival of very real meaning, since at times the red mildew was a terrible scourge, causing heavy damage to the crops. A note in the Praenestine calendar tells that games were held by runners, both men and boys.

16 Tertullian's account of the origin of the games is rather meager and becomes continually terser. As a matter of fact, the reprehensible origin of the Consualia alone is discussed in more detail. Then, after mentioning rather cursorily the Equirria and the games of Mars and Robigo, Tertullian confines himself to naming some kings as 'founders of games.' As for the rest, he refers his readers to his direct source, a work of C. Suetonius Tranquillus on the *History of the Games* (*Historia ludicra*), or 'his sources.'

Chapter 6

(1) The testimony of antiquity is confirmed by that of the succeeding generations. For the titles by which the games still go today betray the nature of their origin. In these titles there is clearly expressed for what idol and for what superstition of one kind or other they were designed. (2) For instance, the games of the Great Mother and Apollo, and also those of Ceres, Neptune, Jupiter Latiaris, and Flora are general festivals;[1] the remaining trace their superstitious ori-

---

[1] In his enumeration of the *ludi,* Tertullian does not aim at completeness. Since his sole interest lies in pointing out their connection with idolatry, he mentions only four of the six great 'public games,' namely, the *ludi Megalenses, Apollinares, Cereales* and *Florales,* and omits the two most important ones, the *ludi Romani* and *ludi Plebei.* The institution of the *ludi Megalenses,* the Games of the Great Mother (finally seven days, April 4-10), is connected with the introduction of the cult of Cybele, known as the Great Mother of the gods, at Rome in 204 B.C. The *ludi Apollinares,* the Games of Apollo (under the Empire, July 6-13), were vowed after the battle of Cannae to insure victory over Hannibal, and given for the first time in 212 B.C. They became a fixed annual festival in 208 B.C. Like all Greek cults, the cult of Apollo increased especially after the second Punic war. The precise date of the institution of the *ludi Cereales* is unknown. From Livy (30.39.8) it appears that they were an annual festival in 202 B.C. (under the Empire, April 12-19). Though they were simply called *ludi Cereales,* two other deities of vegetation, Liber and Libera, shared the festival with Ceres. Though the *ludi Florales* were instituted as early as 238 B.C., they were made annual only in 173 B.C. They were finally extended to six days, April 28 through May 3. Flora, too, was a deity of vegetation. The two remaining games mentioned by Tertullian do not belong to the category of the great public games. The old Roman calendar lists a festival in honor of the Italic Neptune (*Neptunalia*) on July 23. Games on this festival, however, were introduced only later under Greek influence. From the calendar of Philocalus it appears that they were still held in A.D. 354. Concerning games on the festival of Jupiter Latiaris, originally the festival of the allied Latins (*feriae Latinae*), Pliny (*Nat. hist.* 27.6.45) reveals that a chariot race took place on the Capitol in Rome. The *feriae Latinae* belonged to the movable festivals of the Roman calendar.

gin back to birthdays and commemorative celebrations of the emperors, to happy political events, and municipal feasts.² (3) Among them are also the funeral games, established by bequests to render honor to the memory of private persons.³ This, too, is in accordance with ancient custom. For from the very beginning two kinds of games were distinguished: sacred and funereal; that is, games in honor of pagan deities and those in honor of dead persons. (4) But in the question of idolatry, it makes no difference to us under what name and title they are exhibited, as long as the matter concerns the same spirits that we renounce. Whether they exhibit these games in honor of their dead or in honor of their gods, they render the very same honor to their dead as to their gods. On either side you have one and the same situation: it is one and the same idolatry on their part, and one and the same renunciation of idolatry on our part.

---

2 Besides the birthday of the reigning emperor, there were commemorated annually his accession to the throne, memorable events in his life (for instance, the adoption of Antoninus Pius by Hadrian), and great accomplishments of his reign (for instance, Trajan's victory over the Parthians, in remembrance of which the *ludi Parthici* were instituted). To these festival days which were observed throughout the Empire must be added numerous festivals with games, which owed their origin either to a local cult or to important events in the history of a community. The passion of the provincials for games and theatrical performances was hardly less than that of the population of Rome—witness the ruins of theaters and amphitheaters in all parts of the Roman Empire.

3 Reports of funeral games among the Romans are numerous; for instance, Livy 23.30.15: 'In honor of M. Aemilius Lepidus who had been consul and augur, his three sons, Lucius, Marcus and Quintus, exhibited funeral games and twenty-two pairs of gladiators for three days in the Forum.'

Chapter 7

(1) Both kinds of games, then, have a common origin; common, too, are their names, inasmuch as the reasons for their being held are the same. Therefore, also, their equipment must be the same because of the common guilt of idolatry which founded them.

(2) Somewhat greater pomp, however, is displayed in the spectacles in the circus to which the term is properly applied. The *pompa*—'procession'—which comes first, proves in itself to whom it belongs, with the long line of idols, the unbroken train of images, the cars and chariots and conveyances for carrying them, the portable thrones and garlands and the attributes of the gods. (3) Moreover, how many sacred rites are observed, how many sacrifices offered at the beginning, in the course, and at the end of the procession, how many religious corporations, furthermore, how many priesthoods, how many bodies of magistrates are called upon to march in it—each is known to the inhabitants of that city where all the demons have gathered and taken up their abode.[1]

(4) And if in the provinces less care is given to manage-

---

1 Tertullian describes here the religious ceremony that preceded the Circensian Games, namely, the solemn procession which, starting from the Capitol, passed through the Forum and the Velabrum by the Tuscan Street to the Cattle Market, and from there entered the Circus Maximus, which it traversed from end to end. A fuller description of this procession, which was no doubt modeled after the triumphal procession of a victorious general, is found in Dionysius of Halicarnassus' *Roman Antiquities* (7.72). It differs in a number of points from the account given by Tertullian. The variance is probably due to the fact that Tertullian was not interested in giving the exact marching order of the festive procession, but in singling out particular features under the aspect of idolatry. Tertullian is the only ancient author who speaks of the offering of sacrifices at the beginning of the procession. Sacrifices after the procession are mentioned by Dionysius of Halicarnassus (7.72.15).

ment of the games because of less ample funds, all the spectacles in the circus everywhere must be considered as belonging to the model from which they are copied, and are contaminated by the source from which they are drawn. For, also, the small brook from its spring, and the tiny shoot from its stem, contain in them the nature of their origin.

(5) Let splendor and frugality look to it where they come from. The pomp of the circus, whatever its nature, offends God. Even if there be carried but a few idols in procession, it takes only one to have idolatry; even if there be driven but one chariot, it is Jupiter's car; every kind of idolatry, even one meanly or moderately equipped, is still rich and splendid because of its sinful origin.

Chapter 8

(1) In accordance with my plan, I shall deal next with the places. The circus is primarily consecrated to the Sun.[1] His temple stands in the middle of it, and his image shines forth from the pediment of the temple.[2] For they did not think it proper to worship beneath a roof a god whom they see above them in the open.[3] (2) Those who maintain that the first circus show was exhibited by Circe in honor of the Sun, her father, as they will have it, conclude also that the name is derived from her.[4] Plainly, the sorceress undoubtedly

---

1 Probably because the Sun, supposed to ride a car to which four horses were yoked, was the patron of the *quadriga*.
2 That the sun god had an old shrine in the Circus Maximus is also reported by Tacitus (*Annales* 15.74).
3 See the similar explanation concerning the god Consus, p. 61, above.
4 The derivation of the word 'circus' from Circe, the ancient sorceress and lady-poisoner *par excellence*, has all the earmarks of popular etymology. It fits Tertullian's purpose, since it connects the circus with idolatry. *Circus* means originally a circular line, then the circular race course.

transacted the business in behalf of those whose priestess she was, namely, the demons and evil spirits.⁵ How many evidences of idol worship do you recognize accordingly in the decoration of the place? (3) Every ornament of the circus is a temple by itself. The eggs are regarded as sacred to Castor and Pollux by people who do not feel ashamed to believe the story of their origin from the egg made fertile by the swan, Jupiter.⁶ The dolphins spout water in honor of Neptune;⁷ the columns bear aloft images of Seia, so called from *sementatio* ['sowing']; of Messia, so called as deity of *messis* ['reaping']; and of Tutulina, so called as 'tutelary spirit' of the crops.⁸ (4) In front of these are seen three altars for the triple gods: the Great, the Potent, the Prevailing. They think

---

5 By *angeli* evil spirits are meant (see above, p. 51 n.4).
6 On the *spina*, a low wall which ran down the middle of the course, special stands carried seven egg-like objects, one of which was taken down after every round made in the course. In this way the spectators were able to follow the progress of the chariot race, which consisted of the seven rounds of the course. These 'eggs' in the circus are associated with the well-known legend according to which the twins Castor and Pollux were hatched from an egg, laid by Leda, whom Jupiter visited in the form of a swan. Tertullian's main aim is again to show the connection between circus and idolatry.
7 Seven dolphins, placed on high columns, served as a supplement to the counting-apparatus of the 'eggs.' Like the latter, they were taken down, or perhaps simply turned around, according to the number of rounds completed. In some circuses, dolphins also served as gargoyles for basins. It is to such that Tertullian seems to refer here.
8 Instead of the form *Tutulina*, *Tutilina* or *Tutelina* appear elsewhere. A goddess Messia is mentioned only here. But a number of ancient authors describe a similar triad of agrarian deities whose spheres of influence are strictly defined. See, for instance, Augustine, *City of God* 4.8: 'They could not even find a single goddess Segetia to whom alone they might entrust all the crops, but for the sown seed, as long as it lay underground, they would have a goddess Seia, and, from the moment it sprouted to the time of its harvest, a Segetia to act as guardian. When the wheat was gathered and garnered, a Tutulina was to keep it safe.' See also Macrobius, *Saturn.* 1.16.8 and Pliny, *Nat. hist.* 18.2.8. The latter confirms Tertullian's statement that the statues of these three deities could be seen in the Circus Maximus.

these deities are Samothracean.⁹ (5) The huge obelisk,¹⁰ as Hermateles¹¹ maintains, has been set up in honor of the Sun. Its inscription which, like its origin, is Egyptian, contains a superstition. The gathering of the demons would be dull without their Great Mother, so she presides there over the ditch.¹² (6) Consus, as we have mentioned, keeps in hiding underground¹³ at the Murcian Goals. The latter are also the work

---

9 'The triple gods' must belong to the same category of agrarian deities as the above-mentioned three tutelary spirits of the crops. Their statues and altars respectively were, therefore, remainders of an extremely old cult that was once paid to these deities of the earth and of fertility in the valley of the Circus Maximus. With this conclusion there agrees the worship of Consus in the same locality. The identification of the triple gods with the Samothracean deities—an identification based on their names—goes back to the learned speculation of Varro (see *De lingua latina* 5.58).

10 Tertullian refers to the obelisk which Augustus transported from Heliopolis to Rome in 10 B.C. to adorn the *spina* of the Circus Maximus, the first Egyptian obelisk brought to Rome. Pope Sixtus V (1585-1590) removed it to its present place on the Piazza del Popolo. It bears an inscription in hieroglyphs celebrating the glories of King Rameses II.

11 A writer by the name of Hermateles seems to be unknown. This is not the only case where Tertullian makes a slip in quoting a name. Scholars have made several suggestions. Tertullian may have meant Demoteles who, according to Pliny (*Nat. hist.* 36.12.79 and 13.84), wrote on Egypt; or Hermapion from whose work Ammianus Marcellinus (*Res gestae* 17.4.17) transcribes the inscription of the obelisk. Unfortunately, both Demoteles and Hermapion also are very much unknown.

12 For the safety of the spectators Caesar ordered a water ditch to be dug about the arena (Suetonius, *Divus Julius* 39). It was removed by Nero to gain seats for the knights (Pliny, *Nat. hist.* 8.7.21). Later, basins fed by gargoyles (or dolphins) were set up on the *spina*. Finally, the word 'ditch' (*euripus*) was applied to the entire *spina*, as by Tertullian here and in *Adversus Hermogenem* 31.3. With this agrees the phrase that Cybele, the Great Mother of the gods, 'presides' over the ditch, i.e., the *spina*. For the goddess is not infrequently represented as riding on a dashing lion close by the obelisk, i.e., about in the middle of the *spina*.

13 See above, p. 61.

of an idol. For Murcia, as they will have it, is a goddess of love to whom they have dedicated a temple in that part [of the valley].[14]

(7) Take note, O Christian, how many unclean deities have taken possession of the circus. You have nothing to do with a place which so many diabolic spirits have made their own. Speaking of places, this is the appropriate occasion for throwing more light on the subject in order to anticipate a question that some may raise. (8) What will happen, you say, if I enter the circus at some other time? Shall I be then, too, in danger of contamination? There is no law laid down with regard to places as such. For not only these places where people gather for the spectacles but also the temples may be entered by the servant of God without peril to his rule of life, provided that he do so for an urgent and honest reason which has no connection with the business and function proper of the place.

(9) Moreover, there is no place—whether streets or marketplace or baths or taverns or even our own homes—that is completely free of idols: Satan and his angels have filled the whole world. (10) Yet, it is not by our being in the world that we fall away from God, but by taking part in some sins of the world. Therefore, if I enter the temple of Jupiter on the Capitol or that of Serapis as a sacrificer or worshiper, I shall

---

14 In Ch. 5.7 the Murcian Goals are called 'the first goal posts.' They were, therefore, the first which the charioteers had to round. Murcia was an early Roman deity whose very nature was no longer known in historical times. Roman antiquarians advanced the most fanciful etymologies to explain her name. Finally, they related Murcia to Murtea or Myrtea, an epithet of Venus, said to be taken from the myrtle which was sacred to her, and identified Murcia with Venus Murtea, Tertullian's 'goddess of love.' The existence of a shrine of Murcia in the Circus Maximus is confirmed by Varro (*De lingua latina* 5.154).

fall away from God, just as I do if I enter the circus or theater as a spectator. It is not the places in themselves that defile us, but the things done in them, by which the places themselves, as we have contended, are defiled; it is by the defiled that we are defiled.

(11) It is for this reason that we remind you who are those to whom places of this kind are dedicated to prove that what takes place in them is the work of those to whom the very places are sacred.

Chapter 9

(1) Next let us consider the arts displayed in the circus games. In times past, equestrian skill was simply a matter of riding on horseback, and certainly no guilt was involved in the ordinary use of the horse. But when this skill was pressed into the service of the games, it was changed from a gift of God into an instrument of the demons. (2) Accordingly, this kind of exhibition is regarded as sacred to Castor and Pollux, to whom horses were allotted by Mercury, as Stesichorus tells us.[1] Also, Neptune is an equestrian deity, since the Greeks

---

[1] Castor and Pollux, the patrons of horsemanship, were well-known figures to the Romans who were familiar with the old tales according to which the divine twins had appeared on two occasions (after the battle at the Lake Regillus in 497 B.C. and the battle of Pydna in 168 B.C.) at the pool of the water-nymph Juturna in the Roman Forum, riding white horses and bringing news of victory. The divine horsemen were a favorite motif of ancient sculptors. It is highly improbable that Tertullian took directly from Stesichorus, a Greek lyric poet of the sixth century B.C., the story according to which the twins received their horses from Mercury. The passage is found in a number of ancient glossaries. Tertullian may have taken it from some chrestomathy or from some similar work.

call him *Hippios* ['Lord of Steeds'].² (3) Moreover, concerning the chariot, the four-horse team was consecrated to the Sun; the two-horse team, to the Moon.³ But we also read:

Erichthonius first dared to yoke four steeds to the car
And to ride upon its wheels with victorious swiftness.⁴

This Erichthonius, a son of Minerva and Vulcan, fruit of lust, in truth, that fell to earth, is a demon-monster, or, rather, the Devil himself, not a mere snake.⁵ (4) If, however, the Argive Trochilus is the inventor of the chariot, he dedicated this work of his in the first place to Juno. And if, at Rome, Romulus was the first to display a four-horse chariot, he, too, in my view, has been enrolled among the idols himself, provided that he is identical with Quirinus.⁶

---

2 In Ch. 5.5 the same Neptune is identified with Consus; here he is considered the same as the Greek Poseidon. Though the latter's most prominent function was that of sea god, he was also credited with the creation of the horse. When, according to a local Attic legend, Poseidon and Athena competed for the land of Attica, Poseidon produced the first horse and Athena, whom the judges pronounced victor in the contest, planted an olive tree.
3 The Sun was supposed to ride in a four-horse, the Moon in a two-horse, chariot *(Anthologia latina* 1 nr. 197.17). Both motifs occur frequently in ancient art.
4 Virgil, *Georgica* 3.113-114.
5 The story runs as follows. Hephaestus (Vulcan) desired to wed Athena (Minerva). The latter, however, refused and defended herself with her spear. In the ensuing struggle, Hephaestus' seed fell on the earth which was thus fertilized and, in due time, brought forth the semi-serpentiform Erichthonius. The latter's parentage (his mother is Gê, the Earth) and semi-serpent shape show clearly that he was an old spirit of the fertility of the soil. His partly serpentine form may have contributed to Tertullian's belief that Erichthonius was an incarnation of 'the Devil himself.' This belief would also explain Tertullian's scornful and abusive description of the deity.
6 Not satisfied with only one tradition concerning the invention of the chariot, Tertullian adds two more versions. One of them makes Trochilus, the son of the first priestess of Hera (Juno) at Argos, the inventor of the chariot. This may have been the sacred car in which

(5) The chariots having been produced by such inventors, it was only fitting that they clad their drivers in the colors of idolatry. For at first there were only two colors: white and red. White was sacred to Winter because of the whiteness of its snow; red, to Summer because of the redness of its sun. But afterwards, when both love of pleasure and superstition had grown apace, some dedicated the red to Mars, others the white to the Zephyrs, the green to Mother Earth or Spring, the blue to Sky and Sea or Autumn.[7] (6) Since, however, every kind of idolatry is condemned by God, this condemnation certainly applies also to that kind which is impiously offered to the elements of nature.

Chapter 10

(1) Let us pass on to the exhibitions on the stage. We have already shown that they have a common origin with those in the circus, that they bear identical titles, inasmuch as they were called *ludi* ['games'] and were exhibited together

---

the priestess rode from the city of Argos to the temple. The second version ascribes the invention to Romulus, probably because of his instituting the Consualia with its horse-races. The identification of Romulus, the deified founder of the city, with the ancient god Quirinus can be traced back as far as the Ciceronian age. Tertullian is not interested in the credibility of one or the other tradition, but, putting them side by side, by this very accumulation aims at demonstrating the idolatrous character of the circus races.

7 In the course of time the business of providing drivers and horses for the races had been taken over by capitalists or owners of stud-farms. The proverbial Roman passion for races, however, was especially due to the organization of 'parties' or 'factions' (*factiones*), the drivers wearing the colors of the several parties. The original parties were the Whites and the Reds; the Greens and Blues arose under the Empire. The idolatrous character of the colors is seen by Tertullian in the worship which, through them, is offered to the elements of nature.

with equestrian displays.¹ (2) The pageantry is likewise the same, inasmuch as a procession is held to the theater from the temples and altars, with that whole wretched business of incense and blood, to the tune of flutes and trumpets, under the direction of the two most polluted masters of ceremonies at funerals and sacrifices: the undertaker and soothsayer.²

(3) And so, as we passed from the origins of the games to the spectacles in the circus, now we will turn to the performances on the stage. Because of the evil character of the place, the theater is, strictly speaking, a shrine of Venus.³ It was in that capacity, after all, that this type of structure gained influence in the world. (4) For many a time the censors would tear down theaters at the very moment they began to rise. In their solicitude for public morals, they foresaw, no

---

1 Besides the circus games (*ludi circenses*) which had originally been everything, all the great Roman festivals show an increasing measure of dramatic performances (*ludi scaenici*). While Tertullian devotes five chapters (5-9) to the discussion of the circus, there is only one chapter each on the theater (10), *agon* (11) and amphitheater (12). In each case he follows the arrangement of the material he has announced in Ch. 4.4: origin, titles, equipment, places, and presiding deities, finally the arts employed, though the space alloted to each of these subdivisions is rather arbitrary. In the chapter on the theater, for instance, origin, titles, and equipment are disposed of rather cursorily, while the places and the arts employed are discussed more fully.
2 According to this passage, 'the master of ceremonies at funerals' was also in charge of organizing and directing the *pompa* (solemn procession) to the theater. Because of his profession, the undertaker was held in low esteem. The soothsayer (the *haruspex* who foretold the will of the deity by inspecting the entrails of victims killed in sacrifice) took part in the sacrifices before the procession, and was considered by Tertullian as the embodiment of idolatry. Many religious rites, for instance, sacrifices and processions, were accompanied by the music of flutes and trumpets.
3 Cf. Salvian, *De gubernatione dei* 6.11.60 (CSEL 8.142): 'Minerva is worshiped and honored in the gymnasia, *Venus in the theater*, Neptune in the circuses, Mars in the arenas, Mercury in the palaestras.'

doubt, the great danger arising from the theater's lasciviousness.⁴ In this occurrence already, then, the heathens have their own opinion coinciding with ours as evidence, and we have the foreboding situation of a merely human code of morality giving additional strength to our way of life.

(5) So, when Pompey the Great, a man who was surpassed only by his theater in greatness, had erected that citadel of all vile practices, he was afraid that some day the censors would condemn his memory. He therefore built on top of it a shrine of Venus, and when he summoned the people by edict to its dedication, he termed it not a theater, but a temple of Venus, 'under which,' he said, 'we have put tiers of seats for viewing the shows.' (6) In this way he misrepresented the character of a building, condemned and worthy of condemnation, with a temple's name, and employed superstition to make sport of morality.

Venus and Liber [Bacchus], however, are close companions. The two demons of lust and drunkenness have banded together in sworn confederacy. (7) Therefore, the temple of Venus is also the house of Liber. For they appropriately gave the name of Liberalia also to other stage performances which,

---

4 We know of only one such instance. Livy (*Epitome* 48 fin.) tells us that P. Cornelius Scipio Nasica prevented the building of a stone theater, begun by the censors of 154 B.C., as being harmful to the morals of the people. Concerning the resistance to the erection of a stone theater, we must keep in mind the original connection of the dramatic performances with the cult, the god himself being thought to attend the scenic performances that were given in his honor. The *ludi Megalenses,* for instance, took place before the temple of the Great Mother on the Palatine. A wooden stage was erected for the actors and torn down again after the performance. A stone theater, as a permanent site for dramatic performances, would have severed their connection with the god, his cult and temple. In the section immediately following, Tertullian tells how, in building the first stone theater at Rome (55 B.C.), Pompey met this prejudice by erecting a shrine of Venus Victrix on the highest point of the auditorium.

besides being dedicated to Liber (and called Dionysia among the Greeks), were also instituted by him.⁵ (8) And, quite obviously, the arts of the stage are under the patronage of Liber and Venus. Those features which are peculiar to, and characteristic of, the stage, that wantonness in gesture and posture, they dedicate to Venus and Liber, deities both dissolute: the former by sex perversion, the latter by effeminate dress. (9) And all else that is performed with voice and melodies, instruments and script, belongs to the Apollos and the Muses, the Minervas and Mercuries.⁶

You will hate, O Christian, the things whose authors you cannot help but hate.

(10) At this point we intend to make a few remarks concerning the arts and things whose authors we utterly detest in their very names.⁷ We know that the names of dead men are nothing, even as their images are nothing. But we are not unaware of the identity of those who are at work behind those

---

5 The festivals in honor of Dionysus, the Greek god of vegetation, more especially of the vine, were devoted to dramatic performances. Since Tertullian uses the term *Liberalia* as an equivalent of *Dionysia*, he must have in mind not the original Liberalia (see above, p. 59), but the pre-eminently scenic Cerealia which were celebrated in honor of Ceres, Liber and Libera, a triad of deities identified with the Greek Demeter, Dionysus and Kore (see p. 63 n.1).

6 Tertullian mentions additional patron gods of the theater. Apollo, the god of music in general, is called the patron of the human voice; the Muses are in charge of the melodious music at the dramatic performances; Minerva, who was said to have made the first flute and trumpet, is the guardian of the musical instruments; Mercury, who was given credit for having invented letters, is the tutelary god of the script, i.e., the text of the play to be performed.

7 In the remaining part of the chapter, Tertullian makes a digression which is typical of his rigoristic views. Considering the arts only from the point of view of their connection with idolatry, he finds them objectionable on the whole, because they were invented by the demons to seduce and destroy men. It is the demons, too, who inspire the artists.

displayed names and images, who exult in the homage paid to them and pretend to be divine, namely, the evil spirits, the demons. (11) We see then, also, that the arts are consecrated to the honor of those who appropriate the names of the inventors of those arts, and that they are not free from the taint of idolatry when their inventors for that very reason are considered gods. (12) Even more, as far as the arts are concerned, we ought to have gone further back and taken exception to all further arguments, on the ground that the demons, from the very beginning looking out for themselves, contrived, along with the other foul practices of idolatry, also those of the shows in order to turn man from the Lord and bind him to their glorification, and gave inspiration to men of genius in these particular arts. (13) For no one else but the demons would have contrived what was going to redound to their advantage, nor would they have produced the arts at that time through the agency of anyone except those very men in whose names and images and fables they accomplished that fraud of consecration which would work out to their advantage.

To follow our plan, let us now begin the treatment of the contests [*agones*].

SPECTACLES   77

Chapter 11

(1) Their orgin is akin to that of the games.¹ As a result, they, too, are instituted either as sacred or as funereal, and are performed in honor either of the gods of the Gentiles or of the dead.² Accordingly, you have such titles as the Olympian contests in honor of Jupiter (these are called the Capitoline at Rome),³ the Nemean in honor of Hercules, the Isthmian in honor of Neptune;⁴ the rest are various contests to honor the dead. (2) What wonder is it, then, if the whole paraphernalia of these contests are tainted with idolatry—with unholy crowns, priestly superintendents, assistants from the sacred colleges,⁵ and last, but not least, with the blood of bulls?⁶ (3) To add a supplementary remark concerning the place: as you may expect from a place where the arts of the Muses, of Minerva, of Apollo, and even of Mars meet in common, with contest and sound of trumpet they endeavor to equal the

---

1 The athletic and musical contests (*agones*) of Greece, not common under the Republic, became popular under the Empire. Note how Tertullian here also follows carefully the arrangement proposed in Ch. 4.4: origin, titles, equipment, places and presiding deities, finally the arts employed.
2 Again, Tertullian applies the same division to the *agones* as to the *ludi* in general: sacred or in honor of deities, and funereal or in honor of the dead. Of the sacred *agones* he names some of the most important, while the funereal are mentioned in general only.
3 In A.D. 86 Domitian instituted the Capitoline Agon as a Roman counterpart to the quadrennial Olympian Agon in Greece. Its importance may be seen from the fact that it survived to the end of antiquity. The prize (an oak wreath) for Greek and Latin poetry at this Agon was a poet's highest ambition throughout the Empire.
4 Nothing is known about Roman counterparts to the Nemean and Isthmian *agones*.
5 Suetonius' account of the institution of the Capitoline Agon (*Domitianus* 4) is an excellent parallel to Tertullian's description. He, too, mentions the crowns and priestly colleges.
6 A sacrifice of bulls is reported only of the Neronian Agon (Suetonius, *Nero* 12).

circus in the stadium, which is no doubt a temple, too—I mean of the very idol whose festival is celebrated there. (4) The gymnastic arts also had their origin in the teachings of the Castors and Herculeses and Mercuries.⁷

Chapter 12

(1) It still remains to examine the most prominent and most popular spectacle of all. It is called *munus* ['an obligatory service'] from being an *officium* ['a duty']. For *munus* and *officium* are synonyms. The ancients thought they were performing a duty to the dead by this sort of spectacle, after they had tempered its character by a more refined form of cruelty.¹ (2) For in time long past, in accordance with the

---

7 The twins Castor and Pollux were the patron deities of athletic exercises in general: the former, especially of the stadium sprint; the latter, of the boxing match. Hercules was the patron of the *pankration* (game of all powers), a contest that combined both boxing and wrestling; professional athletes especially considered him their patron and called their guilds after him. Mercury is called the teacher of gymnastics by Lucian (*Dialogi deorum* 26.2); the gymnasium and palaestra were sacred to him, and he was considered to have been their founder. Statues of Hercules and Mercury adorned the stadia.

---

1 Originally, *munus* was the term for the gladiatorial show only. When, later, wild-beast hunts (*venationes*) were added, the term was applied to this spectacle, too. Under the Empire the place for both exhibitions was the amphitheater, a building which, duplicating the semi-circular theater, rose above an elliptical arena. Tertullian's statement that, at the beginning, *munus* was a funeral rite is correct. Gladiatorial games, which had their place originally in the cult of the dead in Etruria, were introduced under Etruscan influence in Rome in the third century B.C. For the first time such gladiatorial combats were held at the funeral of Junius Brutus Pera in 264 B.C. They became the most popular form of amusement in the last century of the Republic and under the emperors.

belief that the souls of the dead are propitiated by human blood, they used to purchase captives or slaves of inferior ability and to sacrifice them at funerals.² (3) Afterwards, they preferred to disguise this ungodly usage by making it a pleasure. So, after the persons thus procured had been trained³—for the sole purpose of learning how to be killed!—in the use of such arms as they then had and as best as they could wield, they then exposed them to death at the tombs on the day appointed for sacrifices in honor of the dead. Thus they found consolation for death in murder. (4) Such is the origin of the gladiatorial contest. But gradually their refinement progressed in the same proportion as their cruelty. For the pleasure of these beasts in human shape was not satisfied unless human bodies were torn to pieces also by wild beasts.⁴ What was then a sacrifice offered for the appeasement of the dead was no doubt considered a rite in honor of the dead. This sort of thing is, therefore, idolatry, because idolatry, too, is a kind of rite in honor of the dead: the one and the other is a service rendered to dead persons. (5) It is, furthermore, in the images of the dead that the demons have their abode.

To come to the consideration of the titles also: though this type of exhibition has been changed from being an act in honor of the dead to being one in honor of the living—I mean those entering upon quaestorships, magistracies, flaminates,

---

2 Quoting Varro as his authority, Servius in his *Commentary on Aeneid* 10.519 states that human sacrifice at a tomb was once the custom at Rome, but that in a more humane age the gladiatorial show in honor of the dead was substituted.

3 There was a training school for gladiators in Rome as early as 63 B.C.; similar schools existed outside Rome, for instance, at Pompeii.

4 Tertullian refers to the baitings of animals in the amphitheater. The men who took part in these exhibitions (their general name was *venatores* or *bestiarii*) were, like the gladiators, kept and trained in special schools.

and priesthoods[5]—still, since the guilt of idolatry cleaves to the dignity of the title, whatever is carried out in the name of this dignity shares necessarily in the taint of its origin.

(6) In the same way we must interpret the paraphernalia which are considered as belonging to the ceremonies of these very offices. For the purple robes, the fasces, the fillets, and crowns[6]—finally, also, the announcements made in meetings and on posters,[7] and the pottage dinners given on the eve of exhibitions[8]—do not lack the pomp of the Devil and the invocation of demons.

(7) In conclusion, what shall I say about that horrible

---

5 Gladiatorial combats, originally held in honor of the dead, were sponsored later by higher magistrates, the management of these spectacles being a part of their official duties. In A.D. 47, for instance, Emperor Claudius 'obliged the College of Quaestors to give a gladiatorial show in place of paving the roads' (Suetonius, *Claudius* 24). Outside Rome, the expenses of these entertainments were defrayed by local magistrates (for instance, an aedile) or by the incumbents of certain priesthoods. St. Augustine mentions (*Ep.* 138.19) that Apuleius, the second-century African rhetorician, had to provide gladiatorial combats and wild-animal hunts in his capacity as high priest of the province.

6 The givers of the spectacles had the right to wear the triumphal robe.

7 The spectacles were announced by advertisements painted on the walls of public and private buildings, and even on the tombs along the main roads leading into the towns. One of these advertisements found at Pompeii reads: 'The troupe of gladiators belonging to the Aedile Aulus Suettius Certus will fight at Pompeii on May 31. There will also be animal hunts, and awnings will be provided' (E. Diehl, *Pompeianische Wandinschriften und Verwandtes* [2nd ed., Berlin 1930] nr. 246). The awnings provided highly desirable protection against the sun, since the amphitheater was an uncovered building; they were adjusted from time to time as the sun moved.

8 On the eve of the spectacle, the gladiators and fighters of animals were given a kind of last meal, called 'free banquet.' The fare was luxurious, though a time-honored custom was apparently observed concerning one course. One dish was very simple, consisting of pottage, made of meal, the primitive food of the Romans, which was also used at sacrifices.

place which not even perjurers can bear? For the amphitheater is consecrated to names more numerous and more dreadful than the Capitol, temple of all demons as it is. There, as many unclean spirits have their abode as the place can seat men. And to say a final word about the arts concerned, we know that Mars and Diana are the patrons of both types of games.

Chapter 13

(1) I have, I think, adequately carried out my plan by showing in how many and in what ways the spectacles involve idolatry. I discussed their origins, their names, their equipment, their locations, and their arts—all that we may be certain that the spectacles in no way become us who twice renounce idols. (2) 'Not that an idol is anything,' as the Apostle says, 'but because what they do, they do in honor of demons'[1] who take up their abode there at the consecration of idols, whether of the dead, or, as they think, of gods. (3) It is for this reason, therefore, since both kinds of idols belong to one and the same category (the dead and the gods being the same thing) that we refrain from both types of idolatry. (4) Temples and tombs, we detest both equally; we know neither kind of altar, we adore neither kind of image, we offer no sacrifice, we celebrate no funeral rites. Nor do we eat of what is sacrificed, or offered at funeral rites, because 'we cannot share the Lord's supper and the supper of demons.'[2] (5) If we keep, then, our palate and stomach free from defile-

---
1 Cf. 1 Cor. 8.4; 10.19.
2 Cf. 1 Cor. 10.21.

ment, how much more should we guard our nobler organs, our ears and eyes, from pleasures connected with sacrifices to idols and sacrificers to the dead—pleasures which do not pass through the bowels, but are digested in the very spirit and soul with whose purity God is more concerned than with that of the bowels.[3]

Chapter 14

(1) Having established the charge of idolatry, which in itself should be reason enough for our giving up the spectacles, let us now treat the matter fully from another point of view, chiefly for the benefit of those who delude themselves with the thought that such abstention is not expressly enjoined. (2) The latter excuse sounds as if judgment enough were not pronounced on spectacles, when the lusts of the world are condemned.[1] For, just as there is a lust for money, a lust for high station in life, for gluttony, for sensual gratification, for fame, so there is a lust for pleasure. The spectacles, however, are a sort of pleasure. (3) In my opinion, under the general heading of lust, there are also included pleasures; similarly, under the general idea of pleasures, spectacles are treated as a special class.

---
3 Cf. Matt. 15.11, 17.

1 Cf. Tit. 2.12; 1 John 2.15-17.

Chapter 15

(1) Dealing with the matter of the places, we have already mentioned above that they do not contaminate us of themselves, but on account of what is done in them, that is, once these places have imbibed contamination by such actions, they spit it out again to the same degree on others. So much, then, as we have said, for the main charge: idolatry.

Now let us also point out that the other characteristics of the things which are going on at the spectacles are all opposed to God. (2) God has given us the command both to deal with the Holy Spirit in tranquility, gentleness, quiet, and peace, inasmuch as, in accordance with the goodness of His nature, He is tender and sensitive, and also not to vex Him by frenzy, bitterness of feeling, anger, and grief.[1] (3) How, then, can the Holy Spirit have anything to do with spectacles? There is no spectacle without violent agitation of the soul.[2] For, where you have pleasure, there also is desire which gives pleasure its savor; where you have desire, there is rivalry which gives desire its savor. (4) And where, in turn, you have rivalry, there also are frenzy and bitterness of feeling and anger and grief and the other effects that spring from them, and, moreover, are incompatible with our moral discipline. (5) For, even if a man enjoys spectacles modestly and soberly, as befits his rank, age, and natural disposition, he cannot go to them

---

1 Cf. Eph. 4.30-31.
2 St. Augustine (*Conf.* 6.8) tells about a young Christian who, against his strong objections, was dragged by his fellow students to a performance in the amphitheater. He held his eyelids tightly closed in order not to see the cruel sport, but, when an immense roar from the whole audience struck his ears, he was overcome by curiosity and opened his eyes. Suddenly he was overcome by a mad passion and 'was wounded more seriously in his soul than the gladiator, whom he lusted to observe, had been wounded in the body.' From that time on he went regularly to the spectacles, dragging in others, besides.

without his mind being roused and his soul being stirred by some unspoken agitation. (6) No one ever approaches a pleasure such as this without passion; no one experiences this passion without its damaging effects. These very effects are incitements to passion. On the other hand, if the passion ceases, there is no pleasure, and he who goes where he gains nothing is convicted of foolishness. (7) But I think that foolishness also is foreign to us. Is it, further, not true that a man really condemns himself when he has taken his place among those whose company he does not want and whom, at any rate, he confesses to detest? (8) It is not enough to refrain from such acts, unless we also shun those who commit them. 'If thou didst see a thief,' says holy Scripture, 'thou didst run with him.'³ Would that we did not live in the world with them! Still, we are separated from them in the things of the world. For the world is God's, but the things of the world are the Devil's.

Chapter 16

(1) Since, then, frenzy is forbidden us, we are debarred from every type of spectacle, including the circus, where frenzy rules supreme. Look at the populace, frenzied even as it comes to the show, already in violent commotion, blind, wildly excited over its wagers.¹ (2) The praetor is too slow for them; all the time their eyes are rolling as though in rhythm

---

3 Ps. 49.18.

1 The days preceding the races were filled with eager suspense. People discussed passionately the chances of the different 'factions' and made bets. They even consulted soothsayers and employed all kinds of magic to injure or slacken the speed of the horses and charioteers competing with their favorites.

with the lots he shakes up in his urn.² Then they await the signal with bated breath; one outcry voices the common madness. (3) Recognize the madness from their foolish behavior. 'He has thrown it!' they shout; everyone tells everybody else what all of them have seen just that moment. This I take as a proof of their blindness: they do not see what has been thrown—a signal cloth, they think—but it is the symbol of the Devil hurled headlong from on high.³ (4) Accordingly, from such beginnings the affair progresses to outbursts of fury and passion and discord and to everything forbidden to the priests of peace.⁴ Next come curses, insults without any justified reason for the hatred, and rounds of applause without the reward of affection. (5) What are the partakers in all this —no longer their own masters—likely to achieve for themselves? At best, the loss of their self-control. They are saddened by another's bad luck; they rejoice in another's success. What they hope for and what they dread has nothing to do with themselves, and so their affection is to no purpose and

---

2 The barriers or starting places in the race course, vaulted and roped-in gates by the entrance, were assigned by lot.
3 The presiding magistrate dropped a white handkerchief from his balcony as the signal for the start of the race. Alluding to Luke 10.18, Tertullian sees in the falling handkerchief a symbol of the fall of Lucifer.
4 The characterization of the Christians as 'priests of peace' occurs only here in Tertullian; more frequently he calls them 'the sons of peace' (see, for instance, *De corona* 11.2), an idea taken from the New Testament, where Christ's teaching is described as 'the gospel of peace' (cf., for instance, Eph. 6.15). In a wider sense, all Christians are called 'priests of God and of Christ' in the Apocalypse (6.20). St. Augustine (*City of God* 20.10) comments on this passage as follows: 'Here he [St. John] is speaking not just of bishops and of presbyters (who are now priests in the Church), but of all Christians. For, just as we call all of them Christs by reason of their mystical chrism, we call them all priests insomuch as they are members of the One Priest.'

their hatred is unjust. (6) Or are we, perhaps, permitted to love without cause any more than to hate without cause? God who bids us to love our enemies certainly forbids us to hate even with cause; God who commands us to bless those who curse us does not permit us to curse even with cause.[5] (7) But what is more merciless than the circus, where they do not even spare their rulers or their fellow citizens?[6] If any of these frenzies of the circus become the faithful elsewhere, then it will be lawful also in the circus; but, if nowhere, then neither in the circus.

Chapter 17

(1) In like manner we are commanded to steer clear of every kind of impurity. By this command, therefore, we are precluded also from the theater, which is impurity's own peculiar home, where nothing wins approval but what elsewhere finds approval. (2) And so, the theater's greatest charm is above all produced by its filth—filth which the actor

---

5 Cf. Matt. 5.44; Rom. 12.14.
6 The spectacles where the people assembled *en masse*, often in the presence of the emperor, provided them with an opportunity to make known their attitude and to express wishes and complaints. It was for this very reason, Suetonius (*Tiberius* 47) tells us, that Tiberius 'gave no public shows at all, and very seldom attended those given by others, for fear that some request would be made of him.' Emboldened by the security of numbers, the multitude also directed gibes at the emperor. By demonstrations against fellow citizens Tertullian means probably the outbursts of hatred against Christians who had been led into the arena to die because of their faith. Tertullian himself (*Scorpiace* 10.10) refers to these anti-Christian outbreaks at the shows 'where they readily join in the cry: How long shall we suffer the third race?' By the third race the **Christians** are meant; the first race being the pagans; the second, the Jews.

of the Atellan farces conveys by gestures;[1] filth which the mimic actor even exhibits by womanish apparel, banishing all reverence for sex and sense of shame so that they blush more readily at home than on the stage;[2] filth, finally, which the pantomime experiences in his own body from boyhood in order to become an artist.[3] (3) Even the very prostitutes, the victims of public lust, are brought upon the stage, creatures feeling yet more wretched in the presence of women, the only members in the community who were unaware of their existence; now they are exhibited in public before the eyes of persons of every age and rank; their address, their price, their record are publicly announced, even to those who do not need the information, and (to say nothing of the rest) things which

---

1 The Atellan farce was a very old popular burlesque, called after the small Oscan town Atella in Campania where it had been especially in vogue. Transplanted to Rome at an early time, it grew from amateurish improvisations into a literary genre. It offered coarse, often indecent, scenes taken from daily life, with stock figures such as the dotard, the deceitful soothsayer, the glutton, and the simpleton. Since the actors in the Atellan farce wore masks, lively gesticulation had to serve as a substitute for the play of countenance.
2 The mime was also a farce in which incidents of common life were represented in a ludicrous way. The actors wore no masks. It was the most licentious type of all farces, adultery and love affairs being the main themes. The young actors who played the part of the infatuated or beloved youth appeared on the scene with wavy hair and, both in pose and clothing, strove for womanish gracefulness. In view of the fact that the taste of the general Roman public became increasingly coarser, it is not surprising that this literary genre was especially fashionable under the Empire.
3 In the pantomime entire dramatic scenes were enacted by a single actor who played several parts in succession, male and female, his only medium of expression being clear, effective, and rhythmic movements of the body, while the connective text was sung by a chorus. Since this kind of acting consisted not only in expressive movements of head and hand, but also in bendings and turns and even leaps, it demanded full command of the body, acquired by incessant training and careful diet from early childhood. The pantomime appeared as an independent art in the Augustan Age, soon became very popular, and replaced in a great measure the old drama, especially tragedy.

ought to remain hidden in the darkness of their dens so as not to contaminate the daylight. (4) Let the senate blush, let all the orders blush, let even those very women who have committed murder on their own shame blush once a year when, by their own gestures, they betray their fear of the light of the day and the gaze of the people.[4]

(5) Now, if we must detest every kind of impurity, why should we be allowed to hear what we are not allowed to speak, when we know that vile jocularity and every idle word are judged by God?[5] Why, in like manner, should we be permitted to see that which is sinful to do? Why should things which, spoken by the mouth, defile a man[6] not be regarded as defiling a man when allowed access by the ears and eyes, since the ears and eyes are the servants of the spirit, and he whose servants are filthy cannot claim to be clean himself? (6) You have, therefore, the theater prohibited in the prohibition of uncleanness. Again, if we reject the learning of the world's literature as convicted of foolishness before God,[7] we have a sufficiently clear rule also concerning those types of

---

4 Tertullian is not the only ancient author who tells us about this strange custom at the Floralia (April 28 to May 3): the courtesans appearing in public and enacting a kind of mime which included indecent speech and exposure of the actresses on the stage. Cato the Younger is said to have withdrawn from the theater rather than witness the disgusting spectacle, though he would not interfere with the custom itself (Valerius Maximus 2.10.8). Among the early Christian writers is was especially Lactantius (*Divinae institutiones* 1.20.10) who attacked the licentious character of this custom. To understand it at all, we must keep in mind that, in primitive rituals of vegetation deities, words and actions which would have been repulsive in ordinary life took on a certain meaning: they were thought to promote fertility.
5 Cf. Matt. 12.36; Eph. 5.3.
6 Mark 7.20.
7 Cf. 1 Cor. 3.19. On the basis of this scriptural passage Tertullian spurns the texts of tragedy and comedy as belonging to 'the learning of the world's literature.'

spectacles which, in profane literature, are classified as belonging to the comic or tragic stage. (7) Now, if tragedies and comedies are bloody and wanton, impious and prodigal inventors of outrage and lust, the recounting of what is atrocious or base is no better; neither is what is objectionable in deed acceptable in word.

Chapter 18

(1) Now, if you maintain that the stadium is mentioned in the Scriptures, I will admit at once that you have a point.[1] But as for what is done in the stadium, you cannot deny that it is unfit for you to see—punches and kicks and blows and all the reckless use of the fist and every disfiguration of the human face, that is, of God's image.[2] (2) Never can you approve the foolish racing and throwing feats and the more foolish jumping contests;[3] never can you be pleased with either harmful or foolish exhibitions of strength nor with the cultivation of an unnatural body,[4] outdoing the craftsmanship of of God; you will hate men bred to amuse the idleness of

---

1 Cf. 1 Cor. 9.24.
2 Cf. Gen. 1.27; 9.6. Tertullian refers here especially to the *pankration* (game of all powers), a combination of both boxing and wrestling. In this contest every kind of blow and grip was permitted.
3 These are parts of the *pentathlon,* or five contests, an athletic exhibition which consisted of sprinting, throwing the discus, hurling the spear, leaping, and wrestling (the latter is mentioned in the last section of this chapter).
4 A number of ancient writers speak disdainfully of the gluttony of the pugilists and wrestlers, who fattened their bodies to give them the appearance of unnatural strength.

Greece.⁵ (3) Also, the art of wrestling belongs to the Devil's trade: it was the Devil who first crushed men. The very movements of the wrestler have a snakelike quality: the grip that takes hold of the opponent, the twist that binds him, the sleekness with which he slips away from him. Crowns are of no use to you; why do you seek pleasure from crowns?⁶

Chapter 19

(1) Are we now to wait for a scriptural repudiation of the amphitheater, also? If we can claim that cruelty, impiety, and brutality are permitted us, let us by all means go to the amphitheater. If we are what people say we are, let us take delight in human blood.¹ (2) It is a good thing when the guilty are punished. Who will deny this but the guilty? Yet it is not becoming for the guiltless to take pleasure in the punishment of another; rather, it befits the guiltless to grieve that a man, like himself, has become so guilty that he is treated with such

---

5 Conservative Romans objected to the introduction of Greek gymnastics. Ascribing the fall of Greece chiefly to the idle life in the gymnasia, they feared a similar corruption of the Roman youth by these exercises (cf. especially Plutarch, *Quaestiones Romanae* 40).

6 Tertullian means the crowns, the prizes of victory in the athletic contests. To him the wearing of crowns is a heathen practice connected with idolatry and should, therefore, not be practised by Christians under any circumstances. He deals with this subject in detail in his treatise *De corona*.

---

1 An allusion to one of the false and harmful accusations against the Christians. Their ceremonies while celebrating the Holy Eucharist were distorted by gruesome rumors to the effect that they were akin to cannibalism. Christian phraseology about eating Christ's flesh and drinking His blood led to the notion that the Christians observed cannibalistic rites. Refutation of this accusation in the works of the Christian apologists is quite frequent; see, for instance, Tertullian *Apology* 2.5; 7.1; 8.2,7; Minucius Felix, *Octavius* 9.5.

cruelty. (3) And who is my voucher that it is the guilty always who are condemned to the beasts,² or whatever punishment, and that it is never inflicted on innocence, too, through the vindictiveness of the judge or the weakness of the defense or the intensity of the torture? How much better it is, then, not to know when the wicked are punished, lest I come to know also when the good are destroyed, provided, of course, that there is savor of good in them. (4) Certain it is that innocent men are sold as gladiators to serve as victims of public pleasure.³ Even in the case of those who are condemned to the games, what a preposterous idea is it that, in atonement for a smaller offense, they should be driven to the extreme of murder!

(5) This reply I have addressed to Gentiles. Heaven forbid that a Christian should need any further instruction about the detestableness of this kind of spectacle. No one, however, is able to describe all the details at full length except one who is still in the habit of going to the spectacles. I myself prefer to leave the picture incomplete rather than to recall it.

---

2 One of the most cruel kinds of execution provided for in Roman law was to deliver those sentenced to death either defenseless or insufficiently armed to wild beasts in the arena. The frightful executions in the amphitheater were a center of attraction for the Roman public at large, who had no idea of the sanctity of life.

3 Among the gladiators there were, no doubt, a number of condemned criminals, but the greater part of them consisted of innocent people, prisoners of war, slaves sold by their owners to the arena, free-born men who either were coerced to fight or volunteered, finding the very danger of the profession an incentive. Cf. Lactantius, *Divinae institutiones* 6.20.14: 'Being imbued with this practice [of clamoring for ever-fresh combatants in the amphitheater] they have lost their humanity. Therefore they do not even spare the innocent, but practise upon all what they have learned in the slaughter of the wicked.'

Chapter 20

(1) How foolish, then—rather, how desperate—is the reasoning of those who, obviously as a subterfuge to avoid the loss of pleasure, plead as their excuse that no regulation concerning such an abstinence is laid down in Scripture, in precise terms or in a definite passage, forbidding the servant of God to enter gatherings of this kind. (2) Only recently I heard a novel defense offered by one of these devotees of the games. 'The sun,' he said, 'nay, even God Himself, looks on from heaven and is not defiled.' Why, the sun also sends his rays into the sewer and is not soiled! (3) Would that God looked on at no sins of men that we might all escape judgment! But He looks on at robberies, He looks on at falsehoods and adulteries and frauds and acts of idolatry and at the very spectacles. And it is for that reason that we will not look at them, lest we be seen by Him who looks on at everything. (4) My man, you are putting the defendant on the same footing as the judge: the defendant who is a defendant because he is seen, and the judge who, because he sees, is judge. (5) Do we, perhaps, indulge in frenzy also outside the confines of the circus, outside the gates of the theater give free play to lewdness, outside the stadium to haughty deportment, outside the amphitheater to cruelty, just because God has eyes also outside the covered seats and the tiers and the stage? We are wrong: nowhere and never is there any exemption from what God condemns; nowhere and never is there any permission for what is forbidden always and everywhere. (6) It is the freedom from the change of opinion and from the mutability of judgment that constitutes the fullness of truth and—what is due to truth—perfect morality, unvarying

reverence, and faithful obedience. What is intrinsically good or evil cannot be anything else.

Chapter 21

(1) All things, we maintain, are firmly defined by the truth of God. The heathens who do not possess the fullness of truth, since their teacher of truth is not God, form their judgment of good and evil in accordance with their own opinion and inclination, making what is good in one place evil in another, and what is evil in one place good in another. (2) Thus it happens that the same man who in public will scarcely raise the tunic to ease nature will put it off in the circus in such a way as to expose himself completely to the gaze of all; and the man who protects the ears of his maiden daughter from every foul word will take her himself to the theater to hear such words and see the gestures which accompany them. (3) The same man who tries to break up or denounces a quarrel in the streets which has come to fisticuffs will in the stadium applaud fights far more dangerous; and the same man who shudders at the sight of the body of a man who died in accordance with nature's law common to all will in the amphitheater look down with tolerant eyes upon bodies mangled, rent asunder, and smeared with their own blood. (4) What is more, the same man who allegedly comes to the spectacle to show his approval of the punishment for murder will have a reluctant gladiator driven on with lashes and with rods to commit murder;[1] and the same man who wants every more notorious

---

[1] Reluctant gladiators were driven with whips and hot irons into the arena to fight, while the excited spectators shouted: 'Kill him, lash

murderer to be cast before the lion will have the staff and cap of liberty granted as a reward to a savage gladiator,[2] while he will demand that the other man who has been slain be dragged back to feast his eyes upon him, taking delight in scrutinizing close at hand the man he wished killed at a distance[3]—and, if that was not his wish, so much more heartless he!

Chapter 22

(1) What wonder! Such are the inconsistencies of men who confuse and confound the nature of good and evil through their fickleness of feeling and instability in judgment. (2) Take the treatment the very providers and managers of the spectacles accord to those idolized charioteers, actors, athletes,

---

    him, burn him! Why is he so afraid of facing the sword? Why is he not bold enough to give the death stroke? Why is he not ready enough to die?' (Seneca, *Ep.* 7.4). Cf. Lactantius, *Divinae institutiones* 6.20.13: 'They are even angry with the combatants, unless one of the two is quickly slain; and, as though they thirsted for human blood, they hate delays.'

2 Popular and successful gladiators received a staff (*rudis*) as a sign of their honorable discharge from active service. Though they were exempted from any further obligation to perform, they remained slaves in their gladiatorial school and were promoted to an overseership. Only with the bestowal of the cap of liberty (*pilleus*) did a gladiator win complete freedom. The *pilleus* was a felt cap, shaped like the half of an egg, and made to fit close; it was given to a slave at his enfranchisement as a sign of freedom.

3 Tertullian alludes to a special piece of equipment in the amphitheater. It consisted of a platform in the middle of the arena, on which the wounded victims were placed, thus enabling the spectators to observe more accurately their death-struggle. Such a platform was used, for instance, in the amphitheater of Tertullian's native city, Carthage (cf. *Passion of SS. Perpetua and Felicitas* 21). Cf. a similar allusion in Lactantius, *Divinae institutiones* 6.20.12.

and gladiators, to whom men surrender their souls and women even their bodies, on whose account they commit the sins they censure: for the very same skill for which they glorify them, they debase and degrade them; worse, they publicly condemn them to dishonor and deprivation of civil rights, excluding them from the council chamber, the orator's platform, the senatorial and equestrian orders, from all other offices and certain distinctions.¹ (3) What perversity! They love whom they penalize; they bring into disrepute whom they applaud; they extol the art and brand the artist with disgrace. (4) What sort of judgment is this—that a man should be vilified for the things that win him a reputation? Yes, what an admission that these things are evil, when their authors, at the very peak of their popularity, are marked with disgrace!

---

1 The best performers in the circus, theater, amphitheater, and stadium became popular favorites. At their appearance they were greeted with shouts of applause and good wishes. Often, they received handsome gifts in the form of money, landed property, and fine clothing. Poets sang their praises; commemorative columns and gilded bronze busts and statues perpetuated their fame. Scorpus, a famous charioteer under Domitian, was called by Martial (*Epigr.* 10.53) 'the lustre of the noisy circus, the short-lived delight of Rome and the object of its applause.' The heroes of the arena were especially the ladies' favorites, as can be seen from the *graffiti* (scribblings) on the walls of Pompeii. 'Lord of lassies' (*dominus puparum*) and 'Maidens' sigh' (*suspirium puellarum*) are terms of endearment lavished upon some of these idols. Tertullian's statement that social and legal infamy was attached to all these professions needs some qualification. It applies to the performers in the arena and on the stage. On the other hand, the charioteer was not as contemptible as an actor or gladiator, though, to the Roman way of thinking, exposing oneself for popular pleasure always implied a loss of dignity. Athletes, finally, were hardly affected in their social and legal position. According to the Roman jurists (*Digesta* 3.2.4), they did not follow an actor's trade, but performed only to show their bravery. Morover, the reputation once enjoyed by the athletes in Greece still clung to them.

Chapter 23

(1) Since, then, man reflecting on these matters, even over against the protest and appeal of pleasure, comes to the conclusion that these people should be deprived of the benefits of posts of honor and exiled to some island of infamy, how much more will divine justice inflict punishment on those who follow such professions? (2) Or will God take pleasure in the charioteer, the disturber of so many souls, the minister to so many outbursts of frenzy, flaunting his rostral crown as a priest wears his wreath, dressed up in gay colors like a pimp,[1] attired by the Devil as a ludicrous counterpart of Elias to be swept away in his chariot?[2] (3) Will God be pleased with the man who alters his features with a razor, belying his own countenance and, not content with making it resemble that of Saturn or Isis or Liber, on top of that submits it to the indignity of being slapped,[3] as if in mockery of the Lord's commandment?[4] (4) The Devil, to be sure, also teaches that one should meekly offer his cheek to be struck. In the same way, he also makes the tragic actors taller by means of their

---

1 Tertullian refers to the crown of victory and the many-colored attire of the charioteer. The latter displayed the color of his party in his tunic, the harness, and the adornment of his horses, while the remaining articles of his dress were often of different colors.
2 Cf. 4 Kings 2.11. While Elias was conversing with Eliseus on the hills of Moab, 'a fiery chariot and fiery horses parted them both asunder, and Elias went up by a whirlwind into heaven.' This scriptural passage was used by Christian devotees of the circus to defend the chariot-races (cf. Ps.-Cyprian, *De spectaculis* 2-3).
3 Tertullian means the actor who played the part of the bald-headed and fat-cheeked booby in the mime. Resounding slaps on his ears were regular incidents of the buffoonery. The passage also proves that the travesties of the myths of the gods were favorite subjects of the mime.
4 Cf. Matt. 5.39; Luke 6.29.

high shoes, because 'no one can add a single cubit to his stature.'⁵ He wishes to make Christ a liar. (5) Again, I ask whether this whole business of masks is pleasing to God, who forbids the likeness of anything to be made—how much more of His own image? The Author of truth does not love anything deceitful; all that is counterfeit is a kind of adultery in His eyes. (6) Accordingly, He will not approve the man who feigns voice, sex, or age, or who pretends love, anger, groans, or tears, for He condemns all hypocrisy. Moreover, since in His law He brands the man as accursed who dresses in woman's clothes,⁶ what will be His judgment upon the pantomime who is trained to play the woman? (7) No doubt, also, the artist in punching will go unpunished. For those scars and wales, marks left by boxing gloves and blows, and those growths upon his ears⁷ he got from God when his body was being fashioned; God gave him eyes to have them blinded in fighting! (8) I say nothing of the man who pushes another to the lion lest he seem less a murderer than the fellow who afterwards cuts the same victim's throat.⁸

---

5 Cf. Matt. 6.27; Luke 12.25.
6 Cf. Deut. 22.5.
7 These marks of injury received in fighting are realistically reproduced in the famous bronze figure of the resting pugilist in the Museo delle Terme in Rome. The figure wears the *caestus,* the boxing-glove of ancient pugilists, consisting of strong leather bands loaded with balls of lead or iron, wound around the hands and arms.
8 Tertullian refers to two performers in the *venatio* (animal-baiting). The first, an experienced fighter, shoves the victim (a person sentenced to death) ahead of himself toward the lion. The second, a novice in the profession, gives the victim the finishing stroke on the platform in the middle of the arena (see above, Ch. 21 n 3). A description of such a scene in the amphitheater of Carthage is found in the *Passion of SS. Perpetua and Felicitas* 19-21.

Chapter 24

(1) In how many ways are we expected to prove that none of the things connected with the spectacles is pleasing to God? Or, because it is not pleasing to God, befits His servant? (2) If we have shown that all these things have been instituted for the Devil's sake, and furnished from the Devil's stores (for everything which is not God's or which displeases God is the Devil's), then this represents the pomp of the Devil which we renounce in the 'seal' of faith. (3) No share, however, ought we to have, whether in deed or word, whether by beholding or watching, in what we renounce. Moreover, if we ourselves renounce and rescind the 'seal' by making void our testimony to it, does it remain, then, for us to seek an answer from the heathen? Yes, let them tell us whether it be permitted for Christians to attend a spectacle. Why, for them this is the principal sign of a man's conversion to the Christian faith, that he renounces the spectacles. (4) A man, therefore, who removes the mark by which he is recognized, openly denies his faith. What hope is there left for such a man? No one deserts to the camp of the enemy without first throwing away his weapons, deserting his standards, renouncing his oath of allegiance to his leader, and without pledging himself to die with the enemy.

Chapter 25

(1) Will the man, seated where there is nothing of God, at that moment think of God? He will have peace in his soul, I

suppose, as he cheers for the charioteer; he will learn purity as he gazes with fascination at the mimic actors. (2) No, indeed, in every kind of spectacle he will meet with no greater temptation than that overcareful attire of women and men. That sharing of feelings and that agreement or disagreement over favorites fan the sparks of lust from their fellowship. (3) Finally, no one going to a spectacle has any other thought but to see and be seen. But, while the tragic actor is ranting, our good friend will probably recall the outcries of some prophet! Amid the strains of the effeminate flute-player, he will no doubt meditate on a psalm! And while the athletes are engaged in combat, he is sure to say that a blow must not be struck in return for a blow!¹ (4) He will, therefore, also be in a position to let himself be stirred by pity, with his eyes fixed on the bears as they bite, and the net-fighters as they roll up their nets. May God avert from His own such a passion for murderous delight! (5) What sort of behavior is it to go from the assembly of God to the assembly of the Devil, from sky to sty, as the saying goes?² Those hands which you have lifted up to God, to tire them out afterwards applauding an actor? To cheer a gladiator with the same lips with which you have said 'Amen' over the Most Holy?³ To call out 'for ever and ever'⁴ to anyone else but to God and Christ?

---

1 Cf. Matt. 5.39; Luke 6.29.
2 Cf. A. Otto, *Die Sprichwörter und sprichwörtlichen Redensarten der Römer* (Leipzig 1890) 61.
3 Probably the 'Amen' pronounced by the Christian at receiving the Holy Eucharist; cf. Ambrose, *De sacramentis* 4.5: 'The priest says to you: "The Body of Christ," and you answer: "Amen".'
4 'For ever and ever!' were the words with which victorious gladiators and athletes were cheered.

Chapter 26

(1) Why, then, should such people not also be susceptible to demoniac possession? For we have the case of that woman —the Lord is witness—who went to the theater and returned home having a demon. (2) So, when in the course of exorcism the unclean spirit was hard pressed with the accusation that he had dared to seize a woman who believed, he answered boldly: 'I was fully justified in doing so, for I found her in my own domain.'[1] (3) It is well known, too, that to another woman, during the night following the very day on which she had listened to a tragic actor, a shroud was shown in a dream, and a rebuke called out to her, mentioning the tragic actor by name; nor was that woman still alive after five days.[2] (4) Indeed, how many other proofs can be drawn from those who, by consorting with the Devil at the spectacles, have fallen away from the Lord. For 'no man can serve two masters.'[3] 'What fellowship has light with darkness?'[4] What has life to do with death?

---

1 The passage allows us an insight into Tertullian's demonology. He believes that the theater belongs to the very sphere of action of the Devil, who can take possession of a Christian going there to look at the performances. It must be borne in mind that in the days of the early Christians the air was thought dangerously full of demons, a belief that led a number of early Christian writers to adopt peculiar doctrines in this matter.

2 In *De idololatria* 15.7-8, Tertullian tells another similar story. A Christian was severely chastised through a nocturnal vision because his servants had wreathed the gates of his house at the sudden announcement of a public festivity. Though he himself, being absent, had been unaware of it and had reproved the servants after the event, he was nevertheless rebuked. In view of the fact that the Roman state was especially wedded to the state religion, any action as the above-mentioned could be interpreted as a participation in idolatry.

3 Matt. 6.24.

4 2 Cor. 6.14.

Chapter 27

(1) We ought to hate those gatherings and meetings of the heathen, seeing that there the name of God is blasphemed, there the cry to set the lions upon us is raised every day,[1] there persecutions have their source, thence temptations are let loose. (2) What will you do when you are caught in that surging tide of wicked applause? Not that you are likely to suffer anything there at the hands of men (no one recognizes you as a Christian), but consider how you would fare in heaven. (3) Do you doubt that at the very moment when the Devil is raging in his assembly, all the angels look forth from heaven and note down every individual who has uttered blasphemy, who has listened to it, who has lent his tongue, who has lent his ears to the service of the Devil against God? (4) Will you, therefore, not shun the seats of Christ's enemies, that 'chair of pestilences',[2] and the very air that hangs over it and is polluted with sinful cries? I grant you that you have there some things that are sweet, pleasant, harmless, and even honorable. No one flavors poison with gall and hellebore; it is into spicy, well-flavored, and mostly sweet dishes that he instils that noxious stuff. So, too, the Devil pours into the deadly draught he prepares the most agreeable and most welcome gifts of God. (5) Everything, then, you find there, whether manly or honorable or sonorous or melodious or tender, take it for drippings of honey from a poisoned cake, and do not consider your appetite for the pleasure worth the danger you run from its sweetness.

---

1 Cf. Tertullian, *Apology* 40.1: 'If the Tiber rises as high as the city walls, if the Nile does not rise to the fields, if the weather will not change, if there is an earthquake, a famine, a plague—straightway the cry is heard: "Toss the Christians to the lion!"'
2 Ps. 1.1.

Chapter 28

(1) Let the Devil's own guests stuff themselves with sweets of that sort: the places, the times, and the host who invites are theirs. Our banquet, or marriage feast, has not yet come. We cannot recline with them at table, as they cannot with us. Things in this matter run their course in succession. Now they rejoice, and we are afflicted. (2) 'The world,' holy Scripture says, 'will rejoice, you will be sad.'[1] Let us mourn therefore, while the heathen rejoice, that, when they have begun to mourn, we may rejoice: lest sharing their joy now, then we may be sharing their mourning too. (3) You are too dainty, O Christian, if you desire pleasure also in this world; nay, more, you are a fool altogether if you deem this pleasure. (4) The philosophers at least have given the name 'pleasure' to quiet and tranquility;[2] in it they rejoice, they find their diversion in it, they even glory in it. But you—why, I find you sighing for goal posts, the stage, dust, the arena.[3] (5) I wish you would say plainly: 'We cannot live without pleasure!' Whereas we ought to die with pleasure. For what other prayer have we but that of the Apostle—'to leave the world and find our place with the Lord'?[4] Our pleasure is where our prayer is.

---

1 Cf. John 16.20.
2 Tertullian means the Epicureans. Cf. *Apology* 38.5: 'The Epicureans were allowed to decide upon a different truth regarding the nature of pleasure, namely, tranquility of mind.'
3 Cf. *ibid*. 38.4: 'Our tongues, our eyes, our ears have nothing to do with the madness of the circus, the shamelessness of the theater, the brutality of the arena, the vanity of the gymnasium.'
4 Cf. Phil. 1.23.

Chapter 29

(1) And finally, if you think that you are to pass this span of life in delights, why are you so ungrateful as not to be satisfied with so many and so exquisite pleasures given you by God, and not to recognize them? For what is more delightful than reconciliation with God, our Father and Lord, than the revelation of truth, the recognition of errors, and pardon for such grievous sins of the past? (2) What greater pleasure is there than distaste of pleasure itself, than contempt of all the world can give, than true liberty, than a pure conscience, than a contented life, than freedom from fear of death? (3) To trample under foot the gods of the heathen, to drive out demons, to effect cures,[1] to seek revelations,[2] to live unto God[3] —these are the pleasures, these are the spectacles of the Christians, holy, everlasting, and free of charge. In these find your circus games: behold the course of the world, count the generations slipping by, bear in mind the goal of the final consummation, defend the bonds of unity among the local

---

1 Casting out of demons and healing of the sick belonged together, inasmuch as it was commonly assumed that diseases were sometimes caused by demoniac influences.
2 Though the treatise belongs to Tertullian's early writings, the phrase 'to seek revelations' shows a trait in his character which carried him later from the Church into the sect of the Montanists, who contended that divine revelation had by no means come to a close with Christ and His Apostles, but had reached the stage of full maturity with Montanus and his associates. Tertullian felt himself attracted by this view on ecstatic prophecy, which insisted on the necessity of progressive revelation. 'To seek revelations' was, therefore, something highly commendable. Montanism was proud of the ecstatic experiences of its followers.
3 Cf. Rom. 6.10.

churches, awake at the signal of God, arise at the angel's trumpet, glory in the palms of martyrdom.[4]

(4) If the literary accomplishments of the stage delight you, we have sufficient literature of our own, enough verses and maxims, also enough songs and melodies;[5] and ours are not fables, but truths, not artful devices, but plain realities. (5) Do you want contests in boxing and wrestling? Here they are —contests of no slight account, and plenty of them. Behold impurity overthrown by chastity, faithlessness slain by faith, cruelty crushed by mercy, impudence put in the shade by modesty. Such are the contests among us, and in these we win our crowns. Do you have desire for blood, too? You have the blood of Christ.

Chapter 30

(1) Moreover, what a spectacle is already at hand—the second coming of the Lord, now no object of doubt, now exalted, now triumphant! What exultation will that be of

---

4 Tertullian makes a bold comparison between the pagan circus games and 'the circus games' of the Christians. One feature deserves special mention. In his day there began the slow amalgamation of the circus parties, the factions becoming more and more things of the past. The Christian counterpart of this fusion, Tertullian urges, must be the unity of the universal Church, obtained by the communion of the local churches among themselves. A similar comparison is found in one of the sermons of St. John Chrysostom, *Oratio de circo* (*PG* 59.568-569): Elias with his fiery chariot is the charioteer; the four Gospels form the four-horse team; starting-point and final goal of the race are earth and heaven respectively; the spectators are God and the inhabitants of heaven; the prize of victory is heaven itself.

5 The singing of hymns served in the early Church as a useful vehicle for the propagation of orthodox ideas against the heretics.

SPECTACLES   105

the angels, what glory of the saints as they rise again! What
a kingdom, the kingdom of the just thereafter! What a city,
the new Jerusalem!¹

(2) But there are yet other spectacles to come—that day
of the Last Judgment with its everlasting issues, unlooked
for by the heathen, the object of their derision, when the
hoary age of the world and all its generations will be con-
sumed in one fire. (3) What a panorama of spectacle on
that day! Which sight shall excite my wonder? Which, my
laughter? Where shall I rejoice, where exult—as I see so
many and so mighty kings, whose ascent to heaven used to
be made known by public announcement, now along with
Jupiter himself, along with the very witnesses of their ascent,
groaning in the depths of darkness?² Governors of provinces,
too, who persecuted the name of the Lord, melting in flames
fiercer than those they themselves kindled in their rage
against the Christians braving them with contempt? (4) Whom

---
1 Tertullian gives here a colorful description of the millennium, picturing the feverish expectation of an early return of Christ to establish an earthly kingdom of the just, whose duration is frequently given as one thousand years. The deceased saints will rise again to participate in this glorious reign, during which all powers hostile to God will be rendered impotent. The millennialists thought to find a confirmation of their belief in the description of the New Jerusalem in Apocalypse 20-21. Millenarian expectations were especially strong in the post-apostolic age, but grew less and less in the course of the third century. The reign of Christ on earth with His saints will be followed by the universal resurrection and the Last Judgment which Tertullian describes in the remaining part of this chapter.
2 Since the apotheosis of Julius Caesar it was a common practice of Roman statecraft to recognize departed emperors as gods. The deification was made known by an official decree of the senate. There were always witnesses who vouched for having actually observed the ascension of the deceased emperor. An ex-prator, for instance, testified by oath to have seen the form of Emperor Augustus on its way from the funeral pyre to heaven (Suetonius, *Augustus* 100).

else shall I behold? Those wise philosophers blushing before their followers as they burn together, the followers to whom they taught that the world is no concern of God's, whom they assured that either they had no souls at all or that what souls they had would never return to their former bodies? The poets also, trembling, not before the judgment seat of Rhadamanthus or of Minos,[3] but of Christ whom they did not expect to meet. (5) Then will the tragic actors be worth hearing, more vocal in their own catastrophe; then the comic actors will be worth watching, much lither of limb in the fire; then the charioteer will be worth seeing, red all over on his fiery wheel; then the athletes will be worth observing, not in their gymnasiums, but thrown about by fire—unless I might not wish to look at them even then but would prefer to turn an insatiable gaze on those who vented their rage on the Lord. (6) 'This is He,' I will say, 'the son of the carpenter and the harlot,[4] the sabbath-breaker,[5] the Samaritan who had a devil.[6] This is He whom you purchased from Judas,[7] this is He who was struck with reed and fist, defiled with spittle,[8] given gall and vinegar to drink.[9] This is He whom the disciples secretly stole away to spread the story of His resurrection,[10] or whom the gardener

---

3 In ancient mythology Rhadamanthus, Minos, and Aeacus, the three just men of early days, are the judges of the dead in the lower regions.
4 One of the numerous slanders that were circulated against Christ; see Matt. 13.55.
5 Cf. John 5.18.
6 Cf. John 8.48.
7 Cf. Matt. 26.14,15; Luke 22.4,5.
8 Cf. Matt. 26.67; Mark 14.65.
9 Cf. John 19.29.
10 According to Matt. 28.11-15, the chief priests and elders bribed the soldiers of the guard to spread the story that the disciples had come by night and stolen the body of Christ. Tertullian mentions and refutes the often-repeated story in his *Apology* 21.20-22.

removed lest his lettuces be trampled by the throng of curious idlers.'[11]

(7) What praetor or consul or quaestor or priest with all his munificence will ever bestow on you the favor of beholding and exulting in such sights? Yet, such scenes as these are in a measure already ours by faith in the vision of the spirit. But what are those things which 'eye has not seen nor ear heard and which have not entered into the heart of man'?[12] Things of greater delight, I believe, than circus, both kinds of theater, and any stadium.

---

11 The story of the gardener removing the body of Christ may ultimately go back to John 20.15. Tertullian is the only ancient writer to mention it.
12 1 Cor. 2.9.

THE APPAREL
OF WOMEN

Translated by
EDWIN A. QUAIN, S.J., Ph.D.
Fordham University

INTRODUCTION

N WRITING HIS TWO BOOKS on *The Apparel of Women* (*De cultu feminarum*) Tertullian addresses himself especially to women who have lately become converts to the Christian faith.[1] With solemn sternness, and often with caustic wit, he castigates the luxury and extravagance of dress and adornment which fashion and convention have imposed on the fair sex of his day. He describes these eccentricities of feminine vanity as fitting only for harlots and immodest women, and contrasts them with the virtues with which alone it becomes Christian women to embellish themselves.

The two books do not form a coherent whole in the sense that the second book is a continuation of the first. The second is rather a new and more comprehensive treatment of the subject of the first book which the author left unfinished, apparently considering it unsatisfactory. Originally, the two books were distinct works, the first being entitled *De habitu muliebri*, the second *De cultu feminarum*.[2]

---

1 'Blessed' (*benedictae;* cf. Book 2.4.1; 5.5; 9.4; 13.5) was an appellation given especially to catechumens and neophytes. See above, p. 17 n.1.
2 See the critical apparatus in Kroymann's edition, *Corpus Christianorum,* Series Latina 1.343.

The contents of the first book can be summed up as follows. In the introductory chapter, Tertullian reminds the Christian women that it was through Eve, the first woman, that sin entered into the world; hence, it is rather a penitential garb that is best suited to the daughters of Eve. According to the *Book of Henoch,* ornaments and cosmetics are the inventions of the fallen angels and, therefore, of diabolical origin (Ch. 2). Chapter 3 is devoted to a defense of the genuineness of this apocryphal work. With Chapter 4 the author resumes the treatment of his topic. He proposes to examine female toilet itself, distinguishing between *cultus* (dress which consists of gold, silver, jewels, and clothes) and *ornatus* (make-up which includes care of the hair, skin, etc.). To the first he imputes the crime of ambition; to the second, that of prostitution. In dealing with the first (Ch. 5-7) he tries to show that gold and silver are merely earthy materials like others and hence, in themselves, possess no greater value than other metals. The same is true concerning precious stones and pearls. It is solely their rarity that makes them so desirable. In like manner the dyeing of materials for clothing is unnatural. 'God is not pleased by what He Himself did not produce. We cannot suppose that God was unable to produce sheep with purple or sky-blue fleeces. If He was able, then He chose not to do it; and what God refused to do certainly cannot be lawful for men to make. Therefore, those things cannot be the best by nature which do not come from God, who is the author of nature. Hence, they must be understood to be from the Devil, who is the corrupter of nature' (Ch. 8). The use of God's creatures must be regulated by the distribution the Creator Himself has made of them. Out of immoderate desire for possessing them there grows ambition which, with other vices in its train, may become so powerful 'that one damsel carries the whole income from a large fortune on her small body' (Ch. 9).

Here Tertullian breaks off suddenly, without having even touched upon the second part of his topic (*ornatus*—'make-up'). The topic of the second book is the same, but the author has reversed the arrangement of the subject matter. He deals first with the question of cosmetics, ostentatious dressing of the hair, etc. (*ornatus*), and then with jewelry and dress (*cultus*). He prefaces the book by pointing out that an excessive desire to please does not agree with a Christian woman's principal virtue, which is modesty (Ch. 1). By an inordinate love of admiration the woman can become the object of sinful desires and thus be an accessory to the sins of others (Ch. 2). As 'pursuers of things spiritual,' Christian women may safely scorn all glory that is 'in the flesh' (Ch. 3). Married women have no valid reason for enhancing their natural beauty, since they have to please no one else but their own husbands (Ch. 4). Though there is no virtue in squalor and filth, and proper care ought to be taken of the body, the use of skin creams, rouges, powders and other kinds of cosmetics to improve complexion, amounts to criticizing God's creative workmanship. These artificial devices for enhancing personal appearance have been invented by the Devil, who in his own wily way tempts man to do violence to God Himself (Ch. 5). The same holds true concerning the foolish custom of dyeing the hair and the elaborate styles of head-dress (Ch. 6-7). In order to avoid any accusation of bias against the fair sex, Tertullian makes it clear that his remarks apply in like manner to males. As a matter of fact, he finds any excessive care bestowed by men on their personal appearance more blameworthy, because it is inconsistent with that gravity which is the distinctive mark of the Christian man (Ch. 8).

The Christian woman must not only shun any artificiality in her toilet, but, because of the tribulations of the times, also renounce that elegance in clothing and finery which is allowed and in keeping with her social rank (Ch. 9). After describing the origin of the desire for expensive clothes and jewelry in the same manner as in the first book, the author suggests 'that all these things have been provided by God at the beginning and placed in the world in order that they should now be means of testing the moral strength of His servants so that, in being permitted to use things, we might have the opportunity of showing our self-restraint' (Ch. 10). Simplicity in clothing becomes the Christian woman, because it edifies her fellow men and serves the glorification of God (Ch. 11). Even the mere resemblance of coquetry must be avoided. A Christian woman always wears a modest garb and never that of a harlot (Ch. 12). Passionate love for finery weakens the strength of our faith, makes us reluctant to fulfil our duties as Christians, and renders us incapable of remaining steadfast in persecution. Reminding his readers of the afflictions visited upon the Church of his day, but at the same time holding out to them the stirring hope of final victory, Tertullian exclaims: 'The lives of the Christians are never spent in gold, and now less than ever, but in iron. The stoles of martyrdom are being prepared, and the angels who are to carry us [to heaven] are being awaited.' The book ends with an exhortation that is distinguished by great rhetorical refinement: 'Go forth to meet those angels, adorned with the cosmetics and ornaments of the Prophets and Apostles. Let your whiteness flow from simplicity, let modesty be the cause of your rosy complexion, paint your eyes with reserve, your mouth with silence, hang on your ears the words of God, bind on your neck the yoke of Christ . . . Dress yourselves in the silk of probity, the fine linen of holiness, and the purple of chastity. Decked out in this manner, you will have God Himself for your lover' (Ch. 13).

As we may expect, exaggerations are not lacking in either of the two books. But the second is much milder in tone and more tolerant in its views. The leading idea of both occurs in two of Tertullian's earlier writings, namely, his exhortation *To the Martyrs* and his treatise *Spectacles*: to be a Christian means renunciation of everything pagan and complete surrender to the divine Master whose teachings must be the sole and supreme norm of a Christian's conduct in everyday life. The first book was written after *Spectacles,* since Tertullian explicitly refers to the latter (8.4). Moreover, the way in which he speaks of the dress of women in Chapter 20 of *Prayer,* without mentioning that he has treated the same topic in two special works, seems to indicate that *The Apparel of Women* was composed after the treatise on *Prayer.* There is no trace of Montanistic ideas in either of the two books. They were the main source of St. Cyprian's treatise, *The Dress of Virgins* (*De habitu virginum*).

The text followed in the present translation is that of Aem. Kroymann in *Corpus Christianorum,* Series Latina 1 (Turnholti 1954) 341-370.

SELECT BIBLIOGRAPHY

Texts:

A. Kroymann, *Corpus Christianorum*, Series Latina 1 (Turnholti 1954) 341-370; also, CSEL 70 (1942) 59-95.

J. Marra, *De corona, De cultu feminarum* (Corpus Scriptorum Latinorum Paravianum; Turin 1951).

Secondary Sources:

G. Cortellezzi, 'Il concetto della donna nelle opere di Tertulliano,' *Didaskaleion* (1923) 1.5-29; 2.57-79; 3.43-100.

H. Koch, 'Tertullianisches,' *Theologische Studien und Kritiken* 101 (1929) 469-471.

L. B. Lawler, 'Two Portraits from Tertullian,' *Classical Journal* 25 (1929) 19-23.

J. Quasten, *Patrology* 2 (Westminster, Md. 1953) 294-296.

THE APPAREL OF WOMEN

BOOK ONE

Chapter 1

IF THERE EXISTED upon earth a faith in proportion to the reward that faith will receive in heaven, no one of you, my beloved sisters, from the time when you came to know the living God and recognized your own state, that is, the condition of being a woman, would have desired a too attractive garb, and much less anything that seemed too ostentatious. I think, rather, that you would have dressed in mourning garments and even neglected your exterior, acting the part of mourning and repentant Eve in order to expiate more fully by all sorts of penitential garb that which woman derives from Eve—the ignominy, I mean, of original sin and the odium of being the cause of the fall of the human race. 'In sorrow and anxiety, you will bring forth, O woman, and you are subject to your husband, and he is your master.'[1] Do you not believe that you are [each] an Eve?

---
1 Cf. Gen. 3.16.

(2) The sentence of God on this sex of yours lives on even in our times and so it is necessary that the guilt should live on, also. You are the one who opened the door to the Devil, you are the one who first plucked the fruit of the forbidden tree, you are the first who deserted the divine law; you are the one who persuaded him whom the Devil was not strong enough to attack. All too easily you destroyed the image of God, man. Because of your desert, that is, death, even the Son of God had to die. And you still think of putting adornments over the skins of animals that cover you? (3) Well, now—if, in the very beginning of the world, the Milesians had invented wool by shearing sheep, and if the Chinese had woven the strands of silk, and the Tyrians had invented dye and the Phrygians embroidery and the Babylonians weaving, if pearls had gleamed and rubies flashed with light, if gold itself had already been brought forth from the bowels of earth by man's greed, and finally, if a mirror had already been capable of giving forth its lying image, do you think that Eve, after she had been expelled from Paradise and was already dead, would have longed for all of these fineries? She would not. Therefore, she ought not to crave them or even to know them now, if she desires to be restored to life again. Those things which she did not have or know when she lived in God, all those things are the trappings appropriate to a woman who was condemned and is dead, arrayed as if to lend splendor to her funeral.

Chapter 2

(1) For those, too, who invented these things are condemned to the penalty of death, namely, those angels who

rushed from heaven upon the daughters of men so that this ignominy is also attached to woman.[1] For when these fallen angels had revealed certain well-hidden material substances, and numerous other arts that were only faintly revealed, to an age much more ignorant than ours—for surely they are the ones who disclosed the secrets of metallurgy, discovered the natural properties of herbs, made known the power of charms, and aroused the desire to pry into everything, including the interpretation of the stars[2]—they granted to women as their special and, as it were, personal property these means of feminine vanity: the radiance of precious stones with which necklaces are decorated in different colors, the bracelets of gold which they wrap around their arms, the colored preparations which are used to dye wool, and that black powder which they use to enhance the beauty of their eyes.

(2) If you want to know what kind of things these are, you can easily learn from the character of those who taught these arts. Have sinners ever been able to show and provide anything conducive to holiness, unlawful lovers anything contributing to chastity, rebel angels anything promoting the fear of God? If, indeed, we must call what they have passed on 'teachings,' then evil teachers must of necessity have taught evil lessons; if these are the wages of sin, then there can be nothing beautiful about the reward for something evil. But why should they have taught and granted such things?

(3) Are we to think that women without the material of adornment or without the tricks of beautifying themselves would not have been able to please men when these same

---
1 Cf. Gen. 6.1-2.
2 Cf. *Book of Henoch* 8.1,3.

women, unadorned and uncouth and, as I might say, crude and rude, were able to impress angels? Or would the latter have appeared beggarly lovers who insolently demanded favors for nothing, unless they had brought some gift to the women they had attracted into marriage? But this is hardly conceivable. The women who possessed angels as husbands could not desire anything further, for, surely they had already made a fine match.[3]

(4) The angels, on the other hand, who certainly thought sometimes of the place whence they had fallen and longed for heaven after the heated impulses of lust had quickly passed, rewarded in this way the very gift of woman's natural beauty as the cause of evil, that is, that woman should not profit from her happiness, but, rather, drawn away from the ways of innocence and sincerity, should be united with them in sin against God. They must have been certain that all ostentation, ambition, and love achieved by carnal pleasure would be displeasing God. You see, these are the angels whom we are destined to judge,[4] these are the angels whom we renounce in baptism, these are the very things on account of which they deserved to be judged by men.

(5) What connection, therefore, can there be between their affairs and their judges? What business can there be between the condemned and their judges? I suppose, the same as between Christ and Belial.[5] How can we with good conscience mount that judgment-seat to pronounce sentence against those whose gifts we are now trying to get? You realize, of course, that the same angelic nature is promised to you, women, the selfsame sex is promised to you as to men,[6]

---
3 Cf. Gen. 6.2.
4 Cf. 1 Cor. 6.3.
5 Cf. 2 Cor. 6.15.
6 Cf. Matt. 22.30.

and the selfsame dignity of being a judge. Therefore, unless here in this life we begin to practise being judges by condemning their works which we are destined to condemn in them some day, then they will rather judge us and condemn us.

Chapter 3

(1) I am aware that the Book of Henoch which assigns this role to the angels is not accepted because it is not admitted into the Jewish canon. I suppose it is not accepted because they did not think that a book written before the flood could have survived that catastrophe which destroyed the whole world. If that be their reason, let them remember that Noe was a great-grandson of Henoch[1] and a surviver of the deluge. He would have grown up in the family tradition and the name of Henoch would have been a household word and he would surely have remembered the grace that his ancestor enjoyed before God and the reputation of all his preaching, especially since Henoch gave the command to his son Mathusala that the knowledge of his deeds should be passed on to his posterity. Therefore, Noe could surely have succeeded in the trusteeship of his ancestor's preaching because he would not have kept silent about the wonderful providence of God who saved him from destruction as well as in order to enhance the glory of his own house.

(2) Now, supposing that Noe could not have had this knowledge thus directly, there could still be another reason to warrant our assertion of the genuineness of this book: he could have easily rewritten it under the inspiration of the

---

1 Cf. Gen. 5.21-29.

Spirit after it had been destroyed by the violence of the flood, just as, when Jerusalem was destroyed at the hands of the Babylonians, every document of Jewish literature is known to have been restored by Esdras.

(3) But, since Henoch in this same book tells us of our Lord, we must not reject anything at all which really pertains to us. Do we not read that every word of Scripture useful for edification is divinely inspired?[2] As you very well know, it was afterwards rejected by the Jews for the same reason that prompted them to reject almost all the other portions which prophesied about Christ. Now, it is not at all surprising that they refused to accept certain Scriptures which spoke of Him when they were destined not to receive Him when He spoke to them Himself.[3] To all that we may add the fact that we have a testimony to Henoch in the Epistle of Jude the Apostle.[4]

Chapter 4

(1) Let us assume for the moment that we do not condemn all womanly ornament ahead of time merely because of the fate of those who invented it. Let those angels be blamed only for the repudiation of heaven and their carnal marriage. Let us rather examine the character of these things themselves so that we may learn the reasons why they are so desirable. Female toilet has two possible purposes—dress and make-up. (2) We use the word dress when we refer to what they call womanly grace, whereas make-up is more fittingly called womanly disgrace. Articles of dress are considered gold and

---

2 Cf. 2 Tim. 3.16.
3 Cf. John 1.11.
4 Cf. Jude 14.

silver and jewels and clothes, whereas make-up consists in the care of hair and of the skin and of those parts of the body which attract the eye. On one we level the accusation of ambition; on the other, that of prostitution. I say that now, O handmaid of God, that you may well know what, out of all these, is proper for your behavior, since you are judged by different principles, namely, those of humility and chastity.

Chapter 5

(1) Now, gold and silver, the principal materials of worldly dress, are necessarily the same as that from which they come, namely, earth. To be sure, they are earth of a nobler sort. For, wet with tears of those condemned to penal labor in the deadly foundries of the accursed mines, those 'precious' metals leave the name of earth in the fire behind them and, as fugitives from the mines, they change from objects of torment into articles of ornament, from instruments of punishment into tools of allurement, from symbols of ignominy into signs of honor.

(2) But the basic nature of iron and brass and of other metals, including the cheapest, is the same [as that of gold and silver], both as to their earthy origin and manufacture in the mines, and hence, according to nature itself, the substance of gold and silver is no more noble than theirs. Should, however, gold and silver derive their estimation from the quality of being useful, then certainly the value of iron and brass is higher, since their usefulness has been determined in such a way [by the creator] that they discharge functions of their own more numerous and more necessary for human life, and at the same time lend themselves to the more becoming uses

of gold and silver. We know that rings are made of iron, and the history of antiquity still preserves [the fame of] certain vessels for eating and drinking made of brass. It is no concern of ours if the mad plentifulness of gold and silver serves to make utensils even for foul purposes. (3) Certainly you will never plow a field with a golden plow nor will any ship be held together with silver bolts; you would never drive a golden mattock into the earth nor would you drive a silver nail into a plank. I leave unnoticed the fact that the necessities of our whole life depend upon iron and brass, merely mentioning that those precious materials themselves, requiring both to be dug out of the mines and forged into their specific form to be of any use whatsoever, cannot even be mined without the use of iron and brass.

(4) From this, then, you must already judge why it is that gold and silver enjoy such high estimation as to be preferred to other materials that are related to them by nature and are much more valuable if we consider their usefulness.

Chapter 6

(1) But how shall I explain those precious little stones which share their glory with gold, other than to say that they are only little stones and pebbles and tiny little bits of the selfsame earth? They certainly are not required for laying foundations or for building up walls or supporting pediments or giving compactness to roofs; the only building they seem to erect is this silly admiration of women. They are cautiously cut that they may shine, they are cunningly set that they may glitter, they are carefully pierced so as to hang properly and render to gold a meretricious service in return. (2) Moreover,

whatever love of display fishes up from the seas around Britain or India is merely a kind of shellfish, and its taste is no better than that of the giant mussel. Now, there is no reason why I should not approve of shellfish as the fruit of the sea. If, however, this shellfish produces some sort of growth inside of it, this should be considered a fault rather than a cause for glory. And even though we call this thing a pearl, it certainly must be seen to be nothing else but a hard and round lump inside a shellfish.

There is a tradition that gems also come from the foreheads of dragons, just as we sometimes find a certain stony substance in the brains of fish. (3) This would indeed crown it all: the Christian woman in need of something from the serpent to add to her grace. It is probably in this way that she is going to tread upon the serpent's head[1] while around her neck or even on top of her own head she carries ornaments that come from the head of the Devil!

Chapter 7

(1) The only thing that gives glamour to all these articles is that they are rare and that they have to be imported from a foreign country. In the country they come from they are not highly priced. When a thing is abundant it is always cheap. Among certain barbarians where gold is common and plentiful the people in the workhouses are bound with golden chains and the wicked are weighed down by riches and the richness of their bonds is in proportion to their wickedness. At last a way seems to have been found to prevent gold from

---
1 Cf. Gen. 3.15.

being loved. (2) We ourselves have seen the nobility of jewels blushing before the matrons in Rome at the contemptuous way the Parthians and Medes and the rest of their countrymen used them. It would seem they use jewels for any reason *except* adornment; emeralds lurk in their belts, and only the sword knows the round jewels lie hidden in its scabbard, and the large pearls on their rough boots wish to be lifted out of the mud. In short, they wear nothing so richly jeweled as that which ought not to be jeweled at all; in this way it is not conspicuous, or else is conspicuous only to show that the wearer does not care for it.

Chapter 8

(1) In the same manner, even their servants cause the glory to fade from the colors of our garments. They use as pictures on their walls whole purple and violet and royal hangings which you with great labor undo and change into different forms. Purple among them is cheaper than red. (2) For, what legitimate honor can garments derive from adulteration with illegitimate colors? God is not pleased by what He Himself did not produce. We cannot suppose that God was unable to produce sheep with purple or sky-blue fleeces. If He was able, then He chose not to do it, and what God refused to do certainly cannot be lawful for man to make. Therefore, those things cannot be the best by nature which do not come from God, who is the Author of nature. Hence, they must be understood to be from the Devil, who is the corrupter of nature. (3) Obviously, they cannot come from anyone else if they are not from God, because those things which are not of God must be of His rival. And there is

no other rival of God except the Devil and his angels. Now, even if the material out of which something is made is from God it does not therefore follow that every way of enjoying these things is also of God. We always have to raise the question of not only whence shellfish come, but what task is assigned to them and where they will exhibit their beauty. (4) For it is clear that all those profane pleasures of worldly spectacles about which we have already written a special treatise,[1] and even idolatry itself, derive their material from the creatures of God. (5) But that is no reason why a Christian should devote himself to the madness of the circus or the cruelties of the arena or the foulness of the theater, just because God created horses, panthers, and the human voice; any more than he can commit idolatry with impunity because the incense and the wine and fire which feeds on them, and the animals which are the victims, are God's workmanship, since even the material thing which is adored is God's creature. (6) Thus, then, with regard to the use of the material substances, too; that use is falsely justified on the basis of their origin from God, since it is alien to God and is tainted with worldly glory.

Chapter 9

(1) For, just as certain things which are distributed by God in individual countries or in individual regions of the sea are mutually foreign to one another, so in turn they are considered rare by foreigners but rightfully neglected or not desired at all in their land of origin, because no anxious

---

[1] Tertullian refers to his treatise on *Spectacles*.

longing exists there for a glory which is hardly appreciated by the natives. So, it is merely because of this distribution of possessions which God has arranged as He wished that the rarity and singularity of an object which always finds favor with foreigners stirs up a great desire to possess it for the simple reason of not having what God has given to others. (2) And out of this another vice grows—that of immoderate greed—although a possession may be necessary, moderation must be exercised. This vice will be ambition and the very word 'ambition' must be interpreted in this way that from concupiscence encompassing [*ambiente*] the soul a desire of glory is born—a great desire no doubt, which, as we have said, is not approved either by nature or by truth, but only by a vicious passion of the soul. There exist still other vices that are connected with ambition and glory. Thus it is this vice of ambition that has enhanced the prices of things that by doing so it might add fuel to itself also. (3) For, concupiscence has a way of growing greater in proportion as it sets a higher value upon that which it desires. A large fortune can be lifted out of a little box; a million sesterces can hang from a single thread; one slender neck can be surrounded by jewels worth many forests and islands; two slender lobes of the ears can cost a fortune; and each finger on the left hand puts to shame any money-bag. Such is the power of ambition that one damsel carries the whole income from a large fortune on her small body.

BOOK TWO

Chapter 1

HANDMAIDENS OF THE LORD, my fellow servants and sisters, on the strength of the right of fellow servantship and brother—the right by which I, the very last of you, am counted as one of you—I am emboldened to address to you some words,¹ not, of course, of affection, but paving the way for affection in the cause of your salvation. Salvation, however, and not of women only, but also of men, is especially to be procured in the observance of modesty. For, since we are all temples of God because the Holy Spirit has entered into us and sanctified us,² modesty is the sacristan and priestess of that temple; modesty will prevent anything unclean or profane from entering, lest God who dwells therein should be offended and leave the defiled abode.

(2) But it is not our object now to speak of modesty which the omnipresent divine precepts sufficiently promulgate and prescribe, but I do intend to talk about something that pertains to modesty, that is, the way in which you ought to

---
1 Cf. Eph. 3.8. See the same modest form of reference to himself in *To the Martyrs* 1.2 and *Prayer* 20.1.
2 Cf. 1 Cor. 3.16; 2 Cor. 6.16.

conduct yourselves.³ For, too many women—I trust God will permit me to reprove this very thing by censuring it in all concerned—either in ignorant simplicity or downright dishonesty so conduct themselves as if modesty consisted solely in the integrity of the flesh and the avoidance of actual sin and as if there were no need to care for the externals, I mean about the arrangement of dress and ornament. They go right ahead in their former pursuit of beauty and glamour, showing in their walk the very same appearance as do women of the pagans who are devoid of all understanding of true modesty because there is nothing true in those who do not know God, the Master and Teacher of all truth. (3) For, if any modesty can be assumed to exist among the Gentiles, it is certainly so imperfect and defective that even though it asserts itself to some extent in the way of thinking, it destroys itself by a licentious extravagance in the matter of dress after the manner of the usual perversity of the Gentiles of actually desiring that of which it shuns the effect. How many pagan women are there who do not desire to be pleasing even to strangers? Who is there among them who does not try to have herself painted up in order that when desired she may refuse? In fact, this is a characteristic of Gentile modesty, not actually to fall, but to be willing to do so, or even not to be willing, yet not quite to refuse. Is there any wonder? All things are perverse which are not from God.

(4) Let those women, therefore, look to it, who, by not holding on to the whole good, easily mix with evil even what they do hold fast. It is your obligation to be different from them, as in all other things, so also in your gait, since you ought to be perfect as your heavenly Father is perfect.⁴

---
3 Cf. 1 Thess. 4.1.
4 Cf. Matt. 5.48.

Chapter 2

(1) You must know that perfect modesty, that is, Christian modesty, requires not only that you never desire to be an object of desire on the part of others, but that you even hate to be one. First of all, because the effort to please by external beauty does not come from a sound conscience, since beauty we know to be naturally the exciter of lust. Why, then, excite that evil against yourself? Why invite something to which you profess to be a stranger? Secondly, because we ought not to open the way to temptations. For, although by their vehemence—from which God guard His own—they sometimes lead to greater perfection, they certainly disturb the soul by presenting a stumbling block to it.[1]

(2) We ought, indeed, to walk so in holiness and in the total fullness of our faith that we can be confident and sure in our own conscience, desiring that modesty may abide in us to the end, yet not presumptuously relying on it. For, the one who is presumptuous is less likely to feel apprehension, and he who feels less apprehension takes less precaution, and the one who takes less precaution is in the greater danger. Fear is the true foundation of our salvation, whereas presumption is a hindrance to fear. (3) Therefore, it will be more useful for us if we foresee the possibility that we may fall than if we presume that we cannot fall. For in anticipating a fall we will be fearful, and if fearful we will take care, and if we take care we shall be safe. On the other hand, if we are presumptuous and have neither fear nor take any precautions, it will be difficult for us to achieve salvation. He who acts securely and not at the same time warily does not possess a safe and firm security, whereas he who is wary can truly say that he will be

---

1 Cf. Matt. 18.7.

safe. May the Lord in His mercy always take care of His servants that they may happily be permitted even to presume on His goodness.

(4) But why are we a source of danger to others? Why do we excite concupiscence in others? If the Lord in amplifying the Law[2] does not make a distinction in penalty between the actual commission of fornication and its desire,[3] I do not know whether He will grant impunity to one who is the cause of perdition to another. For he perishes as soon as he looks upon your beauty with desire, and has already committed in his soul what he desires, and you have become a sword [of perdition] to him so that, even though you are free from the actual crime of unchastity, you are not altogether free from the odium [attached to it]. As for instance, when a robbery has been committed on some man's land, the actual crime is not imputed to the master, but, as long as the estate is in bad repute, he also is tinged with a certain amount of infamy.

(5) Are we, then, going to paint our faces in order that others may perish? What about the Scripture which tells us: 'Thou shalt love thy neighbor as thyself.[4] Do not seek only your interests, but those of your neighbor'?[5] Now, no utterance of the Holy Spirit should be restricted only to its present matter, but must be directed and referred to every occasion to which its application is useful. Since, therefore, our own welfare as well as that of others is involved in the pursuit of beauty which is so dangerous, it is time for you to realize that you must not only shun the display of false and studied beauty, but also remove all traces of natural grace by concealment

---

2 Cf. Matt. 5.17.
3 Cf. Matt. 5.28.
4 Matt. 19.19; 22.39; cf. Lev. 19.18.
5 1 Cor. 10.24.

and negligence, as equally dangerous to the glances of another's eyes. (6) For, although comeliness is not to be censured as being a bodily happiness, as an additional gift of the divine Sculptor, and as a kind of fair vestment of the soul, it must be feared because of the affront and violence on the part of those who pursue it. This danger even Abraham, the father of the faith, greatly feared because of his wife's shapely form and, untruthfully introducing Sara as his sister, he purchased his life by her disgrace.[6]

Chapter 3

(1) Now, let it be granted that excellence of form is not to be feared as if it were either harmful to those who possess it or ruinous to those who desire it or dangerous for those who come in contact with it; let us further assume that it is neither an occasion of temptation nor surrounded by danger of scandal[1]—it is enough to say that it is not necessary for the handmaidens of God. For, where modesty exists there is no need of beauty, since, strictly speaking, the normal use and effect of beauty is wantonness, unless, of course, someone can think of some other good that flows from bodily beauty. Let those women enhance the beauty they possess or seek for beauty they do not possess who think that they bestow upon themselves what is demanded from beauty when they exhibit it to others.

(2) But someone will say: Suppose we exclude wantonness and give to chastity its rightful place. Why should we not be permitted to enjoy the simple praise that comes to beauty and

---

6 Cf. Gen. 12.11-13.

1 Cf. Matt. 18.7.

to glory in a bodily good? Let whoever takes pleasure in glorying in the flesh see to that.[2] For us, in the first place, there can be no studious pursuit of glory, since glory is of its very nature a kind of exaltation and, in turn, exaltation is incongruous for those who, according to God's precepts, profess humility.[3] Secondly, if all glory is vain and foolish, how much more so that which is a glorying in the flesh, particularly in us? For, if we must glory in something, let it be in the spirit rather than in the flesh that we wish to please, since we are pursuers of things spiritual.[4]

(3) Let us find our joy in that which is really our business. Let us seek for glory in those things in which we hope for salvation. To be sure, a Christian will also glory in his flesh, but only after it has endured torture for Christ's sake in order that the spirit may be crowned in the flesh rather than that the flesh may attract the eyes and sighs of a young man. Thus, a thing that from every point of view is useless to you, you can safely scorn if you do not possess it and neglect if you do possess it.

Chapter 4

(1) Holy women, let none of you, if she is naturally beautiful, be an occasion of sin; certainly, if even she be so, she must not increase beauty, but try to subdue it. If I were speaking to Gentiles, I would give you a Gentile precept and one that is common to all: you are bound to please no one except your own husbands. And, you will please your husbands in the proportion that you take no pains to please any-

---
2 Cf. Phil. 3.3.
3 Cf. Matt. 11.29; 1 Peter 5.6; James 4.10.
4 Cf. Rom. 8.8,9.

one else. Be unconcerned, blessed sisters: no wife is really ugly to her own husband. She was certainly pleasing to him when he chose to marry her, whether it was for her beauty or for her character. Let none of you think that she will necessarily incur the hatred and aversion of her husband if she spends less time in the adornment of her person.

(2) Every husband demands that his wife be chaste; but beauty a Christian husband certainly does not demand, because we Christians are not fascinated by the same things that the Gentiles think to be good. If, on the other hand, the husband be an infidel, he will be suspicious of beauty precisely because of the unfavorable opinion the Gentiles have of us.[1] For whose sake, then, are you cultivating your beauty? If for a Christian, he does not demand it, and if for an infidel, he does not believe it unless it is artless. Why, then, are you so eager to please either one who is suspicious or one who does not desire it?

Chapter 5

(1) To be sure, what I am suggesting is not intended to recommend to you an utterly uncultivated and unkempt appearance; I see no virtue in squalor and filth, but I am talking about the proper way and norm and just measure in the care of the body. We must not go beyond what is desired by those who strive for natural and demure neatness. We must not go beyond what is pleasing to God. (2) For, surely, those women sin against God who anoint their faces with creams, stain their cheeks with rouge, or lengthen their eye-

---

[1] Tertullian here refers to one of the vulgar accusations made against the Christians by the pagans, that of Oedipean intercourse.

brows with antimony. Obviously, they are not satisfied with the creative skill of God; in their own person, without doubt, they censure and criticize the Maker of all things! Surely they are finding fault when they try to perfect and add to His work, taking these their additions, of course, from a rival artist. (3) This rival artist is the Devil. For, who else would teach how to change the body but he who by wickedness transformed the spirit of man? It is he, no doubt, who prepared ingenious devices of this sort that in your own persons it may be proved that to a certain degree you do violence to God.

(4) Whatever is born, that is the work of God. Obviously, then, anything else that is added must be the work of the Devil. What a wicked thing it is to attempt to add to a divine handiwork the inventions of the Devil! We do not find our servants borrowing something from our foes, nor do soldiers desire anything from the enemy of their general. For, it is certainly a sin for you to solicit a favor from the enemy of Him in whose hands you lie. Can a true Christian really be helped by that evil one in anything? If he is, I do not think he will be a Christian for long, for he will belong to him from whom he strives to learn. (5) How alien are these things to your principles and to your promises—how unworthy of the name of Christian that you bear! To have a painted face, you on whom simplicity in every form is enjoined! To lie in your appearance, you to whom lying with the tongue is not allowed! To seek for that which is not your own, you who are taught to keep hands off the goods of another! To commit adultery in your appearance, you who should eagerly strive after modesty! Believe me, blessed sisters! How can you keep the commandments of God if you do not keep in your own persons the features which He has bestowed on you?

Chapter 6

(1) I see some women dye their hair blonde by using saffron. They are even ashamed of their country, sorry that they were not born in Germany or in Gaul! Thus, as far as their hair is concerned, they give up their country. It is hardly a good omen for them that they wish their hair to be flame-colored and mistake for beauty something which merely stains them. (2) As a matter of fact, the strength of these bleaches really does harm to the hair, and the constant application of even any natural moist substance will bring ruin to the head itself, just as the warmth of the sun, while desirable for giving life and dryness to the hair, if overdone is hurtful. How can they achieve beauty when they are doing themselves harm; how can they make something attractive by means of filth? Shall a Christian woman heap saffron on her hair as upon an altar? For, surely, anything that is normally burned in honor of an unclean spirit, may be considered as a sacrifice to idols, unless it is applied for honest and necessary and wholesome uses for which all of God's creatures were provided. (3) But the Lord has said: 'Which of you can make a white hair black or out of a black a white?'[1] Thus do they refute the word of the Lord. 'Behold,' they say, 'out of white or black we make it blonde, which is surely more attractive.' Why, you will even find people who are ashamed of having lived to old age and try to make their hair black when it is white. Are you not ashamed of such folly? Trying to keep it a secret that you have reached that age for which you longed and prayed, sighing for youth which was a time of sin, missing the chance to show some true maturity! I hope that the daughters of Wisdom will avoid such foolishness. The

---
1 Matt. 5.36.

harder we work to conceal our age the more we reveal it. (4) Or does your eternal life depend on the youthful appearance of your hair? Is that the incorruptibility which we have to put on for the reign that is to come[2]—the incorruptibility promised by the kingdom that will be free from sin?[3] Well, indeed, you speed toward the Lord, well you make haste to be free from this most wicked world, you who find it unpleasant to approach your own end!

Chapter 7

(1) What profit, again, do you derive for your salvation from all the labor spent in arranging your hair? Why can you not leave your hair alone, instead of at one time tying it up, at another letting it hang loose, now cultivating it, now thinning it out? Some women prefer to tie it up in little curls, while others let it fall down wild and disheveled—a hardly commendable kind of simplicity. Besides, some of you affix to your heads I know not what monstrosities of sewn and woven wigs, now in the form of a cap as if it were a casing for the head and a covering for the crown, now in the form of a chignon at the back of the neck. (2) I am surprised that there is no open defiance of the Lord's precepts one of which declares that no one can add anything to his stature.[1] You, however, do add something to your weight anyway by wearing some kind of head-dresses or piling shield-bosses upon your necks! If you are not ashamed of your outrageous behavior, then be at least ashamed of covering yourselves with

---
2 Cf. 2 Cor. 5.2.
3 Cf. 1 Cor. 5.8.

1 Cf. Matt. 6.27.

filth, in the fear that you may be putting on a holy and Christian head the cast-offs of hair of some stranger who was perhaps unclean, perhaps guilty and destined for hell. In fact, why do you not banish all this slavery to beauty from your own free head? It will do you no good to seem beautiful; you are wasting your time looking for the cleverest manufacturers of wigs. God commands women to be veiled. I imagine He does so lest the heads of some of them should be seen!

(3) I certainly hope that I, in the day of Christian joy, miserable man that I am, may be able to raise my head at least as high as your heels. Perhaps I will then see whether or not you will arise with your ceruse, your rouge, your saffron, and all that parade of head-gear; whether it will be women painted up that way whom the angels will carry up to meet Christ in the clouds. If these things are now good and are of God, then they will join your rising bodies and find there again their proper place. But nothing can rise but flesh and spirit sole and pure. Whatever, therefore, does not rise in spirit and flesh is damned, because it is not of God. Have nothing to do now with things that are damned; let God see you today such as He will see you on the day of your final resurrection.

Chapter 8

(1) Of course, I am now merely talking as a man and, jealous of women, I try to deprive them of what is their own! But are there not certain things that are forbidden to us, too, out of regard for the sobriety we should maintain out of fear we owe to God? (2) Now, since, by a defect of nature, there is inborn in men because of women (just as in women

because of men) the desire to please, the male sex also has its own peculiar trickeries for enhancing their appearance: for instance, cutting the beard a bit too sharply, trimming it too neatly, shaving around the mouth, arranging and dyeing our hair, darkening the first signs of gray hair, disguising the down on the whole body with some female ointments, smoothing off the rest of the body by means of some gritty powder, then always taking occasion to look in a mirror, gazing anxiously into it. Are not all of these things quite idle and hostile to modesty once we have known God, have put aside the desire to please others and foresworn all lasciviousness? (3) For, where God is there is modesty, where modesty is there is dignity, its assistant and companion. How shall we ever practise modesty if we do not make use of its normal means, that is, dignity? How shall we ever be able to make use of dignity in practising modesty unless we bear a certain seriousness in our countenance, in our dress, and in the appearance of the entire man?

Chapter 9

(1) In the same manner, therefore, you must be intent on curtailing and rejecting all superfluous elegance in your clothing and the remaining lumber of your finery. For, what good does it do to wear on your face an appearance of propriety and temperance and a simplicity that is in accordance with the divine teaching if the rest of the body is covered with a lot of frilly and foolish pomps and luxuries? (2) To be sure, there is no difficulty in recognizing how close the connection is between these pomps and the business of lasciviousness and how they must interfere with the principles of

modesty: such frills adjoined to fancy dress prostitute the grace of true beauty, so much so that, if they are not worn, natural beauty makes no impression and is hardly noticed as if disarmed and altogether ruined; on the other hand, if natural beauty is not present, the supporting aid of fancy dress supplies grace, as it were, of its own power. (3) Lastly, finery and elegant dress have a tendency to deprive of peace those periods of life which are already blessed with quiet and withdrawn into the harbor of modesty, and to disturb their seriousness by stimulating desires which evidently try to compensate for the coldness of age by the provocative charms of dress.

(4) First, then, blessed sisters, have nothing to do with the lewd and seductive tricks of dress and appearance. Secondly, if some of you, because of wealth or birth or former dignities, are forced to appear in public in overly elaborate dress, as if they had not yet acquired the good sense that is fitting to their age, take heed to temper the evil that is in this thing, lest under pretext of necessity you give rein to unbounded licence. (5) For, how can you fulfill the precept of humility which we profess as Christians if you do not keep in check the use of wealth and finery which so encourage the pursuit of glory? For, glory tends to exalt and not to humble.

(6) 'But,' you will say, 'may we not use what is ours?' Who is forbidding you to use what is yours? No one less than the Apostle who advises us to use this world as if we did not use it. He tells us: 'The fashion of this world is passing away. And those who buy, let them act as though they possessed not.'[1] And why? Because he had previously said: 'The time is growing short.'[2] If, then, he plainly shows that even wives

---
1 1 Cor. 7.30,31.
2 1 Cor. 7.29.

themselves are so to be had as if they be not had, because the times are straitened, what would he think about all these vain appliances of theirs?

(7) In fact, are there not many who do just that, dedicating themselves to be eunuchs and for the kingdom of God voluntarily foregoing a desire which is so strong and, as we know, permitted to us?[3] Are there not some who deny themselves what God has created, abstaining from wine and from dishes of meat, the enjoyment of which provides no particular danger or fear? But they sacrifice to God the humility of their soul in restricting their use of food. Therefore, you have used your wealth and finery quite enough, and you have plucked the fruit of your dowries sufficiently before you came to know the teaching of salvation. (8) For, we are the ones for whom the times were to run their course to the end; we were predestined by God before the world was created for the extreme end of time; and so we are trained by God to castigate and, so to speak, emasculate the world. We are the circumcision of all things both spiritual and carnal, for in both spirit and in the flesh we circumcise the things of this world.

Chapter 10

(1.) Of course, it was God who taught men how to dye wool with the juice of herbs and the slime of shells; it had escaped Him, when He bade all things to come into existence, to issue a command for the production of purple and scarlet sheep! It was God, too, who devised the manufacture of those very garments which, light and thin in themselves, are heavy only in their price; God it was who produced such a

---

3 Cf. Matt. 19.12.

great amount of gold for the careful setting and fitting of jewels; and it was God, too, to be sure, who caused the puncturing of ears and was so interested in tormenting his own creatures as to order suffering to infants with their first breath; and this, in order that from these scars on the body—it seems as if the latter was born to be cut—there might hang some sort of precious stones which, as is well known, the Parthians insert in their shoes in place of studs! (2) As a matter of fact, this gold whose glitter you find so attractive is used by some nations for chains, as pagan literature tells us. And so, it is not because of intrinsic value that these things are good, but merely because they happen to be rare. After artistic skills, however, had been introduced by the fallen angels, who had also discovered the materials themselves, elaborate workmanship, combined with the rareness of these things, brought about the idea of their being precious and stimulated the desire on the part of the women to possess them because of their precious character.

(3) Now, if these very angels who discovered the material substances of this kind as well as their charms—I mean gold and precious stones—and passed on the techniques of working them and taught, among other things, the use of eyelid-powder and the dyeing of cloth, if these angels, I say, are condemned by God, as Henoch tells us,[1] how are we ever going to please God by taking pleasure in things developed by those who because of those acts provoked the wrath and punishment of God?

(4) I will grant you that God foresaw all these things and that He has permitted them, and that Isaias[2] does not object to any purple garments, permits the wearing of an ornament

---
1 Cf. *Book of Henoch* 7.1.
2 Cf. Isa. 3.18-23.

shaped like a bunch of grapes in the hair, and finds no fault with crescent-shaped necklaces. Still, let us not flatter ourselves, as the pagans are accustomed to do, that God is merely the Creator of the world and thereafter pays no attention to the works He has created. (5) Could we not be acting much more usefully and cautiously if we were to presume that all these things have been provided by God at the beginning and placed in the world in order that they should now be means of testing the moral strength of His servants, so that, in being permitted to use things, we might have the opportunity of showing our self-restraint? Do not wise masters purposely offer and permit some things to their servants in order to try them and to see whether and how they make use of things thus permitted, whether they will do so with moderation and honesty? (6) However, is not that servant deserving more praise who abstains totally, thus manifesting a reverential fear of the kindness of his master? Therefore the Apostle concludes: 'All things are lawful, but not all things are expedient.'[3] It will be much easier for one to dread what is forbidden who has a reverential fear of what is permitted.

Chapter 11

(1) Moreover, what reasons have you for appearing in public in fancy dress, since you are automatically removed from the occasions which demand that sort of thing? You do not visit pagan temples nor do you long for the spectacles nor do you keep the holy days of the Gentiles. People only wear fancy dress in public because of those gatherings and the

---

3 1 Cor. 10.23.

desire to see and to be seen,¹ either for the purpose of transacting the trade of wantonness or else of inflating their vanity. You, however, have no cause of appearing in public, except such as is serious. (2) You either visit some sick brethren or attend the sacrifice of the Mass or listen to the word of God. Any one of these functions is an occasion of seriousness and holiness for which there is no need of any extraordinary studiously arranged and luxurious attire. And if you are required to go out because of friendship or duty to some Gentile, why not go dressed in your own armor—all the more, in fact, because you are going to those who are strangers to the faith? It is desirable that there be some way of distinguishing between the handmaids of God and of the Devil so that you may be an example to them and they be edified in you;² as St. Paul says: 'Let God be glorified in your body.'³ God, however, is glorified in your body through modesty; hence, also, through dress that is suitable to modesty.

(3) But some of you may object that the [Christian] name should not be blasphemed in us by making some derogatory change of our former style of dress. Well, let us then continue to practise our former vices! If we must keep the same appearance, let us also maintain the same conduct! Then certainly the pagans will not blaspheme the [Christian] name! It is, indeed, a great blasphemy if it is said of one of you: 'Since she became a Christian she walks in poorer garb'! Are you going to be afraid to appear to be poorer from the time that you have been made richer and to be more shabbily clothed from the time when you have been made more clean?

---

1 Cf. Tertullian, *De spectaculis* 25.3; Ovid, *Ars amatoria* 1.99.
2 Cf. 1 Cor. 10.23.
3 Cf. Phil. 1.20.

In a word, should a Christian walk according to what is pleasing to the pagan or according to what is pleasing to God?

Chapter 12

(1) We should certainly see to it that we never give adequate cause to another to blaspheme. Yet, how much more conducive to blasphemy is it if you who are called the priestesses of modesty go around dressed and painted like those who are immodest! In fact, to what extent could one consider those poor, unhappy victims of organized lust to be beneath you? Even though in the past some laws used to forbid them to adorn themselves as married women or as matrons, now, surely, the corruption of our times which is daily growing worse makes it very difficult to distinguish them from the most honorable women. (2) Yet even the Scriptures suggest to us that the alluring display of beauty is invariably joined with and appropriate to bodily prostitution. That powerful city which rules over the seven mountains and over many waters merited from the Lord the appellation of a prostitute[1] and received that name because of the likeness of dress. Surely she sits in purple and scarlet and gold and precious stones;[2] surely those things are cursed without which an accursed prostitute could not have been described. (3) The only reason why Juda thought that Thamar was sitting [on the cross-road] for hire was because she had painted her face and adorned herself, and thus (because she was hidden beneath her 'veil' and, by the kind of dress she wore, pretended that she was a harlot) he considered her as such, addressed

---
1 Cf. Apoc. 17.1.
2 Cf. Apoc. 17.4.

her as such and bargained with her in the same fashion.³ Thus, we learn that it is our obligation to provide in every way against all immodest associations or even the suspicion of them. For, why is the purity of the chaste mind stained by the suspicion of another? Why is something looked for in me which I abhor? Why does not my garb announce beforehand my character lest my spirit should be wounded through hearing what is said by those who are shameless? Well, it is certainly permitted to you to appear chaste to an unchaste person.

Chapter 13

(1) Some women may say: 'I do not need the approval of men. For I do not ask for the testimony of men: it is God who sees my heart.'¹ We all know that, to be sure, but let us recall what the Lord said through the Apostle: 'Let your modesty appear before men.'² Why would he have said that unless we should be an example and a witness to those who are evil? Or, what did Christ mean by 'let your works shine before men'?³ Why did the Lord call us 'the light of the world'?⁴ Why did He compare us to a city set on a mountain if we were not to shine in [the midst of] darkness and stand out among those who are sunk down?⁵ (2) 'If you hide your light under the measure,'⁶ you will necessarily be lost in darkness and run

---

3 Cf. Gen. 38.14-16.

1 Cf. 1 Kings 16.7.
2 Phil. 4.5.
3 Cf. Matt. 5.16.
4 Matt. 5.14.
5 Cf. Matt. 5.14,15; Mark 4.21; Luke 8.16; 11.33.
6 Cf. *ibid.*

down by many people. It is our good works that make us to be the lights of the world. Moreover, what is good, provided it be true and full, does not love the darkness; it rejoices to be seen and exults in being pointed out by others. (3) It is not enough for Christian modesty merely to be so, but to seem so, too. So great and abundant ought to be your modesty that it may flow out from the mind to the garb, and burst forth from the conscience to the outer appearance, so that even from the outside it may examine, as it were, its own furniture —a furniture that is suited to retain the faith forever. We must, therefore, get rid of such delicacies as tend by their softness and effeminacy to weaken the strength of our faith. (4) Otherwise, I am not so sure that the wrist which is always surrounded by a bracelet will be able to bear the hardness of chains with resignation; I have some doubts that the leg which now rejoices to wear an anklet will be able to bear the tight squeeze of an ankle chain; and I sometimes fear that the neck which is now laden with strings of pearls and emeralds will give no room to the executioner's sword.

(5) Therefore, my blessed sisters, let us think of the hardships to come, and we will not feel them. Let us abandon luxuries and we will never miss them. Let us stand ready to endure every violence, having nothing which we would be afraid to leave behind. For, these things are really the bonds that hold down the wings of our hope. Let us cast away the ornaments of this world if we truly desire those of heaven. (6) Do not love gold—that substance which caused the very first sins of the people of Israel to be branded with infamy.[7] You should hate that which ruined your fathers, that gold

---

7 Cf. Exod. 32.7-35; Josue 7.10-26.

which they adored when they abandoned God, for even then gold was food for the fire.⁸

But the lives of Christians are never spent in gold, and now less than ever, but in iron. The stoles of martyrdom are being prepared,⁹ and the angels who are to carry us [to heaven] are being awaited. (7) Go forth to meet those angels, adorned with the cosmetics and ornaments of the Prophets and Apostles. Let your whiteness flow from simplicity, let modesty be the cause of your rosy complexion; paint your eyes with demureness, your mouth with silence; hang on your ears the words of God,¹⁰ bind on your neck the yoke of Christ;¹¹ bow your heads to your husbands¹²—and that will be ornament enough for you. Keep your hands busy with spinning and stay at home—and you will be more pleasing than if you were adorned in gold. Dress yourselves in the silk of probity, the fine linen of holiness, and the purple of chastity. Decked out in this manner, you will have God Himself for your lover.

---
8 Cf. Exod. 32.20.
9 Cf. Apoc. 6.11.
10 Cf. Jer. 9.20.
11 Cf. Matt. 11.29.
12 Cf. Eph. 5.22,23.

PRAYER

Translated by
SISTER EMILY JOSEPH DALY, C.S.J., Ph.D.
College of St. Rose
Albany, N. Y.

INTRODUCTION

WITH NO DIMINUTION of zeal but with considerably less intensity and aggressiveness than appear in most of his writings, Tertullian sets forth to the catechumens, presumably in his native city of Carthage, his instructions on *Prayer*. No traces of unorthodoxy are present to detract from these inspiring exhortations. Consequently, it may be concluded that the composition of this work falls within the early years of Tertullian's conversion (about 198-200).

In many of his writings, Tertullian's violent character and impassioned delivery have interfered with a well-ordered presentation of his material. Such is not the case with *Prayer*, which, after a brief introduction, presents a commentary, phrase by phrase, on the Lord's Prayer (Ch. 2-9). There follow (Ch. 10-28) the most varied admonitions regarding prayer: the attitude of heart and mind required; the modest and humble demeanor required of the one who prays; the kiss of peace; station days; the dress of women and the question of whether virgins should have their heads veiled; the time and place for prayer. The treatise ends in an enthusiastic exposition of the power and efficacy of prayer (Ch. 29).

Not only for the inspiring exhortations which it contains but also for its stylistic qualities the treatise merits special attention. From the opening sentence, with its striking rhetorical figures,[1] to the final chapter with its eulogy of prayer so reminiscent of Cicero's famous passage in the *Pro Archia,* the exceptional literary genius of the author is in evidence. There is an inescapable feeling that the work was a sermon:[2] the sentences are composed and arranged in oratorical style; balance, assonance, rhetorical questions, touches of ironical humor,[3] and, in general, a certain directness of manner strengthen this impression.

As in his other ascetical and moral works, quotations from both Old and New Testament abound. Of classical writers only Herodotus—an author whom Tertullian often cites—is quoted once. It is particularly interesting to note the prominence of terminology culled from the world of business (Ch. 7), military life (Ch. 19), and the courts. The catechumens who received the exhortations in *Prayer* formed a cross-section of the metropolis and would find their teacher using an idiom familiar to them in their various pursuits. Even the neophyte, long accustomed to the pagan ritualistic ceremonies, would discover that the material victim of pagan sacrifice was supplanted in Christian worship by the spiritual offering

---

1 Translation fails to reproduce the impact and effectiveness of the anaphora, chiasmus, and polyptoton of this sentence: *Dei spiritus et dei sermo et dei ratio, sermo rationis et ratio sermonis et spiritus utriusque, Iesus Christus, dominus noster, novis discipulis novi testamenti novam orationis formam determinavit.*

2 Cf. Ch. 22.10 . . . *constanter super meum modulum pronuntiare contestarique possum velandas* . . . : 'I can *declare* and *avow* this with more than my usual firmness: their heads should be covered . . . ' Both verbs are most commonly used of *spoken* expression.

3 E.g., the reference to Paul's cloak (Ch. 15.2) and the *ridiculum ad absurdum* arguments of Ch. 16.1-4.

which manifested, on a supernatural plane, all the qualities specified by Roman law (Ch. 28.4).

Foremost among the significant features of this work is the contribution which it makes to the history of the development of the liturgy. There is an allusion (Ch. 3) to the beginning of the Preface and Sanctus of the Mass: 'Certainly it is right that God should be blessed in all places and at all times because it is every man's duty to be ever mindful of His benefits . . . To Him the hosts of angels cease not to say: "Holy, holy, holy!" Therefore, we, too—the future comrades of the angels, if we earn this reward—become familiar here on earth with that heavenly cry of praise to God and the duty of our future glory.' There is reference (Ch. 3-4) to the use of the Lord's Prayer at Mass, and Tertullian's statement that we prepare for this prayer *cum memoria praeceptorum* (Ch. 10) suggests the liturgical introduction of this prayer in the Mass. Elsewhere (Ch. 14) there is a reference to the Mass as the Sacrifice which repeats the Passion of Christ. From Chapter 18 it is learned that there was a kiss of peace after prayer with the brethren. This was usual in all public prayers. Some people wanted to omit the kiss on fast days. Tertullian allows this omission only on Good Friday (which he calls *dies paschae*). In Chapter 19 he refers to station days and in 27 to the practice of the people singing the Alleluia and verses of the Gradual psalms.

The treatise of St. Cyprian, *De oratione Dominica,* is proof of the high esteem in which he held Tertullian's *Prayer*. He adheres closely to the pattern established by Tertullian. While the verbal reminiscences are few,[4] there is in both works a preliminary admonition against ostentatious display of one's

---

[4] A notable exception is Cyprian's *'Deus non vocis sed cordis auditor est'* (*De oratione dominica* 4), which is taken verbatim from Tertullian (17.3).

piety, followed by consideration of the sevenfold petitions of the *Pater Noster*. Cyprian's tract is not, however, the stylized, rhetorical work that his African predecessor has produced.

The present translation is based on the critical text of G. F. Diercks in the *Corpus Christianorum*, Series Latina 1 (Turnholti 1954) 255-274.

SELECT BIBLIOGRAPHY

Texts:

A. Reifferscheid and G. Wissowa, CSEL 20 (1890) 180-200.
R. W. Muncey, *Q. S. F. Tertulliani De oratione*, edited with introduction and notes (London 1926).
G. F. Diercks, *Corpus Christianorum*, Series Latina 1 (Turnholti 1954) 255-274.

Secondary Sources:

F. J. Dölger, 'Das Niedersitzen nach dem Gebet. Ein Kommentar zu Tertullian, De oratione 16,' *Antike und Christentum* 5 (1936) 116-137.
W. Haller, 'Das Herrengebet bei Tertullian,' *Zeitschrift für praktische Theologie* 12 (1890) 327-354.
G. Loeschke, *Die Vaterunsererklärung des Theophilus von Antiochien. Eine Quellenuntersuchung zu den Vaterunsererklärungen des Tertullian, Cyprian und Hieronymus* (Berlin 1908).
J. Moffat, 'Tertullian on the Lord's Prayer,' *Expository Times* 18 (1919) 24-41.
J. Quasten, *Patrology* 2 (Westminster, Md. 1953) 296-298.
B. Simovic, 'Le pater chez quelques pères latins,' *France Franciscaine* 21 (1938) 193-222;245-264.
O. Schäfer, 'Das Vaterunser, das Gebet des Christen. Eine aszetische Studie nach Tertullian De oratione,' *Theologie und Glaube* 35 (1943) 1-6.

PRAYER

Chapter 1

JESUS CHRIST OUR LORD—the Spirit of God and the Word of God and the Reason of God—the Word [which expresses] the Reason, and the Reason [which possesses] the Word, and the Spirit of both[1]—has prescribed for His new disciples of the New Testament a new form of prayer. For in this matter, also, it was fitting that new wine be stored in new wine skins and that a new patch be sewed upon a new garment.[2] Whatever had prevailed in days gone by was either abolished, like circumcision, or completed, like the rest of the Law, or fulfilled, like the prophecies, or brought to its perfection, like faith itself. (2) Everything has been changed from carnal to spiritual by the new grace of

---
1 If Tertullian here and elsewhere calls the Son of God also the Spirit of God, he does so only to describe His essence, without intending to identify Him with the third Person who alone bears this name. Tertullian almost combines the two meanings of the word λόγος, which in Greek means both 'word' and 'thought.' Therefore, he calls the λόγος 'sermo' (word), and 'ratio' (reason), the 'intellectus' (or νοῦς) of God. Cf. *Adversus Hermogenem* 18; 45; *Apology* 17; 21.10-11; 23.12; *De carne Christi* 19.
2 Cf. Matt. 9.16,17; Mark 2.21,22; Luke 5.36,37.

God which, with the coming of the Gospel, has wiped out the old completely; and in this grace it has been proved there is the Spirit of God and the Word of God and the Reason of God, Jesus Christ our Lord; as the Spirit wherein He prevailed, the Word whereby He taught, and the Reason for which He came. Consequently, the prayer formulated by Christ consists of three elements: the spirit whereby it can have such power, the word by which it is expressed, and the reason why it produces reconciliation. (3) John, too, had taught his disciples to pray, but everything that John did was a preparation for Christ, until He would increase—even as John himself announced[3] that He [Christ] must increase, but he himself must decrease—and the entire work of the servant would pass over, along with the spirit itself, to the Master. Hence it is that the words in which John taught men to offer their prayer are not extant, for the earthly have given place to the heavenly. 'He who is from the earth,' He says, 'of the earth speaks, and he who comes from heaven bears witness to that which he has seen.' And what that is of Christ the Lord is not of heaven, as is also this instruction concerning prayer?

(4) Let us then, my blessed ones,[4] consider His heavenly wisdom, in the first place with regard to the admonition to pray in secret. By this, He demanded of man the faith to believe that he is seen and heard by Almighty God even when he is within the house and out of sight; and He desired a modest reserve in the manifestation of his faith so that he would offer his homage to God alone who he believed was listening and observing everywhere. (5) The next recommendation in the following precept would, then, pertain to

---

3 Cf. John 3.30-32.
4 'Blessed' (*benedicti*) was an appellation given especially to catechumens; see *To the Martyrs* 1.1.

faith and the proper display of faith; we should not think that the Lord is to be approached with a barrage of words since we are certain that of His own accord He has regard for His creatures. (6) Yet, that concise phrase which forms the third point of His teaching rests for support upon a profound and effective figure of speech: the thought compressed within such few words carries a flood of meaning to the mind. For not only does it embrace the proper duties of prayer, namely, worship of God and man's act of supplication, but practically every word of the Lord, the whole content of His teaching, so that, really, in [the Lord's] Prayer, there is contained an abridgement of the entire Gospel.

Chapter 2

(1) It begins with a proof of [our belief in] God and a meritorious act of faith when we say, 'Father, who art in heaven.'[1] For we adore God and prove our faith, of which this form of address is the result. It is written: 'To them that believe in God He gave the power to be called the sons of God.'[2] (2) Our Lord very frequently spoke to us of God as a Father; in fact, He even taught us to call none on earth 'father,' but only the one we have in heaven.[3] Therefore, when we pray like this we are observing this precept, too. (3) Happy they who know the Father! This is the reproach made

---

1 Tertullian's text of the *Pater Noster* is as follows: *Pater qui in caelis es, sanctificetur nomen tuum. Fiat voluntas tua in caelis et in terra. Veniat regnum tuum. Panem nostrum quotidianum da nobis hodie. Dimitte nobis debita nostra, [sicut] nos quoque remittimus debitoribus nostris. Ne nos inducas in temptationem, sed devehe nos a malo.*
2 Cf. John 1.12.
3 Cf. Matt. 23.9.

against Israel, when the Spirit calls heaven and earth to witness saying: 'I have begotten sons and they have not known me.'⁴ (4) Moreover, when we say 'Father,' we also add a title to God's name. This form of address is one of filial love and at the same time one of power. (5) In the Father, the Son is also addressed. For Christ said, 'I and the Father are one.'⁵ (6) Nor is Mother Church passed over without mention,⁶ for in the Son and the Father the Mother is recognized, since upon her the terms 'Father' and 'Son' depend for their meaning. (7) With this one form, then, or word, we honor God with His own, we heed His precept, and we reproach those who are unmindful of the Father.

Chapter 3

(1) The title 'God the Father' had not been revealed to anyone. Even Moses who had inquired about God's name had heard a different one.¹ It has been revealed to us in His Son. For, before the Son [came] the name of the Father did not exist. 'I have come,' said Christ, 'in the name of my Father.'² And again: 'Father, glorify thy name.'³ And, more explicitly: 'I have manifested thy name to men.'⁴ (2) We ask that this name be hallowed; not that it would be the proper thing for men to wish God well as if He were [just]

---

4 Cf. Isa. 1.2.
5 Cf. John 10.30.
6 The notion of the Church as a mother occurs in Tertullian for the first time in Latin Christian literature; see above, p. 17 n. 2.

---

1 Cf. Exod. 3.13,14.
2 Cf. John 5.43.
3 *Ibid.* 12.28.
4 *Ibid.* 17.6.

another man and we could express some wish in his regard; or as if it would hurt Him if we did not express the wish. Certainly it is right that God should be blessed in all places and at all times because it is every man's duty to be ever mindful of His benefits, but this wish takes the form of a benediction. (3) Moreover, when is the name of God not holy and blessed in itself, when of itself it makes others holy? To Him the attending hosts of angels cease not to say: 'Holy, holy, holy!'[5] Therefore, we, too—the future comrades of the angels, if we earn this reward—become familiar even while here on this earth with that heavenly cry of praise to God and the duty of our future glory.

(4) So much for the glory we give to God. Over and above that, there is reference to our own petition when we say: 'Hallowed be thy name.' We are asking that it be sanctified in us who are in Him, as well as in all other men for whom the grace of God is still waiting. In this, too, we obey the precept by praying for all men, even our enemies. And thus, by an ellipsis, we say, not: 'May Thy name be hallowed among us,' but, we say: 'Among all men.'

Chapter 4

(1) Next, we add this phrase: 'Thy will be done in heaven and on earth.' Not that anyone could prevent the fulfillment of God's will and we should pray that His will be successfully accomplished, but we pray that in everything His will may be done. For, by a figure of speech, under the symbol of flesh and spirit we represent heaven and earth. (2) But, even if

---

5 Isa. 6.3; Apoc. 4.8. An allusion to the beginning of the Preface and the Sanctus of the Mass.

this is to be understood literally, the sense of the petition is the same, namely, that the will of God be done in us on earth, in order that it may be done [by us] also in heaven. Now, what does God will but that we walk according to His teaching? We ask, therefore, that He grant us the substance and riches of His will, for our salvation both in heaven and on earth, since the sum total of His will is the salvation of those whom He has adopted as His children.

(3) This is the will of God which our Lord accomplished by His teaching, His works, and His sufferings. For, if He Himself said that He did not His own will, but the will of His Father,[1] without a doubt what He did was the will of His Father, to which we are now summoned as to a model, that we, too, may teach and work and suffer even unto death. That we may accomplish this there is need of God's will.[2]

(4) Likewise, when we say: 'Thy will be done,' we thereby wish well to ourselves because there is no evil in God's will, even if some adversity be inflicted upon one according to his deserts.

(5) Now, by this phrase we forearm ourselves for patient endurance since our Lord, too, willed to point out in His own flesh under the intensity of His Passion the weakness of the flesh. 'Father,' He said, 'remove this cup from Me,' and then, after reflection, He added: 'Yet not my will but thine be done.'[3] He Himself was the will and power of the Father, yet He surrendered Himself to the will of His Father to indicate the patient endurance which is rightly due.

---

1 John 6.38.
2 I.e., God's gracious assistance.
3 Luke 22.42.

Chapter 5

(1) The phrase, 'Thy kingdom come,' also refers to the same end as 'Thy will be done,' namely, [May Thy kingdom come] in ourselves. For, when does God not reign, 'in whose hand is the heart of every king'?[1] But, whatever we wish for ourselves, we direct our hope toward Him, and we attribute to Him what we expect from Him. Well, then, if the realization of our Lord's kingdom has reference to the will of God and to our uncertain condition, how is it that some ask for an extension of time, as it were, for this world, since the kingdom of God—for the coming of which we pray—tends toward the consummation of the world? Our hope is that we may sooner reign, and not be slaves any longer. (2) Even if it were not prescribed to ask in prayer for the coming of His kingdom, we would, of our own accord, have expressed this desire in our eagerness to embrace the object of our hope. (3) With indignation the souls of the martyrs beneath the altar cry aloud to the Lord: 'How long, O Lord, dost thou refrain from avenging our blood on those who dwell on the earth?'[2] For, at least from the end of the world vengeance for them is ordained. (4) Indeed, as quickly as possible, O Lord, may Thy kingdom come! This is the prayer of Christians; this shall bring shame to the heathens; this shall bring joy to the angels; it is for the coming of this kingdom that we are harassed now, or rather, it is for this coming that we pray.

---
1 Prov. 21.1.
2 Apoc. 6.10.

Chapter 6

(1) With what exquisite choice has divine Wisdom arranged the order of this prayer that, after the matters which pertain to heaven—that is, after the name of God, the will of God, and the kingdom of God—it should make a place for a petition for our earthly needs, too! For our Lord has taught us: 'Seek first the kingdom, and then these things shall be given you besides.'[1] (2) However, we should rather understand 'Give us this day our daily bread' in a spiritual sense. For Christ is 'our bread,' because Christ is Life and the Life is Bread. 'I am,' said He, 'the bread of life.'[2] And shortly before: 'The bread is the word of the living God who hath come down from heaven.'[3] Then, because His Body is considered to be in the bread: 'This is my body.'[4] Therefore, when we ask for our daily bread, we are asking to live forever in Christ and to be inseparably united with His Body.

(3) But, since there is admitted also an interpretation of this phrase according to the flesh, it cannot be devoid of religious sense and spiritual instruction. Christ commands that we ask for bread, which, for the faithful, is the only thing necessary, for the pagans seek all other things. Thus, too, He impresses His teaching by examples and He instructs by parables, saying, for example: 'Does a father take bread from his children and cast it to the dogs?'[5] And again: 'If his son asks him for a loaf, will he hand him a stone?'[6] He indicates what children expect from their father. That caller, too, who

---

1 Matt. 6.33; Luke 12.31.
2 John 6.35.
3 *Ibid* 6.33.
4 Matt. 26.26; Mark 14.22; Luke 22.19.
5 Matt. 15.26; Mark 7.27.
6 Matt. 7.9; Luke 11.11.

knocked upon the door in the night was asking for bread.⁷
(4) Moreover, He has rightly added: 'Give us this day' in view of what He had previously said: 'Do not be anxious about tomorrow, what you shall eat.'⁸ To this idea He also referred in the parable of that man who, when his crops were plentiful, laid plans for an addition to his barns and a long-range program of security—though he was destined to die that very night.⁹

Chapter 7

(1) Having considered God's generosity, we pray next for His indulgence. For, of what benefit is food if, in reality, we are bent on it like a bull on his victim?¹ Our Lord knew that He alone was without sin.² Therefore, He taught us to say in prayer: 'Forgive us our trespasses.' A prayer for pardon is an acknowledgment of sin, since one who asks for pardon confesses his guilt.³ Thus, too, repentance is shown to be acceptable to God, because God wills this rather than the death of the sinner.⁴

(2) Now, in Scripture, 'debt' is used figuratively to mean sin, because of this analogy: When a man owes something to a judge and payment is exacted from him, he does not escape the just demand unless excused from the payment of the debt,

---

7 Luke 11.5.
8 Matt. 6.34.
9 Luke 12.16-21.

---

1 I.e., consider it our only end.
2 Cf. John 8.46.
3 By *exomologesis* Tertullian means, according to the definition given in *De paenitentia* 12, the exterior act of penitence, whereas here and in Ch. 9.2 there predominates the etymological meaning of 'confession.'
4 Ezech. 33.11.

just as the master forgave the debt to that servant. Now, this is the point of the whole parable: Just as the servant was freed by his lord, but failed in turn to be merciful to his debtor and therefore, when brought before his lord, was handed over to the torturer until he paid the last penny,[5] that is, the least and last of his faults, [Christ] intended by this parable to get us, also, to forgive our debtors. (3) This is expressed elsewhere under this aspect of prayer; 'Forgive,' He said, 'and you shall be forgiven.'[6] And when Peter asked if one should forgive his brother seven times, our Lord said, 'Rather, seventy times seven times,'[7] that He might improve upon the Law, for in Genesis vengeance was demanded of Cain seven times, of Lamech seventy times seven.[8]

Chapter 8

(1) To complete the prayer which was so well arranged, Christ added that we should pray not only that our sins be forgiven, but that they be shunned completely: 'Lead us not into temptation,' that is, do not allow us to be led by the Tempter. (2) God forbid that our Lord should seem to be the tempter, as if He were not aware of one's faith or were eager to upset it! (3) That weakness and spitefulness belongs to the Devil. For, even in the case of Abraham, God had ordered the sacrifice of his son not to tempt his faith, but to prove it, that in him He might set forth an example for His precept whereby He was later to teach that no one should hold his

---

5 Matt. 18.25-35.
6 Luke 6.37.
7 Matt. 18.21,22.
8 Gen. 4.15; 24.

loved ones dearer than God.¹ (4) Christ Himself was tempted by the Devil and pointed out the subtle director of the temptation. (5) This passage He confirms [by His words to His Apostles] later when He says: 'Pray that you may not enter into temptation.'² They were so tempted to desert their Lord because they had indulged in sleep instead of prayer. (6) Therefore, the phrase which balances and interprets 'Lead us not into temptation' is 'But deliver us from evil.'

Chapter 9

(1) How many utterances of the Prophets, Evangelists, and Apostles; how many of our Lord's sermons, parables, examples, and precepts are touched in the brief compass of a few little words! How many duties are fulfilled! (2) The honor due to God in the word 'Father'; a testimony of faith in the very title used; the offering of obedience in the mention of God's will; the remembrance of hope in the mention of His kingdom; a petition for life in the mention of bread; the confession of sins in asking for pardon; solicitude regarding temptation in the request for protection. (3) Yet, why be surprised? God alone could teach us how He would have us pray. The homage of prayer, then, as arranged by Him and animated by His Spirit at the very moment it went forth from His divine lips, because of the prerogative granted to Him, ascends to heaven, recommending to the Father what the Son has taught.

---

1 Luke 14.26.
2 Luke 22.46.

Chapter 10

(1) Since, however, our Lord, who saw the needs of men, after giving them the method of prayer, said: 'Ask and you shall receive,'[1] and since every man has petitions to make according to his own circumstances, everyone first sends ahead the prescribed and customary prayer which will, so to speak, lay the ground work for his additional desires. He then has the right to heap upon this [substructure] petitions, over and above—ever keeping in mind, however, the prescribed conditions, that we may be no farther from the ears of God than from His teachings.

Chapter 11

(1) The remembrance of these teachings paves the way for our prayers to reach heaven, and the first of these is not to approach the altar of God without settling any controversy or quarrel we may have contracted with our brethren. For, how can one approach the peace of God without peace, or the forgiveness of sin when he nurses a grudge? How will he please his Father if he be angry with his brother, when all anger has been forbidden us from the beginning? (2) For Joseph, sending his brothers home to bring their father, said: 'Do not quarrel on the way!'[1] He was, in fact, admonishing us—for elsewhere our manner of life is called our 'way'—that on the way of prayer that has been set up we must not approach the Father if we are angry. (3) Furthermore, our

---
1 Matt. 7.7; Luke 11.9.

---
1 Gen. 45.24.

Lord, clearly enlarging upon the Law, adds anger with one's brother to the sin of murder. He does not permit even an evil word to be expressed; even if one must experience anger, it should not outlast the setting of the sun, as the Apostle reminds us.[2] How foolhardy it is, moreover, either to pass a day without prayer, while you fail to give satisfaction to your brother, or to pray to no avail since your anger persists!

Chapter 12

(1) Since the attention of our prayer is bestowed by and directed to the same Spirit, it should be free not only from anger, but from any and every disturbance of the mind. For the Holy Spirit does not acknowledge an impure spirit, neither is a sad spirit recognized by the Spirit of Joy, nor a spirit that is bound by one that is free. No one extends a welcoming hand to an opponent; no one admits another unless he is a kindred spirit.

Chapter 13

(1) Furthermore, what is the sense of approaching prayer with hands that have been cleansed but with a spirit that is stained? Why, even the hands themselves need a spiritual cleansing that they may be raised to heaven cleansed of falsehood, murder, cruelty, poisoning, idolatry, and all other stains which, conceived in the spirit, are accomplished by the operation of the hands. This is the real cleansing, not the kind which many, in superstitious anxiety, attend to, taking

---

2 Eph. 4.26.

water at every prayer, even when they come after a complete bath! (2) When I pondered this in detail and sought an explanation, I found it told of Pilate that he washed his hands in the act of surrendering Christ. We adore Christ, we do not surrender Him. Surely, we ought rather to follow a course of conduct different from that of the traitor and for that very reason *not* wash our hands; except to wash them because of some stain resulting from our dealings with men, for our conscience's sake; but the hands are sufficiently clean which we have washed once and for all, together with the whole body, in Christ.

Chapter 14

(1) Though Israel may wash all its members every day, it is never clean. Its hands, at least, are always stained, forever red with the blood of the Prophets and of our Lord Himself. Conscious, therefore, of this hereditary stain of their fathers, they do not dare to raise their hands to the Lord, lest some Isaias cry out,[1] lest Christ abominate them. In our case, not only do we raise them, we even spread them out, and, imitating the Passion of our Lord, we confess Christ as we pray.

Chapter 15

(1) Now, since we have mentioned one detail of religious observance that is foolish, we shall not be loathe to censure the others, too, in which vanity deserves to be reproved, inas-

---
1 Isa. 1.15.

much as they are without the authority of any precept, either on the part of our Lord or any of the Apostles. Practices such as this are to be considered superstition rather than devout homage; affected and forced and indicative of scrupulosity rather than of a rational service; at any rate, constrained to match those of the pagans. (2) Take, for example, the practice some have of laying aside their cloaks when they pray. This is the way pagans approach *their* idols. Now certainly, if this were necessary, the Apostles would have included it in their instructions about the dress for prayer; unless there are some who think that it was during his prayer that Paul left his cloak with Carpus![1] I suppose that the God who heeded the prayer of the three holy youths in the furnace of the Babylonian king when they prayed in their wide oriental trousers and turbans[2] would not listen to those who wear their cloaks during prayer!

Chapter 16

(1) Similarly, regarding the custom some have of sitting down when their prayer is ended: I see no reason for it except that they are acting like children.[1] What do I mean? If that Hermas, whose writings generally bear the title 'The Shepherd,' had not sat upon his bed when his prayer was finished, but had done something else, would we adopt this practice, too?[2] Certainly not! (2) For the phrase, 'When I

---

1 Cf. 2 Tim. 4.13.
2 Cf. Dan. 3.94.

---

1 I.e., they do everything they see anyone else do.
2 Hermae Pastor, *Vis.* 5.1.

had offered my prayer and had seated myself on the bed,' was set down simply and solely in the course of the narrative, not as a point of discipline. (3) Otherwise, we would not be obliged to offer prayers anywhere except where there was a bed! (4) On the other hand, it would be violating his directions to sit upon a chair or bench! (5) Furthermore, since this is what the pagans do—sit down before the images of the gods which they adore—it is on this score that what is done before idols deserves to be reproved in us. (6) For this reason it is set down as a charge of irreverence, and would be so understood, even by those pagans, if they had any understanding. For, if it is disrespectful to sit down in the presence and sight of one whom you hold in very high esteem and honor, how much more is it the height of disrespect to do so in the presence of the living God with the angel of prayer standing beside Him? Unless we are offering a reproach to God because our prayer has wearied us!

Chapter 17

(1) On the other hand, when we offer our prayer with modesty and humility, we commend our petitions to God all the more, even though our hands have not been raised very high in the air, but only slightly and to a proper position, and even though our gaze has not been lifted up in presumption. (2) For, even the publican who, not only in his words but in his countenance as well, was humble and prayed with downcast eyes went away justified rather than the haughty Pharisee.[1] (3) The tone of voice, too, should be lowered; otherwise, what lungs we will need, if being heard depends

---
1 Luke 18.10-14.

upon the noise we make! But God is not one who heeds the voice; rather, it is the heart which He hears and beholds.² (4) 'Even the speechless I hear, and the silent petition I answer.' So runs an oracle of the Pythian demon.³ Do the ears of God await a sound? If they did, how could Jonas' prayer from the depths of the whale's belly have made its way to heaven, up through the organs of such a great beast from the very bottom of the sea, up through such a vast amount of water? (5) As for those who pray in such a loud voice, what else will they attain but the annoyance of their neighbors? Let us say, rather, when they thus publicize their petitions, what else are they doing but praying in public?

Chapter 18

(1) There is another custom which has now become established: when those who are fasting have finished their prayer with their brethren, they withhold the kiss of peace; yet this is the seal of prayer.¹ (2) But, when is the kiss of peace to be given to our brethren if not when our prayer ascends to heaven, made more worthy of praise because of our charity? So that they themselves may share in our charity, who have contributed to it by passing on their peace to their

---

2 Cf. Cyprian, *De oratione dominica* 4.
3 Herodotus 1.47.

---

1 In the early African liturgy, the kiss of peace, termed the *signaculum orationis*, was associated with the *Pater Noster*. Some suggested that the kiss be omitted on fast days, but Tertullian strenuously objected to this practice. The kiss of peace was not associated exclusively with the Mass. This is an important point to note, for it seems that generally there has been attached to this ceremony too great an importance as characteristic of the Mass. In reality, Tertullian tells us, no prayer, no service is complete without the 'peace.'

brother. (3) What prayer is complete without the bond of a holy kiss? (4) With whom does the kiss of peace interfere in his service of the Lord? (5) What kind of sacrifice is it from which one departs without giving the kiss of peace? (6) Whatever the reason may be, it will not outweigh the observance of the precept whereby we are bidden to conceal our fasting. For, when we refrain from the kiss, it is recognized that we are fasting. But, even if there is some reason for it, still, that you may not be guilty of transgressing this precept, you may, if you wish, dispense with the kiss of peace at home, since there you are among those from whom it is not entirely possible to conceal your fasting. But, wherever else you can conceal your acts of mortification, you ought to remember this precept; in this way you will satisfactorily comply with religious discipline in public, and with ordinary usage at home. (7) Thus, too, on Good Friday, when the fasting is a general and, as it were, a public religious obligation, we rightly omit the kiss of peace, having no anxiety about concealing that which we are doing along with everyone else.

Chapter 19

(1) Similarly, with regard to the station days, many do not think that there should be any attendance at the prayers of sacrifice, because the station should be ended when the Lord's Body is received. (2) Has the Eucharist, then, dispensed with a duty vowed to God, or does it place upon us a greater obligation to God? (3) Will not your station be more solemn if you stand at the altar of God? (4) When the Body of our

PRAYER   175

Lord is received and reserved, both are preserved: the participation in the sacrifice and the fufillment of a duty.¹ (5) Since 'station' has taken its name from military procedure (for we are God's militia), certainly no joy nor sadness which befalls the camp releases the soldiers on guard duty. For, in joy one will perform his duty more readily, and, in sadness, more conscientiously.

Chapter 20

(1) As regards dress—I refer only to that of women—the difference of custom since the time of the holy Apostle¹ has caused me, though a man of no rank [in the Church],² to deal with this matter, which is a daring thing to do; except that it is not so daring if we deal with it as did the Apostle. (2) As for the modesty of their attire and adornment, the admonition of Peter, too, is clearly expressed.³ Using the same

---

1 The Christian week was consecrated by two days of fast and penance over and above Sunday, namely, Wednesday and Friday. These were days of special prayer called 'station days.' Some rigorists mistakenly believed that the faithful should refrain from receiving Holy Communion on these days. Tertullian was righteously indignant at such an idea. He pointed out that one who feared that the communion would break the fast could reserve the Eucharist until the hour when the station was ended.

---

1 Cf. the recommendations of Paul, 1 Tim. 2.9; 1 Cor. 11.3ff.
2 This phrase suggests that Tertullian was not a priest when he wrote *Prayer*. With the use of the modest term of reference to himself (*nullius loci homines*) cf. his use of *postremissimus*, in *De cultu feminarum* 2.1.1.
3 1 Peter 3.3.

words as Paul, because inspired by the same Spirit, he imposes restraint regarding ostentation in their dress, the proud display of gold, and the overcareful, meretricious arrangement of their hair.[4]

Chapter 21

(1) A point which must be treated, since in general, throughout the Church, it is regarded as a matter of dispute, is the question of whether or not virgins should be veiled.[1] (2) Those who grant to virgins the right of having their heads uncovered seem to support their position by the fact that the Apostle designated specifically, not that virgins, but that women, are to be veiled;[2] that is, he referred not to the sex, using the generic term 'females,' but to one group within the sex, saying 'women.'[3] (3) For, if he had specified the [entire] sex by the term 'females' he would have laid down an absolute law relating to every woman; but since he designates one group within the sex, he sets it apart by his silence regarding another group. (4) For, they say, he could have included them in the general term 'females.'

---

4 Cf. 1 Tim. 2.9. Tertullian makes no mention of his *De cultu feminarum,* an indication that his two books on *The Apparel of Women* originated after *Prayer.*

1 Upon this question Tertullian later composed the violent polemic *De virginibus velandis.*
2 1 Cor. 11.5.
3 Cf. *De virginibus velandis* 3.5.

Chapter 22

(1) Those who take this stand ought to give some thought to the basic meaning of this word. What does 'woman' mean right from the first pages of holy Scripture?[1] They will discover that it is the term used to designate the sex, not a group within the sex; for God called Eve, although she had not yet known man, both woman and female: female, as an over-all term for the sex; woman, with special reference to a stage of life within the sex. Thus, since Eve, who up to that time was still unmarried, was designated by the term 'woman,' this term came to be commonly applied to a virgin, also. No wonder, then, if the Apostle, actuated by the same Spirit which has inspired all the sacred Scriptures as well as that Book of Genesis, used this same word, 'woman,' which, because of its application to the unmarried Eve, means also a virgin.

(2) Everything else, then, is in agreement. For, by the very fact that he has not named virgins, just as is the case in another passage, where he is teaching about marriage, he makes it clear that he is speaking about all women and the entire sex and that there is no distinction between a woman and a virgin since he does not mention the latter at all. For, since he did not forget to make a distinction in another passage where the difference demands it (he distinguishes both classes by designating each with its proper term), in a passage where he does not distinguish, since he does not name each, he does not intend any distinction.

(3) But what of the fact that in the Greek, in which the Apostle wrote his epistles, the ordinary usage is to speak of 'women' rather than 'females,' that is, γυναῖκας rather than

---

1 Gen. 2.23.

θηλείας? Well, if this word is the one commonly used to designate the sex, then the Apostle, in saying γυναῖκα, referred to the [entire] sex [by using] a word which, in translation, means 'females.' But in the [entire] sex the virgin, too, is included.

(4) The form of expression is unmistakable: 'Every woman,' he says, 'praying or prophesying with her head uncovered disgraces her head.'[2] What is the meaning of the expression 'every woman' except women of every age, every rank, and every circumstance? In saying 'every,' he excepts no member of the female sex, even as he does not command that men should have their heads covered. For then he would say 'every man.' Therefore, as in the reference to the male sex, under the term 'man' he forbids that even unmarried men should have their heads covered, similarly, in reference to the female sex, under the term 'woman' he commands that even a virgin should have her head covered. Without discrimination, in the case of both sexes, the younger should follow the rule for the elder; or else unmarried men should have their heads covered, too, if unmarried women should not have *their* heads covered; for the former are not specifically named in the regulation; let the [married] man be different from the unmarried if the woman is different from the virgin.

(5) Of course, it is on account of the angels, he says, that the woman's head is to be covered,[3] because the angels revolted from God on account of the daughters of men. Who, then, would contend that it is only women, that is, married women no longer virgins, that are a source of temptation? Unless, of course, unmarried women may not present an

---
2 1 Cor. 11.5.
3 1 Cor. 11.10.

attractive appearance and find their lovers? Rather, let us see whether it was virgins alone whom they desired when Scripture speaks of the 'daughters of men'; for it could have used the terms 'men's wives' or 'women' indifferently. (6) But, since it says: 'And they took to themselves wives,'[4] it does so because they took as their wives those without husbands. Scripture would have used a different expression for those who had husbands. Now, they could be without husbands either because they were widows or virgins. So, in naming the sex in general by the term 'daughters,' he embraced species in genus.

(7) Likewise, when he says that nature itself teaches that women should cover their heads[5] because it has bestowed hair on woman both as a covering and an adornment, has not this same covering and this same adornment for the head been bestowed upon virgins as well? If it is a disgrace for a woman to have her hair shorn, it is for a virgin then, also.

(8) Since, then, one and the same condition is attributed to each in regard to the head, then one and the same regulation regarding the head is imposed upon them—even upon those virgins whom their tender age protects. For, right from the start she is included in the term 'woman.' Finally, Israel has the same regulation. But even if it did not, our law, amplified and supplemented, would demand an addition, imposing a veil upon virgins, also. Granted that at the moment that period of life which is unaware of its own sex should be excused. (Granted that it should retain the privilege of its innocence; for both Eve and Adam, when realization came to them, immediately covered what they had come to know.) At any rate, in the case of those who have left child-

---
4 Gen. 6.2.
5 1 Cor. 11.14,15.

hood, their age ought to confer much both by way of nature and of discipline. For women are revealed by their members and their duties. No one is a virgin from the time she is of marriageable age, since the age now in her has become the bride of its own partner, that is, time.

(9) 'But [suppose that] someone has consecrated herself to God.' Nevertheless, from this time on, she rearranges her hair and changes her whole appearance to that of a woman. Therefore, let her be earnest about the whole business and present the complete appearance of a virgin; what she conceals for God's sake let her keep completely out of sight. It is to our interest to entrust to the knowledge of God alone what is done for the sake of God, lest we bargain with men for what we hope to receive from God. Why do you expose before the eyes of God what you cover in the presence of men? Will you be more modest in the public street than in church? If it is a gift from God and 'thou hast received it, why dost thou boast,' says the Apostle, 'as if thou hadst not received it?'[6] Why do you condemn other women by this exhibition of yourself? Or are you inviting others to good by your vanity? Yet you are in danger of losing it yourself if you boast of it, and you force others to the same dangers. That is easily destroyed which is assumed with an inclination to vanity. Virgin, cover your head if you are a virgin, for you ought to blush for shame! If you are a virgin, avoid the gaze of many eyes. Let no one look in admiration upon your face. Let no one realize your deceit. It is praiseworthy for you to create the false impression that you are married by covering your head. Rather, it will not be a false impression you are creating; for you are the bride of Christ. To Him you have surrendered your body; act according to the instructions of

---

6 1 Cor. 4.7.

your Spouse. If He bids other men's brides to cover their heads, how much more His own!

(10) 'But [suppose that] someone thinks the arrangement of his predecessor should not be changed.' Many apply their own ideas and persistence in the same to the custom established by another. Granted that virgins should not be forced to cover their heads; at any rate, those who are willing to do so should not be prevented.[7] If some cannot deny that they are virgins, they should be content, for the sake of preserving their conscience before God, to risk their reputation.[8]

However, in regard to those who are betrothed, I can declare and avow this with more than my usual firmness: their heads should be covered from the day when they first trembled at the kiss and handclasp of their future husband. For, in these symbols they have pledged every bit of themselves—their life throughout its full development, their flesh throughout their lifetime, their spirit through their understanding [of the contract], their modesty through the exchange of a kiss, their hope through their expectation, and their mind through their willingness. For us, Rebecca stands as sufficient example; when her future husband had been pointed out to her, she covered her head with her veil merely because she knew she was to marry him.[9]

---

7 This view is considerably less vigorous than the one he holds in *De virginibus velandis*. His reference to changing the regulations of one's predecessor prompts the suspicion that the present incumbent of the episcopal see of Carthage did not favor the views held by Tertullian on this subject.
8 Textual difficulties render the passage very obscure.
9 Cf. Gen. 24.65.

Chapter 23

(1) With regard to kneeling, too, prayer allows a difference in custom because of certain ones—a very few[1]—who stay off their knees on the Sabbath, an opposing point of view which is just now strongly defending itself in the churches. (2) The Lord will give His grace so that either they will yield, or else maintain their own opinion without giving scandal to others. As for ourselves, according to our tradition, only on the day [which commemorates] our Lord's Resurrection should we refrain from this custom; and not only from this, but from every sign that bespeaks solicitude and every ceremony arising therefrom. This includes deferring business, lest we give any opportunity to the Devil. The same holds for the season of Pentecost, which is marked by the same joyous celebration. (3) But who would hesitate every day to prostrate himself before God for at least the first prayer with which we approach the light of day? (4) Moreover, during the periods of fasting and on the station days no prayer should be said except on the knees and with every other sign of a humble spirit. For we are not merely praying, but beseeching and offering satisfaction to God our Lord.

Chapter 24

(1) Regarding the time for prayer there has been no regulation at all, except that we are to pray at all times and everywhere. But how can we pray everywhere when we are forbidden to pray in public? 'In every place,'[1] He said, which

---

1 Probably of Jewish descent.

1 1 Tim. 2.8.

circumstance or even necessity provides. For it is not considered that when the Apostles, within the hearing of their guards, prayed in prison and sang to God they were acting contrary to the precept any more than was Paul when, aboard ship, in the sight of all, he gave thanks to God.[2]

Chapter 25

(1) With regard to the time, the outward observance of certain hours will not be without profit.[1] I refer to those hours of community prayer which mark the main divisions of the day, namely, Terce, Sext, and None. These, it can be found, are mentioned in holy Scripture as being more deserving of note. (2) It was at the third hour—Terce—when the disciples were assembled, that the Holy Spirit was infused into them for the first time.[2] (3) It was at the sixth hour—Sext—on the day when he had the vision of all creatures in the sheet that Peter had climbed to a higher spot in order to pray.[3] (4) Similarly, it was at the ninth hour—None—that he went into the Temple with John where he restored the paralytic to health.[4] (5) Although these incidents simply happen without any precept of observing [these hours], it would be good to establish some precedent which would make the admonition to pray a binding force to wrest us violently at times, as by a law, from our business to such an obligation so that we may

---

2 Acts 27.35.

1 *Otiosa.* Cf. *De baptismo* 1.1 for a recurrence of *otiosum* in this meaning. With this passage, cf. *De ieiunio* 10; Cyprian, *De orat. dom.* 34.
2 Acts 2.15.
3 Acts 10.9.
4 Acts 3.1-7.

offer adoration no less than three times a day at least, being debtors to the three divine Persons, Father, Son and Holy Spirit. And this, too, we read was observed by Daniel according to the rites of Israel.[5] Of course, we are excepting the appropriate prayers which are due without any admonition at the approach of dawn and evening. (6) It is befitting for the faithful not to take food and not to bathe before saying a prayer. For the refreshment and food of the spirit are to be put before [the needs] of the flesh, because the things of heaven are to be put before those of the earth.[6]

Chapter 26

(1) When a brother has entered your home, do not let him go away without a prayer. ('You have seen,' He said, 'a brother; you have seen your Lord').[1] Particularly should this be observed in the case of a stranger, lest he should happen to be an angel. (2) But, even after one has been welcomed by his brethren, you should not attend to earthly refreshment before the heavenly. For immediately will your faith be revealed. Or how can you say, according to the precept, 'Peace to this house,'[2] unless you exchange the kiss of peace with those who are in the house?

---

5 Dan. 6.10.
6 Cf. *Ad martyras* 1.1.

1 Many consider this a corruption of a Biblical citation; cf. Matt. 25.40; Gen. 18.3; 19.2; Heb. 13.2.
2 Luke 10.5.

Chapter 27

(1) Those who are more exact about prayer are in the habit of adding to their prayers an 'Alleluia' and psalms of such a character that those who are present may respond with the final phrases. Assuredly, the practice is excellent in every respect which by its high praise and reverence of God is competent to offer Him, as a rich victim, a prayer that has been filled out in every detail.

Chapter 28

(1) Now, this is the spiritual victim which has set aside the earlier sacrifice. 'To what purpose do you offer me the multitude of your victims,' saith the Lord? 'I am full, I desire not holocausts of rams, and fat of fatlings, and blood of calves and goats. For who required these things at your hands?'[1] (2) The Gospel teaches what God demands. 'The hour is coming,' He says, 'when the true worshipers will worship the Father in spirit and in truth. For God is spirit,'[2] and therefore He requires that His worshipers be of the same nature. (3) We are the true worshipers and true priests who, offering our prayer in the spirit, offer sacrifice in the spirit—that is, prayer—as a victim that is appropriate and acceptable to God; this is what He has demanded and what He has foreordained for Himself. (4) This prayer, consecrated to Him

---

1 Isa. 1.11,12.
2 John 4.23,24.

with our whole heart,[3] nurtured by faith, prepared with truth—a prayer that is without blemish because of our innocence, clean because of our chastity—a prayer that has received the victor's crown because of our love for one another—this prayer we should bring to the altar of God with a display of good works amid the singing of psalms and hymns and it will obtain for us from God all that we ask.

Chapter 29

(1) For what will God refuse to the prayer that comes to Him from the spirit and in truth, since this is the prayer He has exacted? What proofs of its efficacy do we read of and hear of and believe! To be sure, the prayer of old would save one from fires and wild beasts and starvation; yet, it had not received its form from Christ. But how much more is wrought by Christian prayer! It does not cause an angel of dew to appear in the midst of fire, nor does it stop the mouths of lions nor take the breakfast of country folk to the hungry; it does not destroy all sense of pain by the grace that is conferred;[1] but by patient endurance it teaches those who suffer,

---

3 The Roman religion required that the animal for sacrifice (*hostia*) be offered according to ritualistic formula (*devota*); it must be fattened and made ready for the altar (*pasta et curata*); it must be without blemish (*integra*), and clean (*munda*); it must be adorned with a fillet, sometimes also wreathed with a garland of flowers (*coronata*). Preceded by the sacrificing magistrate or priest and their attendants, the victims were led in solemn procession (*pompa*) with singing and music to the altar. Tertullian adroitly parallels all these features required for pagan sacrifice with those of Christian prayer by employing a terminology which is equally applicable to both.

1 As happened in the Old Covenant; cf. Dan. 3.20-50; 6.16-23; the cases of Habacuc, Job, the three young men in the fiery furnace, etc.

those who are sensitive, and those who have sorrow; by virtue it increases grace that our faith may know what comes from the Lord and understand what it suffers for the name of God.

(2) Then, too, in the past, prayer would impose stripes, set loose the armies of the enemy, and prevent the beneficent effects of rain. But now, the prayer of justice averts the wrath of God, is on the alert for enemies, and intercedes for persecutors. What wonder if it could wrest water from the heavens,[2] when it could even ask for fire and obtain it! Prayer alone overcomes God; but Christ has willed that it work no evil, upon it He has conferred all power for good. Therefore, it has no power except to recall the souls of the dead from the very path of death, to make the weak recover, to heal the sick, to exorcise demons, to open prison doors, to loosen the chains of the innocent. It likewise remits sins, repels temptations, stamps out persecution, consoles the fainthearted, delights the courageous, brings travelers safely home, calms the waves, stuns robbers, feeds the poor, directs the rich, raises up the fallen, sustains the falling, and supports those who are on their feet.

(3) Prayer is the wall of faith, our shield and weapons against the foe who studies us from all sides. Hence, let us never set forth unarmed. Let us be mindful of our guard-duty by day and our vigil by night. Beneath the arms of prayer let us guard the standard of our general, and let us pray as we await the bugle call of the angel.

(4) All the angels pray, too; every creature prays; the beasts, domestic and wild, bend their knees, and as they go forth from their stables and caves they look up to heaven with no idle gaze. Even the birds, upon rising in the morning,

---

2 Cf. *Apology* 5.6, to which incident Tertullian is perhaps referring here.

mount into the sky and stretch out their wings as a cross in place of hands and say something which might seem to be a prayer. What need, then, is there of further discussion of the duty of prayer? Even our Lord Himself prayed, to whom be honor and power forever and ever.

PATIENCE

Translated by
SISTER EMILY JOSEPH DALY, C.S.J., Ph.D.
College of St. Rose
Albany, N. Y.

INTRODUCTION

IN CONTRAST TO the impassioned rhetoric which stamps so distinctively the bulk of Tertullian's writings, the homily on *Patience* presents an urgent, but gentle, exhortation to the practice of this truly Christian virtue. 'I confess,' he begins, 'to the Lord my God that I certainly have courage, not to say presumption, to have dared to write on patience, a virtue which I am utterly unfit to practise, being, as I am, a man of no account.' Such a disarming admission, followed by a humble acknowledgment of the need of divine assistance in order to attain to patience, together with the relatively mild and pleasing tone of the entire treatise, sets it apart as rather rare in the work of the great controversialist. However, he finds a degree of consolation in speaking of something he does not possess, even as the sick, deprived of health, constantly speak of the value of health. Patience, he points out, has its origin in God, just as impatience comes from the Devil. This latter is the mother of all sins; patience is the fulfillment of the Law. Various stumbling-blocks to this virtue and the joy which attends the exercise of it are outlined. Toward the end (Ch. 15), Tertullian describes in beautiful language the sublime daughter of heaven in her exterior

appearance and pictures her as the type of the ideal Christian.
Undoubtedly, it was for himself as well as for the catechumens that the author intended this attractive essay. It was probably written between 200 and 203.

The present translation is based on the critical text of J. G. Ph. Borleffs in the *Corpus Christianorum,* Series Latina 1 (Turnholti 1954) 297-317.

SELECT BIBLIOGRAPHY

Texts:

Aem. Kroymann, CSEL 47 (1906) 1-24.
J. G. Ph. Borleffs, *Corpus Christianorum,* Series Latina 1 (Turnholti 1954) 297-317.

Secondary Sources:

M. L. Carlson, 'Pagan Examples of Fortitude in the Latin Christian Apologists,' *Classical Philology* 43 (1948) 93-104.
R. Kaderschafka, *Quae ratio et rerum materiae et generis dicendi intercedere videatur inter Cypriani libellum* 'De bono patientiae' *et Tertulliani librum* 'De patientia,' Programm des Gymnasiums Pilsen 1913.

PATIENCE

Chapter 1

CONFESS TO THE LORD my God that I certainly have courage, not to say presumption, to have dared to write on patience, a virtue which I am utterly unfit to practise, being, as I am, a man of no account. For, those who undertake to set forth and recommend any virtue should first give some evidence of practising this virtue, and they should give proper direction to their constant admonition by the example of their own conduct, lest they be put to the blush at the discrepancy between their words and deeds. (2) And would that the blushing brought an improvement, that the shame [we feel] at not doing what we have suggested to others would teach us to do it! But, of course, it is with certain virtues as with certain vices: their greatness is so overwhelming that only the grace of divine inspiration can help us to attain and practise them. (3) For, that which is in the highest sense good belongs in the highest degree to God, and no one dispenses it save He who possesses it, to each one as He sees fit. (4) It will be, then, a comfort to discuss that which it is not granted us to enjoy, somewhat in the manner of the sick, who, when deprived of health, cannot refrain from proclaiming its blessings. (5) Thus, in my pitiable state, ever suffering from the fever of impatience, I must sigh after the health of patience which I do not possess, and I must beg and beseech it, remembering and reflecting, as I consider my weakness, that one does not easily attain the good health of faith and the soundness of the discipline of the Lord unless patience lends assistance thereto. (6) Patience has been given such pre-eminence in matters pertaining to God that no one can fulfill any precept or perform any work pleasing to the Lord without patience.

(7) Even those who do not possess it pay recognition to its excellence by giving it the honorable title of 'the highest virtue.' In fact, the philosophers, who are regarded as creatures possessing some degree of wisdom, attribute such value to it that, while there are disagreements among them because of the various inclinations of the schools and their opposing tenets, they are, nevertheless, of one mind with regard to patience alone, and in this alone of their interests they enter into agreement. With regard to this they are in accord: for this they band together, with one mind they apply themselves to it in their efforts to attain virtue; every display of wisdom they usher in with a show of patience. (8) A great compliment it is to this virtue to be the moving force behind even the vain pursuits of the world to their praise and renown! Or is it rather an insult that divine things are involved in the doings of the world? (9) Let them see to it who will one day be ashamed of their wisdom when it is destroyed and brought to disgrace along with this world![1]

---

1 Isa. 29.14; 1 Cor. 1.19.

Chapter 2

(1) There has been given to us as a model in the practice of patience no [merely] human product fashioned of the dullness of Cynic indifference, but the divine ordinance of a life-giving and heavenly way of life which points out as an exemplar of patience God Himself. (2) Long has He been scattering the brilliance of this light [of the sun] upon the just and unjust[1] alike and has allowed the deserving as well as the undeserving to enjoy the benefits of the seasons, the services of the elements, and the gifts of all creation. (3) He endures ungrateful peoples who worship the trifles fashioned by their skill and the works of their hands, who persecute His name and His children, and who, in their lewdness, their greed, their godlessness and depravity, grow worse from day to day; by His patience He hopes to draw them to Himself. There are many, you see, who do not believe in the Lord because for so long a time they have no experience of His wrath [directed] against the world.

Chapter 3

(1) This is, indeed, a picture of the divine patience which exists, so to speak, far away from us, the patience, we might say, which prevails on high. But what about that patience which exists openly among men on earth, which is, as it were, within our reach? (2) God allows Himself to become incarnate: in His mother's womb He awaits [the time of birth] and after His birth suffers Himself to grow into manhood, and, when an adult, shows no eagerness to become

---
1 Cf. Matt. 5.45.

known, but bears reproaches and is baptized by His own servant and by His words alone repels the attacks of the Tempter. (3) When He, [begotten] of the Lord, becomes a master[1] teaching man how to avoid death, He teaches him for his own good how to offer reparation to outraged patience. (4) He did not wrangle or cry aloud; neither did anyone hear His voice in the streets; a bruised reed He did not break, a smoking wick He did not quench.[2] (Now, the Prophet—or, rather, the testimony of God Himself, placing His own spirit in His Son with all patience—has not lied!) (5) He did not force one who was unwilling to stay close to Him; He scorned no one's table or dwelling; in fact, He ministered personally to His disciples by washing their feet. (6) He did not despise sinners or publicans, He showed no anger even toward that city which refused to receive Him, even when the disciples wished fire from heaven to fall upon such a shameful town;[3] He healed the ungrateful, yielded to His persecutors. (7) More than this, He even kept in His company the one who would betray Him and did not firmly denounce him. Why, even when He is betrayed, when He is led like a beast to the slaughter—for thus [is it written]: 'He does not open His mouth any more than does a lamb in the power of its shearer'[4]—He who could have had if He wished, at a single word, legions of angels from heaven to assist Him[5] did not approve of an avenging sword on the part of even one of His disciples.[6] (8) It was the forbearance of the Lord

---

1 Cf. John 3.2.
2 Cf. Isa. 42.2,3; Matt. 12.19,20.
3 Cf. Luke 9.52-56.
4 Isa. 53.7.
5 Matt. 26.53.
6 Matt. 26.51; John 18.10.

that was wounded in [the person of] Malchus.⁷ And so, He actually cursed for all time the works of the sword and by healing him whom He had not Himself struck,⁸ He made satisfaction by forbearance, which is the mother of mercy. (9) I say nothing about His crucifixion; it was for this that He had come. Still, did there have to be such insults attending the death He must undergo? No; but as He went forward to His death, He willed to have His fill of joy in suffering: He is spat upon, beaten, mocked, disgracefully clothed, and even more disgracefully crowned. (10) Marvel at the constancy of His meekness: He who had proposed to escape notice in the guise of man has in no degree imitated man's impatience. For this reason particularly, you Pharisees, you should have recognized the Lord! Patience such as this no mere man had ever practised!

(11) Such were the manifestations [of His patience], the very magnitude of which is the reason why pagan nations reject the faith; for us they are its rational foundation. For those to whom there has been granted the gift of faith they suffice to make it very clear, not only by the words our Lord used in His precepts, but also by the sufferings which He endured, that patience is the very nature of God, the effect and manifestation of a certain connatural property [of His being].

Chapter 4

(1) Now, if we see that all servants of righteous character and good disposition live according to the mind of their lord

---
7 Matt. 26.52.
8 Luke 22.51.

—obedience, as you know, is a facility in rendering service, but the principle of obedience is compliant submission—how much more does it behoove us to be found modeled upon our Lord! Servants indeed we are of the living God whose sway over His [creatures] consists not in manacles or the granting of the slave's cap,[1] but in alloting everlasting punishment or salvation. (2) To escape His severity or to invite His liberality one needs diligence in obeying which is proportionate to the threats uttered by His severity or the promises made by His liberality. (3) Yet, we ourselves exact obedience not only from men who are bound to us by the bonds of slavery or who, because of some other legal bond, are under obligation to us, but also from our flocks and even from the wild animals. We understand that they have been provided and granted by the Lord for our purposes. (4) I ask you: in the practice of obedience, shall those creatures which God has made subject to us surpass us? In a word, creatures which obey [their masters] acknowledge [their condition as creatures]: do we hesitate to heed Him to whom alone we are subject, namely, the Lord? Why, how unjust it would be, and in addition how ungrateful, for you not to make a return of what you have obtained from others through the kindness of a third party, to him through whom you obtained it!

(5) But, no more about the manifestation of the obedience which we owe to the Lord our God. For, in the act of recognition of God one understands sufficiently what is incumbent upon him. However, lest we seem to have inserted something irrelevant to this discussion of obedience, [let me

---

[1] The *pilleus* was a felt cap shaped like the half of an egg, and made to fit close; it was given to a slave at his enfranchisement as a sign of his freedom.

remark that] obedience itself also stems from patience: never does one who is impatient obey nor does a patient man ever refuse obedience. (6) Who, then, could deal adequately with the value of that patience which the Lord our God, the model and patron of all that is good, has displayed in Himself? Who would doubt that those who belong to God have an obligation to strive with their whole soul for every good, since it has reference to God? By these considerations our recommendation and exhortation on the subject of patience is briefly established in a summary, as it were, of the prescribed rule.

Chapter 5

(1) Now, to thrash out a question about essential points of faith is not wearisome, since it is not without profit. Verboseness, though a fault at times, is no fault when it tends to edification. (2) Therefore, if some good is being discussed, the matter demands that we examine also the evil which is its opposite. You will throw a better light upon what one should strive for if you discuss in connection with it what should be avoided. (3) Let us, then, with regard to impatience, consider whether, as patience [exists] in God, its opposite was born and discovered in our adversary. From this it will appear how impatience, more than anything else, is opposed to faith. (4) For, that which is conceived by God's rival[1] is certainly not a friend to the things of God. There is the same hostility in the things as there is in their authors. Furthermore, since God is infinitely good, and the Devil, on

---

1 *Aemulus Dei* ('God's rival') as well as *adversarius* of the preceding sentence are frequently used by patristic writers with reference to Satan.

the other hand, is superlatively evil, by their very difference they bear witness that neither one effects anything for the other; it can no more seem to us that some good is produced from evil than some evil from good.

(5) Now, I find the origin of impatience in the Devil himself. Even when the Lord God subjected to His own image, that is, to man, all the works He had made,[2] the Devil bore it with impatience. (6) For, he would not have grieved, had he endured it, nor would he have envied man, had he not grieved; he deceived man because he envied him; he envied him because he grieved; he grieved because he certainly had not borne it with patience. (7) What the angel of perdition was first—I mean, whether he was first evil or impatient—I do not bother to inquire; it is clear that, whether impatience had its beginning in evil or evil in impatience, they entered into combination and grew as one in the bosom of one father. (8) For, as soon as he perceived that it was through his impatience that he had committed the first sin, having learned from his own experience what would assist in wrong-doing, he availed himself of this same impatience to lead men into sin. (9) Without delay, and I would say not without forethought, he contrived a meeting with the woman, and simply and solely through their conversation she was touched by his breath, already infected with impatience. But never would she have sinned at all had she preserved her patience according to the divine command! (10) And what of the fact that she could not endure having met [the Devil] alone but, being unable to remain silent about it in the presence of Adam—he was not yet her husband, nor as yet under any obligation to lend her his ear—she makes him the carrier of that which she had imbibed from

---

2 Gen. 1.26.

the Evil One? (11) Thus, a second member, too, of the human race falls through the impatience of the first; and his fall, too, results from his own impatience committed in two ways: with regard to the forewarning of God, and with regard to the deceit of the Devil; for he was unable to observe the former or to oppose the latter. (12) Condemnation began with him in whom sin originated; God's anger began with him by whom man was induced to offend Him. God's patience began with him who had aroused His indignation; for at that time He was content with simply cursing him and He refrained from inflicting punishment upon the Devil. (13) What sin previous to this sin of impatience can be imputed to man? He was innocent and a close friend of God and a tenant dwelling in paradise. But, when once he yielded to impatience, he ceased to relish God and could no longer endure the things of heaven. (14) From that time on, as a man delivered up to the earth and cast away from the eyes of God, he began to serve as an easy instrument for impatience to use for everything that would offend God. (15) For, immediately, that impatience which was conceived by the seed of the Devil with the fecundity of evil gave birth to a child of wrath and instructed its offspring in its own arts. Since it had plunged Adam and Eve into death, it taught their son, also, to commit the first murder. (16) Vain were it for me to ascribe this sin to impatience, had Cain, the first homicide and the first fratricide, accepted it with equanimity and without impatience when his offerings were refused by the Lord; if he had not been angry with his brother; if, in fine, he had killed no one. (17) Therefore, since he could not commit murder unless he were angry, and could not be angry unless he were impatient, it proves that what he did in anger is to be referred to that which prompted the anger.

(18) Such was the cradle of impatience which was then, so to speak, in its infancy. But to what proportions it soon grew! And no wonder: if it was the prime source of sin, it follows that, being the prime source, it was therefore also the sole fashioner of all sin, pouring forth from its own abundant resources the varied channels of crimes. (19) Homicide has already been mentioned. It sprang originally from anger, and whatever causes it finds for itself afterwards, it ascribes them to impatience at its origin. For, whether one commits this crime through enmity or for some gain, the original cause is that one is overwhelmed by hatred or greed. (20) Whatever is the motivating force, a crime could not be perpetrated unless one lacks patience. Who has ever attempted adultery save one who was unable to withstand his lustful desires? Even the fact that [disgrace] is forced upon [some] women for a price, that sale of one's honor is certainly set in order by an inability to set at naught despicable gain. (21) Impatience is, as it were, the original sin in the eyes of the Lord. For, to put it in a nutshell, every sin is to be traced back to impatience. Evil cannot endure good. No unchaste person but is intolerant of chastity; no scoundrel but is irked by righteousness; no negligent person but resents his obligations; no agitator but is impatient of peace. Although anyone may become evil, not everyone can persevere in good.

(22) Why, then, should not this hydra-like generator of sins[3] offend the Lord, who condemns all wickedness? Is it not clear that Israel itself, through its impatience, was ever sinning against God? (23) Forgetting the heavenly arm whereby it had been rescued from the afflictions of the Egyp-

---

3 I.e., the hydra, which ever begets from itself new sins.

tians,⁴ it demanded of Aaron gods to be its leaders, while it poured its contributions into an idol of its own gold. For, it had borne without patience the delay necessitated by Moses' meeting with the Lord.⁵ (24) After the rain of manna as food, after the water that followed and flowed from the rock, they gave up hope in the Lord,⁶ unable to endure a three-days' thirst. For this, too, they were charged with impatience by the Lord. (25) But, not to range over individual instances: never would they have been destroyed had they not fallen into sin by impatience. Why did they lay hands on the Prophets, except that they could not bear to listen to them? And more than that: they laid hands upon the Lord Himself, being unable to endure even the sight of Him. But had they acquired patience, they would now be free.

Chapter 6

(1) Such is the patience which is both subsequent to and antecedent to faith. Accordingly, Abraham believed in God and it was credited to him by God as justice.¹ Now, he proved his faith by patience, when he was commanded to offer in sacrifice his son²—I do not say for a trial, but rather for a typical attestation, of his faith. (2) But God knew the man whom He had reputed for his justice. This severe command, which the Lord did not intend should be carried out,

---

4 Cf. Exod. 32.1-4.
5 Exod. 16.14; cf. Exod. 17.6 and 1 Cor. 10.4.
6 Exod. 15.22-25.

1 Gen. 15.6.
2 Gen. 22.2.

Abraham heard with patience and, had God so willed, he would have fulfilled it. Rightly, then, is he blessed because he was faithful; and rightly was he faithful because he was patient.[3] (3) Thus faith was illuminated by patience, since it was sown among the heathens by the seed of Abraham which is Christ and added grace to the Law, and it has made patience its helpmate in amplifying and fulfilling the Law, because in times past this was the only thing lacking to the teaching of justice. (4) Heretofore, men demanded an eye for an eye and a tooth for a tooth[4] and they returned evil for evil. As yet, patience was not found upon the earth, for as yet, you see, there was not faith. Meanwhile, impatience was enjoying the opportunities occasioned by the Law. It was easy when the Lord and Teacher of patience was not on hand. (5) But after He came and united the grace of faith with patience, no longer was one permitted to do injury with so much as a word, or even say 'Thou fool!' without being in danger of the judgment.[5] Wrath was forbidden, passions were kept in check, unruly hands were restrained, the poison of the tongue was removed. (6) The Law acquired more than it lost when Christ said: 'Love your enemies and bless those who curse you and pray for those who persecute you, so that you may be children of your Father in heaven.'[6] Just see what a Father patience acquires for us!

---

3 Gen. 22.17,18; Rom. 4.3.
4 Cf. Exod. 21.24.
5 Matt. 5.22.
6 Matt. 5.44,45.

PATIENCE

Chapter 7

(1) The entire practice of patience is compressed within this fundamental precept whereby not even a lawful injury is permitted. But now, as we run through the causes of impatience, all the other precepts, too, will correspond in their own context. (2) Is the mind disturbed by the loss of property? In practically every passage of the holy Scriptures one is admonished to despise the world, and no greater exhortation is there to an indifference toward money than that our Lord Himself is without it. (3) He always justifies the poor and condemns the rich. Thus He has set disdain for wealth ahead of the endurance of losses, pointing out through His rejection of riches that one should make no account of the loss of them. (4) Hence, we need not seek wealth, since our Lord did not seek it; and we ought to bear the deprivation of even the theft of it without regret. (5) The Spirit of the Lord, through the Apostle, has called the desire of money the root of all evils.[1] We may infer that this consists not only in the desire for that which belongs to another; even that which seems to be our own belongs to another; for nothing is our own, since all things belong to God to whom we, too, belong. (6) Therefore, if we feel impatient when we suffer some loss, we will be found to possess a desire for money, since we grieve over the loss of that which is not our own. We are seeking what belongs to another when we are unwilling to bear the loss of that which belongs to another. (7) The man who is upset and unable to bear his loss sins, you might say, against God Himself by preferring the things of earth to those of heaven. For, the soul which he has received from the Lord is upset by the attractiveness of worldly goods.

---

1 1 Tim. 6.10.

(8) Let us, then, with glad hearts, relinquish earthly goods that we may preserve those of heaven! Let the whole world fall in ruins provided I gain the patience to endure it! In all probability, a man who has not resolved to bear with fortitude a slight loss occasioned by theft or violence or even by his own stupidity will not readily or willingly touch what he owns for the sake of charity. (9) For, what man who refuses to undergo any operation at all at the hands of another puts a knife to his own body? Patience to endure, shown on occasions of loss, is a training in giving and sharing. He who does not fear loss is not reluctant to give. (10) Otherwise, how would one who has two tunics[2] give one of them to him who is destitute, unless the same is one who can offer his cloak as well to the one going off with his tunic?[3] How will we make friends for ourselves with mammon[4] if we love him only to the extent that we do not share in his loss? We shall be damned together with the damned. (11) What do we find here where we have [only something] to lose? It is for pagans to be unable to sustain all loss; they would set worldly goods before their life perhaps. (12) And they do this when, in their eager desire for wealth, they engage in lucrative but dangerous commerce on the sea; when, for money's sake, they unhesitatingly engage in transactions also in the forum, even though there be reason to fear loss; they do it, in fine, when they hire themselves out for the games and military service or when, in desolate regions, they commit robbery regardless of the wild beasts. (13) On the other hand, in view of the difference between them and ourselves, it befits us to give up not our life for money but money for our life, either by voluntary charity or by the patient endurance of loss.

---

2 Luke 3.11.
3 Matt. 5.40.
4 Luke 16.9.

PATIENCE

Chapter 8

(1) Our very life and our very body we have exposed in this world as a target for all manner of injury and we endure this injury with patience; shall we, then, be vexed by the deprivation of lesser things? Far be such shame from the servant of Christ, that his patience, trained by greater trials, should fail in trifling ones! (2) If one tries to provoke you to a fight, there is at hand the admonition of the Lord: 'If someone strike thee,' He says, ' on the right cheek, turn to him the other also.'[1] Let wrong-doing grow weary from your patience; whoever be struck, the one who strikes, weighed down by pain and shame, will suffer more severely from the Lord; by your meekness you will strike a more severe blow to the wrong-doer; for he will suffer at the hands of Him by whose grace you practise meekness. (3) If a spiteful tongue bursts out in cursing or wrangling, recall the saying: 'When men reproach you, rejoice.'[2] The Lord Himself was accursed before the Law,[3] yet He alone is blessed. Let us, then, His servants, follow our Lord and patiently submit to maledictions that we may be blessed! (4) If, with slight forbearance, I hear some bitter or evil remark directed against me, I may return it, and then I shall inevitably be bitter myself. Either that, or I shall be tormented by unexpressed resentment. (5) If, then, I retaliate when cursed, how shall I be found to have followed the teaching of our Lord? For it has been handed down that a man is not defiled by unclean dishes, but by the words which proceed from his mouth;[4] and, what is more,

---

1 Matt. 5.39.
2 Matt. 5.11.
3 Cf. Deut. 21.23; Gal. 3.13.
4 Cf. Mark 7.15.

that it remains for us to render an account for every vain and idle word.[5] (6) It follows, then, that our Lord forbids us to do certain acts, but at the same time admonishes us to endure with meekness the same treatment at the hands of another.

(7) [We shall speak] now of the joy which comes from patience. For every injury, whether occasioned by the tongue or the hand, coming in contact with patience, will meet the same end as a weapon which is flung and dashed upon a hard, unyielding rock. An ineffectual and fruitless action will lose its force immediately and will sometimes vent its passion and strike with the force of a boomerang upon him who sent it forth. (8) This is true, of course, since one insults you with the intention of causing you pain, because the one who inflicts the injury reaps his reward in the pain of the one injured. Consequently, if you cheat him of his reward by not showing any pain, he will himself inevitably feel pain because he has lost his reward. (9) Then *you* will go off, not only uninjured (which of itself should suffice for you) but over and above that you will have the pleasure of seeing your enemy frustrated while you yourself are preserved from pain. Herein lies the advantage of patience and the joy which derives from it.

Chapter 9

(1) Not even that form of impatience which results from the loss of our dear ones is excused, although in this case a sort of rightful claim to grieve justifies it. Observance of the precept of the Apostle must be put first: 'Grieve not,' he says,

---

5 Matt. 12.36.

'over one who has fallen asleep even as the gentiles who have no hope.'¹ (2) And rightly so. For, if we believe in the resurrection of Christ, we believe in our own, also, since it was for us that He died and rose again. Therefore, since there is sure ground for faith in the resurrection of the dead, there is no grief associated with death, and no inability to bear grief. (3) Why should you grieve if you believe that [the loved one] has not perished utterly? Why should you show impatience that one has been taken away for the time being if you believe he will return? That which you think of as death is merely the beginning of a journey.² He who has gone ahead is not to be mourned, though certainly he will be missed. But this lonesomeness must be alleviated by patience. Why should you be inconsolable over the departure of one whom you are soon to follow? (4) Moreover, impatience in such things is a sad indication of our own hope and gives the lie to our faith. Likewise, we injure Christ when we fail to accept with resignation [the death of] those whom He has called, as though they were to be pitied. (5) 'I desire,' says the Apostle, 'to be welcomed home now and to be with the Lord.'³ How much better a prayer he holds forth! As for the Christians' prayer, then, if we bear it with impatience and grief that others have attained their goal, we ourselves do not want to attain our goal!

---

1 1 Thess. 4.12.
2 In early Christian literature death is often referred to as a journey to the Lord (*migratio ad Dominum*); cf. A. C. Rush, *Death and Burial in Christian Antiquity* (Washington, D. C. 1941) 54-71.
3 Phil. 1.23.

Chapter 10

(1) There is another, and very strong, motive which gives rise to impatience, namely, the desire for revenge, which busies itself in the interest of either reputation or wrong-doing. Now, reputation is everywhere empty, and evil never fails to be hateful to the Lord, especially in this situation when, occasioned by wrong-doing on the part of another, it takes the upper hand in executing vengeance and, in paying back the evil, does twice as much as was done in the first place. (2) Revenge mistakenly appears to be a soothing of one's pain, but in the light of truth it is seen to be only evil contending with evil. What difference is there between the one who provokes and the one provoked except that the one is caught doing wrong sooner than the other? Nevertheless, before the Lord each is guilty of having injured a fellow man and the Lord forbids and condemns every act of wrong-doing. (3) There is no hierarchical arrangement in wrong-doing, nor does position make any distinction in that which similarity makes one. Therefore, the precept is unequivocally laid down: evil is not to be rendered for evil.[1] Like deed merits like treatment. (4) But how shall we observe this precept if, in loathing [evil], we have no loathing for revenge? What tribute of honor shall we offer to the Lord our God if we assume to ourselves the right to inflict punishment? (5) We who are matter subject to decay, vessels of clay,[2] are grievously offended when our servants take it upon themselves to seek revenge from their fellow slaves; as for those who show us patience, we not only praise them as slaves who are conscious of their lowly position, men attentive to the respect

---
1 Rom. 12.17.
2 2 Cor. 4.7.

they owe their lord, but we recompense them even more than they had themselves anticipated. Is there any risk for us in such a course when we have a Lord so just in His judgments, so powerful in His deeds? (6) Why, then, do we believe Him a judge, but not also an avenger? Of this He assures us when He says: 'Revenge is mine and I will repay them,'[3] that is: 'Have patience with Me and I will reward your patience.' (7) When He says: 'Do not judge, that you may not be judged,'[4] is He not demanding patience? What man will refrain from judging another except one who will forego [the right] of self-defense? What man judges with the intention of forgiving? And if he does forgive, he has but shied away from the impatience of a man who judges and has usurped the honor of the true Judge, that is, God!

(8) What misfortunes has such impatience, as a rule, brought upon itself! How often has it regretted its self-defense! How often has its obstinacy become worse than the occasions which provoked it! Now, nothing undertaken through impatience can be transacted without violence, and everything done with violence has either met with no success or has collapsed or has plunged to its own destruction. (9) If you are too mild in your self-defense, you will be acting like a madman; if your defense is excessive, you will be depressed. Why should I be concerned about revenge when I cannot regulate its extent because of my inability to endure pain? Whereas, if I yield and suffer the injury, I shall have no pain; and if I have no pain, I shall have no desire for revenge.

---
3 Deut. 32.35.
4 Matt. 7.1.

Chapter 11

(1) Now that we have, to the best of our ability, set forth these principal provocations to impatience in the order of their intensity, with which of the rest that [we encounter] at home and in public life should we concern ourselves? Widespread and extensive are the workings of the Evil One who extends innumerable incentives to impatience which, at times, are slight, at times very great. (2) The slight ones you should ignore for their insignificance; to the great you should yield in view of their invincible power. When the injury is not very important, there is no need for impatience, but when the injury is more serious, then there is greater need for a remedy against the injury, namely, patience. (3) Let us strive, then, to bear the injuries that are inflicted by the Evil One, that the struggle to maintain our self-control may put to shame the enemy's efforts. If, however, through imprudence or even of our own free will we draw down upon ourselves some misfortune, we should submit with equal patience to that which we impute to ourselves. (4) But if we believe some blow of misfortune is struck by God, to whom would it be better that we manifest patience than to our Lord? In fact, more than this, it befits us to rejoice at being deemed worthy of divine chastisement: 'As for me,' He says, 'those whom I love I chastise.'[1] Blessed is that servant upon whose amendment the Lord insists, at whom He deigns to be angry, whom He does not deceive by omitting His admonition!

(5) From every angle, then, we are obliged to practise patience, because we meet up with our own mistakes or the wiles of the Evil One or the warnings of the Lord alike. Great is the recompense for practising it, namely, happiness.

---

1 Apoc. 3.19; Prov. 3.12.

(6) Whom has the Lord declared happy? Those who are patient; for He said:[2] 'Blessed are the poor in spirit, for theirs is the kingdom of heaven.' Assuredly, no one but the humble man is poor in spirit. And who is humble but the man who is patient? No one can take a position of subjection without patience, the prime factor in subjection. (7) 'Blessed,' He says, 'are those who weep and mourn.' Who can endure such things without patience? To such, then, is consolation and joy promised. (8) 'Blessed are the meek.' Certainly, in this word one cannot by any means include the impatient. Likewise, when He applies this same title of happiness to the peace-makers and calls them the children of God, I ask you: Do the impatient share in this peace? Only a fool would think so! (9) And when He says: 'Rejoice and exult when men reproach you and persecute you because your reward is great in heaven,' certainly this promise of great joy is not made to the impatient, for no one will rejoice in adversity unless he has first come to despise it; no one will despise it unless he possesses patience.

Chapter 12

(1) As for what pertains to the practice of this peace so pleasing to God [I ask you]: What man, completely given over to impatience, will forgive his brother, I will not say seven times and seventy times seven times, but even once?[1] (2) What man, taking his case with his adversary to a judge, will settle his trouble to the accommodation of the other

---
2 Matt. 5.3-12.
---
1 Cf. Matt. 18.22; Luke 17.4.

party, unless he first puts an end to his wrath, his resentment, his harshness and bitterness, that is, his impatient disposition? (3) How will you forgive and experience forgiveness[2] if you cling to your injury through a total lack of patience? No one whose mind is violently disturbed against his brother will complete his offering at the altar unless first he has been reconciled to his brother through patience.[3] (4) If the sun goes down upon our anger, we are in danger.[4] We may not live a single day without patience. Yet, since patience governs every aspect of a salutary way of life, what wonder that it also paves the way for repentance which, as a rule, comes to the assistance of those who have fallen? (5) What benefits it produces in both parties when, in spite of their forbearance from their marriage rights—provided it be only for that reason which makes it lawful for a man or woman to persist in their separation—it waits for, hopes for, wins by its prayers repentance for those who will eventually be saved. It purifies the one without causing the other to become an adulterer!

(6) So, too, in those examples in our Lord's parables[5] there is a breath of patience: it is the patience of the shepherd that seeks and finds the straying sheep (for impatience would readily take no account of a single sheep, whereas patience undertakes the wearisome search) and he carries it on his shoulders, a patient bearer of a forsaken sinner. (7) In the case of the prodigal son, too, it is the patience of his father that welcomes him and clothes him and feeds him and finds an excuse for him in the face of the impatience of his angry brother. The one who had perished is rescued, therefore,

---
2 Cf. Luke 6.37.
3 Cf. Matt. 5.23,24.
4 Cf. Eph. 4.26.
5 Cf. Luke 15.4-6, 11-32.

because he embraced repentance; repentance is not wasted because it meets up with patience!

(8) Consider now charity, the great bond of faith, the treasure of the Christian religion, which the Apostle extols with all the power of the Holy Spirit: how is it learned except by the exercise of patience? (9) 'Charity,' he says, 'is magnanimous.'[6] It derives this from patience. 'It is kind.' Patience works no evil. 'It does not envy.' Envy is certainly a characteristic of impatience. 'It is not pretentious.' It has derived its contentment from patience. 'It is not puffed up, is not ambitious,' for that does not befit patience. 'It is not self-seeking.' It suffers [the loss of] its own goods provided that it be to another's advantage. 'It is not provoked.' What, then, would it have left to impatience? Therefore, he says, 'charity bears with all things, endures all things.' Of course it does, because it is itself patient. (10) He is correct, then, in stating that it will never fall away. Everything else will pass away and come to an end. Tongues, knowledge, prophecies are made void, but there persist faith, hope, and charity: faith, which the patience of Christ has instilled; hope, to which the patience of man looks forward; charity, which patience accompanies, according to the teaching of God.

Chapter 13

(1) Thus far [we have been speaking], however, of a patience which constitutes simply and uniformly and solely an operation of the soul, whereas in various ways we should strive for this same patience also in the body in order to

---

6 Cf. 1 Cor. 13.4-13.

attain the good pleasure of the Lord, inasmuch as it was practised by the Lord Himself as a virtue also of the body; for the soul, as the directing agent, readily shares the inspirations of the Spirit with that wherein it dwells. (2) What, then, is the operation of patience in the body? Primarily, mortification of the flesh as a sacrifice acceptable to the Lord. This is an offering of [one's] humility, since it offers to the Lord a sacrifice of mourning dress along with meager rations, contenting itself with plain food and a drink of clear water, joining fast with fast[1] and persevering in sackcloth and ashes. (3) This patience on the part of the body contributes to the value of our petitions and strengthens our prayers for deliverance. It opens the ears of Christ our God, dispels His severity, elicits His mercy.[2] (4) Thus, after offending the Lord, the King of Babylon lived for seven years in squalor and filth, an exile from human society. By this offering of the patient endurance of bodily [discomfort] not only did he

---

1 Tertullian uses the expressions *ieiunia coniungere* (*De patientia* 13.2) and [*ieiunium*] *continuare* (*De ieiunio* 14.3) to describe the practice of extending the fast beyond the usual time—the ordinary fast ended at 6 P.M. It meant a total abstention from food for two, three, and even more days. The technical term for this practice was *superpositio* (sc. *ieiunii*). These lengthy and continuous fasts, which were also called *biduanum* (sc. *ieiunium*), *triduanum, quatriduanum*, were in vogue especially among the ascetics.

2 The sense of the passage is certainly that 'bodily patience,' which manifests itself above all in the mortification of the flesh by penance done in sackcloth and ashes and the observance of vigorous fasts (see the preceding sentence!), *recommends our prayers to God, gives additional strength to our prayers against evil, and opens the ears of God*. The idea that prayer can be strengthened and made more effective by combining it with mortification of the flesh occurs also in Tertullian's *De exhortatione castitatis* 10.2, where he says: 'For this reason the Apostle added the counsel of temporary abstinence for the sake of recommending our prayers' to God (*Ideo apostolus temporalem purificationem orationum commendandarum causa adiecit*).

regain his kingdom, but—and this is even more desirable in a man—he made satisfaction to God.³

(5) Now, if we go on to consider the higher and more blessed degrees of bodily patience, [we see that] it turns continence, too, into an opportunity for sanctity: this it is which preserves the widow [in her state], places its seal upon the virgin, and raises to the kingdom of heaven one who of his own free will embraces a life of celibacy.⁴

(6) That which derives from the power of the soul finds its fulfillment in the flesh. In persecutions the endurance of the flesh engages in battle. If flight besets one, the flesh surmounts the hardships of flight. If imprisonment precludes flight, it is the flesh which submits to the chains, the block of wood, and the bare ground. It is the flesh which endures both the scanty light [of the dungeon] and the deprivation of worldly comforts. (7) But, when one is led forth to the ordeal that will prove his happiness, to the opportunity to renew one's baptism, to the very ascent to the throne of divinity, there is nothing [which avails] more in that situation than endurance on the part of the body. If the spirit is willing but the flesh— without patience—weak,⁵ where is there salvation for the spirit as well as for the flesh itself? (8) On the other hand, when the Lord speaks thus of the flesh and declares it weak, He points out what is needed for strengthening it, namely, patience in the face of everything that is ready to overthrow our faith and impose a penalty for it, that one may bear with constancy stripes, and fire, the cross, wild beasts, or the sword as the Prophets and Apostles bore them and won the victory.

---

3 Cf. Dan. 4.25-30.
4 Cf. Matt. 19.12.
5 Cf. Matt. 26.41.

Chapter 14

(1) In virtue of his power of endurance, Isaias, though cut in pieces, does not refrain from speaking of the Lord.¹ Stephen, as he is stoned, prays for pardon for his enemies.² (2) Happy, too, was that man who displayed every manner of patience against every vicious attack of the Devil!³ His flocks were driven away, his wealth in cattle destroyed by lightning,⁴ his children killed at a single stroke when his house collapsed,⁵ his own body, finally, was tortured by painful sores —yet, by none of these was he lured from his patience and the trust he owed the Lord. Though the Devil struck him with all his strength, he struck in vain! (3) Far from being turned away by so many misfortunes from the reverence which he owed to God, he set for us an example and proof of how we must practise patience in the spirit as well as in the flesh, in soul as well as in body, that we may not succumb under the loss of worldly goods, the death of our dear ones, or any bodily afflictions. (4) What a trophy over the Devil God erected in the case of that man! What a banner of His glory He raised above His enemy when that man let fall from his lips no other word than 'Thanks be to God!' as each bitter message reached him; when he severely rebuked his wife who, weary by now of misfortunes, was urging him to improper remedies.⁶ (5) How God laughed, and how the Evil One was split asunder, when Job, with perfect calm, would wipe

---

1 Cf. *Ascensio Isaiae* 5.14.
2 Cf. Acts 7.59.
3 Cf. Job 1.15-19.
4 The reading of the text is doubtful and the translation here follows the emendation of Engelbrecht; cf. Job 1.16.
5 Cf. Job 1.19.
6 Cf. Job 2.9-10.

away the discharge oozing from his ulcer and, with a jesting remark, would call back to the cavity and sustenance of his open flesh the tiny creatures that were trying to make their way out! (6) Thus did that hero who brought about a victory for his God beat back all the darts of temptation and with the breastplate and shield of patience soon after recover from God complete health of body and the possession of twice as much as he had lost.[7] (7) Had he wanted his sons to be restored, too, he would once again have heard himself called 'father.' But he preferred that they be restored to him on the last day; placing all his trust in the Lord, he deferred that great joy; for the present, he was willing to endure the loss of his children that he might not live without something to suffer!

Chapter 15

(1) God is fully capable of being the trustee of our patience: if you place in His hands an injustice you have suffered, He will see that justice is done; if a loss, He will see that you receive compensation; if a pain, He acts as healer; if death, He restores life. How much is granted to patience that it should have God for a debtor! (2) And not without reason. For it pays attention to all His prescriptions, it becomes surety for all His commands: it strengthens faith, governs peace, sustains love, instructs humility, awaits repentance, places its seal upon the discipline of penance, controls the flesh, preserves the spirit, puts restraint upon the tongue, holds back the [violent] hand, treads under foot temptations,

---

7 Job 42.10.

pushes scandal aside, consummates martyrdom. (3) In poverty it supplies consolation; upon wealth it imposes moderation; the sick it does not destroy, nor does it, for the man in health, prolong his life;[1] for the man of faith it is a source of delight. It attracts the heathen, recommends the slave to his master, the master to God. It adorns a woman, perfects a man. It is loved in a child, praised in a youth, esteemed in the aged. In both man and woman, at every age of life, it is exceedingly attractive.

(4) Now, then! If you will, let us try to grasp the features and appearance of patience. Its countenance is peaceful and untroubled. Its brow is clear, unruffled by any lines of melancholy or anger. The eyebrows are relaxed, giving an impression of joyousness. The eyes are lowered, in an attitude rather of humility than moroseness. (5) The mouth is closed in becoming silence. Its complexion is that of the serene and blameless. It shakes its head frequently in the direction of the Devil, and its laughter conveys a threat to him. The upper part of its garment is white and close-fitting so that it is not blown about or disturbed [by the wind]. (6) It sits on the throne of its spirit which is extremely mild and gentle and is not whipped into a knot by the whirlwind, is not made livid by a cloud, but is a breeze of soft light, clear and simple, such as Elias saw the third time.[2] For where God is, there, too, is the child of His nurturing, namely, patience.

(7) When the Spirit of God descends, patience is His inseparable companion. If we fail to welcome it along with the Spirit, will the latter remain within us at all times? As a matter of fact, I rather think the Spirit would not remain

---
1 The tranlation follows the emendation of Kroymann, who interchanges *consumit* ('destroy') and *extendit* ('prolong life').
2 Cf. 3 Kings 19.12.

PATIENCE

at all. Without its companion and assistant it would feel very uncomfortable anywhere and at any time. It could not endure, all by itself, the blows which its enemy inflicts, if stripped of the means which helps it to endure.

Chapter 16

(1) This is the theory, this the practice, this the operation of the patience which is divine and true, namely, Christian; a patience not like the patience practised by the peoples of the earth, which is false and disgraceful. (2) For, that the Devil might rival the Lord in this respect, also, and be really on an equal footing with Him as it were (except that good and evil are extremes of equal magnitude) the Devil also taught his own a special brand of patience. (3) It is a patience, I say, which renders subject to the power of their wives husbands who are purchased by a dowry or who negotiate with panderers; a patience in virtue of which [a wife] bears, with feigned affection, all the irritation resulting from a forced association so that, as a childless widow, she may lay hands upon her husband's estate; a patience which sentences gormandizers to sacrifice their freedom and become disgraceful slaves to their gluttony. (4) Such are the goals of patience as the heathens know it and by such despicable efforts they appropriate the name of so noble a virtue; they live in patient endurance of their rivals, the wealthy, and their hosts; it is only God alone whom they cannot endure. But let their patience and the patience of their chief take care: there is fire beneath the earth awaiting this kind of patience. (5) Let us, then, love the patience that is of God, the

patience of Christ; let us return to Him that which He expended for us; let us who believe in the resurrection of the flesh and of the spirit offer Him both the patience of the spirit and the patience of the flesh.

THE CHAPLET

Translated by
EDWIN A. QUAIN, S.J., Ph.D.
Fordham University

INTRODUCTION

THE TREATISE on *The Chaplet* is an occasional writing, prompted by an incident which is briefly described in the introductory chapter. On the death of Emperor Septimius Severus on February 4, 211, his two sons and co-rulers Caracalla and Geta followed the time-honored custom of bestowing on each soldier of the army a gift of money (the so-called *donativum*). When the gift was distributed in the camp, the soldiers wore, according to the regulations, a crown of laurel on their heads, except one of them who refused to wear the wreath on the ground that, being a Christian, he was not allowed to conform to a heathen rite. Thereupon he was arrested and thrown into prison, to await death. The incident attracted notice. Many Christians disapproved of the soldier's action, calling it an imprudent and unnecessary provocation which, after a period of peace, could easily lead to another persecution of the Christian religion.

By this time Tertullian had wandered farther and farther away from the Church whose cause he had so vigorously upheld against pagans and heretics alike in the first years after his conversion to Christianity. His violent and excessive character had led him to adopt Montanism. In the teachings of Montanus and his associates he saw not only the realization of his yearnings for a revival of the charismatic gifts which had blossomed in the life of the early Church, but he found there also a moral code which was reassuring to the rigor of his puritanism. Thus it is not surprising that the great polemist, always ready for combating faint-heartedness and censuring human failings, praised and extolled the soldier's action as the heroic deed of a true soldier of God.

His arguments may be summed up as follows. It is an unwritten Christian tradition not to wear crowns (Ch. 2). In all instances, however, in which holy Scripture is mute, every Christian is in duty bound to follow the unwritten tradition of Christianity (Ch. 3-4). The rational basis of this tradition is supported by the laws of nature. Flowers are meant to be enjoyed by the senses of sight and smell. They are not to be placed on the head which can neither appreciate their beautiful color nor inhale their sweet odor (Ch.5). Such clear indications given by nature, however, are equivalent to express divine laws, as we may see from the example of St. Paul, who frequently appeals to the law of nature (Ch. 6). The custom of wearing crowns is of pagan origin and intimately connected with idolatry. For, it was Satan and his minions who introduced and attached this custom to the worship of idols (Ch. 7). The objection that there exist many things in daily life which are used by pagans and Christians alike can easily be rejected. For apart from the fact that they meet the necessities of life, they are free from the taint of idolatry (Ch. 8). Neither in the Old nor in the New Testament is mention ever made of the practice of wearing crowns (Ch. 9). The arguments adduced so far are applicable to the use of crowns in general (Ch. 10). As to the military crown in particular, a Christian must not be a soldier, because he knows only one oath of allegiance, his baptismal vow (Ch. 11). However this may be, there exists no instance in military service in which the wearing of a crown has not had some connection with idolatry (Ch. 12). The same holds true of all other instances either in public or private life, in which all sorts of crowns are worn (Ch. 13). The foregoing arguments should be sufficient to convince every Christian that it is unfitting for him to wear a crown of idolatry, especially since his divine Master was crowned with thorns to save him from eternal damnation (Ch. 14). The Christian should, instead, look forward to receiving the crown of life which has been laid up in heaven for every faithful servant of God (Ch. 15).

The very subject discussed in the treatise had already been touched upon by Tertullian in his *Apology* (42.6). To be sure, the satirical description he gives there of the custom of wearing crowns shows that, even in the early years of his Christian life, everything that seemed to savor of paganism was hateful to this stern moralist and found no favor with him. But now his severity has increased and taken on a fierce bitterness. He condemns the use of any sort of crowns at any time and on any occasion. Moreover, it is no longer the pagans alone who are the target for his scathing invectives, but rather the Catholic Christians whom he accuses of condoning heathen practices and betraying the ideal of primitive Christianity's austere virtue. Again, in his *Apology* (42.3) Tertullian had mentioned the fact that Christians were serving in the army. He had not yet dared to object to the practice of the Church which did not prohibit a Christian from choosing the soldier's profession, or from continuing in that career after receiving baptism. In *The*

Chaplet (Ch. 11), however, and another work of the same time, entitled *Concerning Idolatry* (Ch. 19), he bluntly asserts that military service is incompatible with the profession of Christianity.

These comparisons are instructive: they show how, through contact with Montanism, Tertullian's severe and rigid asceticism has been carried to the extreme. It is not only the lax and tepid members of the Church he censures, but the Catholic Church as a whole that now comes under his attack, including the bishops, whom he accuses of cowardice in the face of danger (see Ch. 1.5). The warning of moderate-minded brethren expressing fear that the rash action of the Christian soldier might provoke another persecution is disposed of by the spiteful remark: 'Maybe they were not all Christians, but they certainly talked very much like pagans' (1.4). More malicious still is the additional remark: 'Yes, I should not be surprised if such people were not figuring out how they could abolish martyrdom in the same way as they rejected the prophecies of the Holy Spirit.' The prophecies of the Holy Spirit mentioned here are, of course, the oracular utterances of Montanus and his two companions, the prophetesses Maximilla and Prisca (or Priscilla), who claimed that, through them, the 'Paraclete' was manifesting himself to the world.

Chapter 3 contains a number of noteworthy liturgical and devotional practices which were observed by the Christians in Tertullian's day. He lists them to show that the principle of tradition, to which he appeals, applies not only to doctrines but to religious practices as well, and that whatever is in common use in the Church contains its justification in itself, even without scriptural evidence. Custom (*consuetudo*) had always been considered by the Roman jurists as one of the sources of law. Tertullian, himself a lawyer, now applies this principle to certain instances in which Scripture is either mute or ambiguous, and a certain tradition seems to favor his own opinion. To be sure, the sophistical arguments he then produces against the use of flowers for making crowns are rather strange. They can be explained only on the ground that to Tertullian the wearing of a crown is something specifically pagan and idolatrous. Accordingly, he considers the use of this heathen symbol by a Christian as equivalent to apostasy.

The treatise is generally assigned to the year 211. The text followed in the present translation is that of Aem. Kroymann in *Corpus Christianorum*, Series Latina 2 (Turnholti 1954) 1037-1065.

SELECT BIBLIOGRAPHY

Texts:

Aem. Kroymann, *Corpus Christianorum*, Series Latina 2 (Turnholti 1954) 1037-1065; also, CSEL 70 (1942) 125-152.

J. Marra, *De corona, De cultu feminarum* (Corpus Scriptorum Latinorum Paravianum; Turin 1951).

Secondary Sources:

R. H. Bainton, 'The Early Church and War,' *Harvard Theological Review* 13 (1946) 190-212.

K. Baus, *Der Kranz in Antike und Christentum: Eine religionsgeschichtliche Untersuchung mit besonderer Berücksichtigung Tertullians* (Bonn 1940).

P. Franchi De'Cavalieri, 'Sopra alcuni passi del *De corona* di Tertulliano,' *Note agiographiche* Fasc. 8 (Studi e Testi 65; Città del Vaticano 1935) 357-386.

J. Köchling, *De coronarum apud antiquos vi atque usu*, Religionsgeschichtliche Versuche und Vorarbeiten 14.2 (Giessen 1914).

G. De Plinval, 'Tertullien et le scandale de la Couronne,' *Mélanges Joseph De Ghellinck* (Gembloux 1951) 183-188.

E. A. Ryan, 'The Rejection of Military Service by the Early Christians,' *Theological Studies* 13 (1952) 1-32.

E. Vacandard, 'La question du service militaire chez les chrétiens des premiers siècles,' *Etudes de critique et d'histoire religieuse*, deuxième série (Paris 1910) 127-175.

THE CHAPLET

Chapter 1

A SHORT TIME AGO a largess, granted by our most excellent emperors, was distributed in the camp.¹ As the roll was called, the soldiers came forward crowned with laurel. One of them, a truer soldier of God and more steadfast than the rest of his comrades who imagined that they could serve two masters,² was nobly conspicuous when his name was called. For he was the only one whose head was bare; holding the useless crown in his hand, by this characteristic mode of action alone he was at once known to everyone as a Christian. (2) Thereupon all began to single him out: those in the rear ranks mocked him, those in the front uttered threats. Since the murmur did not abate, his

---

1 It was customary with the Roman emperors to bestow on each soldier of the army a gift of money (called *donativum*) on special occasions, such as their accession, or in their wills. The emperors referred to above are Caracalla and Geta who succeeded their father, Septimius Severus, in 211. Tertullian does not give the name of the camp. While some scholars have thought of Carthage, where the treatise was written, others have suggested Lambaesis, an important Roman camp in Numidia, the headquarters of the 3rd Augusta Legion.
2 Cf. Matt. 6.24; Luke 16.13.

name and particular offense were reported to the tribune.³ When the soldier had stepped out of line, the tribune at once asked him: 'Why are you not wearing the crown like everyone else?' The soldier replied: 'Maybe it is all right for them, but I cannot wear it.' When the tribune asked his reason, he stated: 'Because I am a Christian.'

There was a true soldier of God for you! The soldiers clamored for the punishment of the offender and the case was referred to a higher tribunal; the offender was led to the prefects.⁴ (3) Glad to be rid of the burden, he let fall his heavy military cloak, he took off the uncomfortable boots he had worn as a scout,⁵ beginning to set foot on holy ground;⁶ he returned the sword which, too, he did not need to defend

---

3 In the Republican army the command of each legion was vested in six military tribunes, who commanded in rotation. In the imperial army a senior officer of experience, styled *legatus legionis,* commanded each legion, a practice which had been introduced by Caesar. The office of legionary tribune was still continued, but the duties were less responsible. The tribunes attended to the exercises and drills, granted discharges and furloughs, kept the military rolls, and were occasionally entrusted with the command on the march. As a rule, in the imperial army the tribunate in the legion was reserved for young men of the nobility starting their public career.

4 When, from the time of Domitian onward, each legion regularly had its own permanent quarters *(castra stativa)*, a new important command, that of 'camp prefect' *(praefectus castrorum)*, was established. It was mostly reserved for soldiers of long experience who had been promoted from the rank of centurion. Being in charge of fortifications, buildings, and supplies, the camp prefect was a kind of divisional officer. From Septimius Severus onward he was usually styled 'prefect of the legion.' Moreover, the same emperor gave the command of three newly raised legions *(legiones Parthicae I-III)* not to *legati,* but prefects. Emperor Gallienus (260-268) substituted prefects for *legati* in all the legions.

5 The scouts *(speculatores)* were legionaries detailed for special duties such as carrying dispatches, acting as military police, etc.

6 Tertullian wants to say that the ground on which a martyr sets foot begins to be holy even before the supreme sacrifice of his life. Cf. Exod. 3.5; Acts 7.33.

his Lord,[7] and dropped the laurel crown from his hand.

Now the only purple cloak he had was the hope of shedding his blood; his feet were shod with the readiness of the Gospel,[8] and he girt about himself the word of God, keener than any sword.[9] Thus fully armed according to the Apostle's advice,[10] and hoping to be crowned more worthily with the white laurel crown of martyrdom, he awaited in prison the reward of Christ. (4) It was then that the gossips started: maybe they were not all Christians, but they certainly talked very much like pagans! 'Why does he have to make so much trouble for the rest of us Christians over the trifling matter of dress? Why must he be so inconsiderate and rash and act as if he were anxious to die? Is he the only brave man, the only Christian among all his fellow soldiers?'

Yes, I should not be surprised if such people were not figuring out how they could abolish martyrdom in the same way as they rejected the prophecies of the Holy Spirit.[11] (5) In a word, they grumble because our soldier was endangering the long and comfortable peace they had been enjoying.[12] Nor do I doubt that some of them will cite holy Scripture and be on the alert to leave their homes, preparing their baggage and girding themselves for flight from city to city;[13] in fact, that is the only text of the Gospel that they remember. I also

---

7 Cf. John 18.11; Matt. 26.52.
8 Cf. Eph. 6.15.
9 Cf. Heb. 4.12; Eph. 6.14.
10 Cf. Eph. 6.14-16.
11 Tertullian upbraids the Catholic Christians for not accepting the 'Paraclete' of Montanus.
12 After a period of persecution by provincial governors, whose most illustrious victims, SS. Perpetua, Felicitas, and their companions, had been put to death in the amphitheater of Carthage on March 7, 203, the Church enjoyed relative tranquility in Africa during the last years of the reign of Septimius Severus.
13 Cf. Matt. 10.23.

know their shepherds! When things are quiet, they are lions, but in time of danger they are frightened deer. The questions, however, concerning our moral obligation to confess the faith, I shall discuss somewhere else.[14]

(6) Seeing that they also produce the following objection: 'But where [in the Gospel] are we forbidden to wear a crown?'—I will, at this time, rather turn my attention to this point, as more appropriate to be dealt with here, since it is, in fact, the essence of the present contention. I will do this in order to enlighten those inquirers who are really concerned about their ignorance as well as to refute those who try to defend such sinful conduct. By the latter I mean especially those laurel-crowned Christians who console themselves with saying: 'It is merely a question of debate.' As if such conduct could be regarded as either no trespass at all, or at least a doubtful one that may be made the subject of an investigation! But I will show them that it is a real offense and not merely a doubtful one.

Chapter 2

(1) It is my contention that not one of the faithful ever wears a crown except in a time of trial. Everyone, from catechumens to confessors, martyrs, and even apostates, observes this custom. The important point here and now is the authority of this custom. Now, when you inquire into the validity of a custom, you implicitly admit its existence. Hence, an action which is committed against a practice that is its own justification and is further validated by the acceptance it

---

14 Tertullian fulfilled the promise by writing *Flight in Time of Persecution*.

has long enjoyed can neither be regarded as no offense nor as one which is doubtful. (2) To be sure, we ought to inquire into the reason for an established custom, but without prejudice to the practice; not for the purpose of undermining the custom, but rather of strengthening it, so that the observance in question may be solidified when you have made sure of the reason behind it.

What are we to think of people who raise the question concerning the validity of an observance then when they have rejected it? Who inquire into the origin of an observance just when they no longer honor it? The only reason they bring the matter up is to justify their own dereliction; by the very same token they admit they were wrong in observing a custom in which they did not believe. (3) If there is no sin in accepting the crown today, then he was wrong when he refused it in the past. Therefore, the following discussion is not for those who have no right to inquire into the matter, but for those who, with a sincere desire of enlightenment, start no debate but look for advice. True inquiry is always promoted by such a desire, and I have nothing but praise for the faith that believes before it has learned the reason for it.

(4) To be sure, it is very easy to ask: 'Where in Scripture are we forbidden to wear a crown?' But, can you show me a text which says we should be crowned? When men demand the support of a scriptural text for a view they do not hold, they ought to be willing to subject their own stand to the same test of holy writ. If they try to say that we may be crowned because the Scriptures do not forbid it, then they leave themselves open to the retort that we may not be crowned because Scripture does not prescribe it. What should be the official ruling on that? Accept both as if neither were prohibited? Or reject both, on the ground that neither is

enjoined? But 'Whatever is not forbidden is, without question, allowed.' Rather do I say: 'Whatever is not specifically permitted is forbidden.'

Chapter 3

(1) Now, how long shall we saw away along the same line on this question, when we have a long-standing practice, which by anticipation has all but settled the question? Even though no scriptural passage prescribes it, it is strengthened by custom which certainly arose from tradition. How can anything become normal practice if it has not first been handed down to us? But, you tell me: 'You must always have a written source if you are going to plead the force of tradition.'

(2) Let us look into the matter, then, whether or not a tradition without a written source should be accepted. The answer will certainly be 'No' if we cannot adduce examples of other observances which are without written source in Scripture, and rest solely on the the basis of tradition and yet have come to have the force of custom. To begin, for instance, with baptism: When we are about to enter the water, and, as a matter of fact, even a short while before, we declare in the presence of the congregation before the bishop that we renounce the Devil, his pomps, and his angels.[1] (3) After that, we are immersed in the water three times,[2] making a

---
1 Cf. *Spectacles* 4.1.
2 Immersion was the most ancient form usually employed in conferring baptism. The candidate was immersed thrice in the name of the Trinity. In the case of the sick and dying, however, the sacrament was conferred by pouring or aspersion. Pouring gradually prevailed in the Western Church.

somewhat fuller pledge than the Lord has prescribed in the Gospel.³ After this, having stepped forth from the font, we are given a taste of a mixture of milk and honey⁴ and from that day, for a whole week, we forego our daily bath. We also receive the sacrament of the Eucharist which the Lord entrusted to all at the hour for supper,⁵ at our early morning meetings, and then from the hand of none but the bishops. Further, we make offerings for the dead on their anniversary to celebrate their birthday [of eternal life].⁶

(4) We consider fasting, or kneeling during service, on Sundays to be unlawful, and we enjoy the same privilege from Easter until Pentecost. We also are upset if any of our bread or wine falls to the earth [at the Lord's Supper]. Lastly, we make the sign of the cross on our foreheads at every turn, at our going in or coming out of the house, while dressing, while putting on our shoes, when we are taking a bath, before and after meals, when we light the lamps, when we go to bed or sit down, and in all the ordinary actions of daily life.

---

3 Tertullian probably means that the answers of the candidate to the interrogations on his faith go somewhat beyond the baptismal formula given by Christ to His disciples in Matt. 28.19.
4 Cf. 1 Cor. 3.2; 1 Peter 2.2; Heb. 5.12-14. The custom of giving to the newly baptized a mixture of milk and honey survived in Africa, Egypt, and Italy until the fifth century.
5 Cf. 1 Cor. 11.23-25; Matt. 26.27; Mark 14.23.
6 The offering for the dead is the Eucharistic sacrifice. The early Christians looked upon death as a birth and upon the day of death as the birthday for heaven. The day of St. Polycarp's martyrdom, for instance, is called his 'birthday' (*The Martyrdom of Polycarp* 18.3). Cf. A. C. Rush, *Death and Burial in Christian Antiquity* (Washington, D.C. 1941) 72-87.

Chapter 4

(1) Now, if you demand a precise scriptural precept for these and other practices of church discipline, you will find none. Tradition, you will be told, has created it, custom has strengthened it, and faith has encouraged its observance. And you will yourself understand (or someone who has experienced it will tell you) that reason generally lies behind such traditions, customs and faith. In the meantime, take it for granted that there is some reasonable basis for óbserving the custom.

(2) I will add still one example from the Old Testament, since it is fitting to draw lessons from there, too. It is so customary among the Jews that their women are veiled that we can recognize them by this sign. What law prescribed that? (Here, I'm not considering St. Paul.)[1] If Rebecca lowered her veil when she recognized her betrothed in the distance,[2] this one modest action of an individual could not constitute a general law. Or, as she did this because of the particular situation in which she found herself, let virgins alone be veiled, and this only when they are coming to be married, and not until they have recognized their future husbands.

(3) And if Susanna be adduced as an argument for wearing a veil, because it was removed at her trial,[3] I can say here also: 'That veil was a matter of choice.' She came as the accused, ashamed of her disgrace and properly hiding her beauty, or because she feared to be pleasing any more. Surely she would not have walked veiled on the paths of her hus-

---
1 Cf. 1 Cor. 11.5.
2 Cf. Gen. 24.64,65.
3 Cf. Dan. 13.32.

band's garden if she wished to please.⁴ But, let us assume that she always wore a veil: in this case, or in any other one, I demand to be shown a law prescribing dress.

(4) If I find nowhere such a law, it follows that it is tradition that has raised this fashion into a custom, which later was to find its justification in the command of the Apostle,⁵ from a reasonable interpretation. Therefore, from these few examples, it will be clear that, because of its being observed, also a non-written tradition can be defended, if it is confirmed by custom, which is itself a valid witness to an approved tradition from the mere fact that it has gone on for a long time.

(5) Moreover, also in the domain of civil law, custom is accepted in place of law when a law is wanting,⁶ and it makes no difference whether it is merely based on reason or on some written word, since reason is, in fact, the basis of law. Besides, if reason is the basis of law, then whatever is based on reason will automatically become law, whosoever its author may be. Do you not believe that every one of the faithful is permitted to originate and establish a law, as long as it is pleasing to God, promotes discipline, and is helpful to salvation, since

---

4 Cf. Dan. 13.4,7,15-20,25,26,36,38.
5 Cf. 1 Cor. 11.4-15.
6 Tertullian, well versed in the field of jurisprudence, follows a principle of the Roman jurists who considered custom (*consuetudo*) as one of the sources of civil law. Cf., for instance, *Auctor ad Herennium* 2.13.19: 'The constituent parts [of law] are the following: nature, statute, custom, previous judgments, equity, and agreement; Cicero, *De inventione* 2.54.162: 'Customary law is either a principle that is derived only in a slight degree from nature and has been fed and strengthened by usage—religion, for example—or any of the laws which . . . we see proceed from nature but which have been strengthened by custom, or any principle which lapse of time and public approval have made the habit or usage of the community'; *Digesta* 1.3.32: 'A custom kept for a long time is justly regarded as a law.'

the Lord says: 'Why even of yourselves do you not judge what is right'?'[7]

(6) The Apostle speaks further, not merely of a judgment of a just man, but of every decision in matters which we have to examine: 'If you are ignorant on any point, this also will God reveal to you,'[8] since he himself was accustomed to give counsel, when he had no precept of the Lord, and to establish some rules on his own authority,[9] since he was in possession of the Spirit of God,[10] the guide to all truth.[11] Thus, a counsel and rule of his became equivalent to a divine precept through the support given by divine reason. (7) Ask, then, this divine reason, while maintaining a respect for tradition, no matter what its source, not considering the author but the authority behind it, and especially that of the custom itself, which on this very account should be revered, lest we be without an interpreter of its rational basis. So, that, if reason, too, is God's gift, you may then learn, not whether you should observe a custom, but why.

Chapter 5

(1) The rational basis of Christian customs is strengthened when it is supported by nature, which is the prime rule by which all things are measured. Now, nature is the first to bring an exception against crown and head being adapted for each other. It seems to me that the Lord of nature, our God,

---
7 Luke 12.57.
8 Cf. Phil. 3.15.
9 Cf. 1 Cor. 7.25.
10 Cf. 1 Cor. 7.40.
11 Cf. John 16.13.

so created man and endowed him with certain powers of sensation that he may desire, appreciate, and enjoy the fruits of nature, by giving him, so to speak, specific bodily instruments; thus, He planted hearing in the ears, He lit the light of sight in the eyes, He hid the power of taste in the mouth, He wafted the power of smell to the nostrils and fixed the power of touch in the hands.

(2) By these instruments of the outer man, which act as servants for the inner man, the enjoyments of the divine gifts are conveyed by the senses to the depths of the soul. Now, what in flowers gives you enjoyment? For, it is the flowers of the field which form the peculiar, or at least the chief, material of crowns. You answer rightly: 'Either their fragrance, or their color, or both together.' Now, what other senses, save that of sight and smell, are supposed to smell and see? And, what sense organs are supposed to accomplish that, if not the eyes and the nose? Therefore, make use of the flowers with sight and smell, for these are the senses by which they are meant to be enjoyed; use the eyes and the nose which are the organs of these senses. The thing, you have from God; while the mode of using it is determined by the [community of men in the] world.

(3) An extraordinary mode of using a thing, however, is no hindrance to its ordinary use. Use flowers, then, when they are tied together and twisted [into a crown] with thread and rush, just the same way as you would when they are free and loose, that is, things to be looked at and smelled. Count it a crown, let me say, when a bunch of flowers is tied together in a series, so that you can carry many of them at the same time and enjoy them all at once. If they are so pure, then lay them on your breast; or spread them on your bed, if they are so soft; or even dip them in your cup if they are so

harmless. Enjoy them in each of the ways in which they affect the senses.

(4) But what do you have in your head to relish a flower, to feel a crown, except its band? Your head is able neither to distinguish the color of flowers, nor to inhale their sweet odor, nor to appreciate their softness. It is just as much against nature to long for a flower with your head as to crave food with your ear or sound with your nose. But, anything that is against nature deserves to be branded as monstrous among all men; we, surely, should also consider it as a sin of sacrilege against God the Master and Author of nature.

Chapter 6

(1) If you demand a divine law, you have that common one prevailing all over the world, written on the tablets of nature, to which, also, St. Paul is accustomed to appeal. Thus he says concerning the veiling of women: 'Does not nature teach you this?'[1] Again, in saying in his letter to the Romans that the Gentiles do by nature what the Law prescribes,[2] he hints at the existence of natural law and a nature founded on law. In the preceding chapter of the same epistle[3] he says that male and female have changed among themselves the natural function of the creature and descended to unnatural practices. And, since he understands this very sin as the punishment visited upon them for their error, he evidently supports the natural function [of the creature]. (2) We come to the knowledge of God first by the teachings of

---
1 1 Cor. 11.14.
2 Cf. Rom. 2.14.
3 Cf. Rom. 1.25-27.

nature. We call Him, for instance, God of gods, we assume that He is benevolent, and we invoke Him as Judge.

Perhaps you have some doubt as to whether we should allow nature to be our guide in the enjoyment of God's creatures? To be sure, there is a danger that we be led astray in the direction in which God's rival has corrupted, along with man himself, the whole of creation which had been made over to man for certain services. Hence it is that the Apostle says that 'creation was made subject to vanity, but not by its own will,'[4] first being subverted by vain, then by vile, wicked and ungodly use. Take, for instance, the pleasures derived from the spectacles. The creature is dishonored by those who have a natural feeling that all the components that make up the spectacles come from God, but lack the knowledge to understand that all these things have been changed by the Devil. But on this subject, I have written fully in Greek, for the benefit of our lovers of the shows.[5]

Chapter 7

(1) Let those advocates of crowns, then, acknowledge in the meantime the authority of nature, as men who are heirs of our common wisdom. Let them also do this as a testimony to their own religion, as intimate friends and worshipers of the God of nature,[1] and let them thus, as it were, super-

---

4 Rom. 8.20.
5 Tertullian wrote with equal facility in Greek and Latin. Of his treatise on *Spectacles,* to which he refers here, he made a Greek and Latin edition. The former has been lost. In Ch. 2 of the treatise Tertullian refutes the objection that everything used in the spectacles comes from God and hence is good. People who make this objection disregard the fact that Satan corrupted, along with man, the whole material world.

---

1 Cf. *Spectacles* 2.5, where Tertullian says that, while the heathen know God only by the law of nature and from afar, the Christians know Him by right of friendship and from intimate association.

abundantly recognize the other reasons which forbid us especially to wear crowns on the head, and indeed, crowns of every sort. (2) For, I see myself compelled to turn from the teaching of nature, which we share with mankind in general, to the specific Christian teachings which alone must now be defended in relation to all the other kinds of crowns which seem to be intended for other uses, since they are made of different materials. The crowns (for instance, this laurel crown of the soldiers) are not made of flowers, the use of which nature has designated, and one might think they do not come under the ban of Christian religion, since they have escaped any objection of nature.

I realize that I must deal with this matter with the greatest care and in detail, from its beginnings, through the successive stages of its growth, down to its present condition. (3) For this purpose I shall have to draw on pagan literature; profane things should be established from their own documents. What little I know [of pagan literature] will, I imagine, be sufficient.

If there ever was such a person as Pandora whom Hesiod[2] tells us was the first woman, she was the first one who ever wore a crown. She received it from the Graces, at the time

---

2 The story of Pandora, told by Hesiod in *Works and Days* 50-105, is a part of the Prometheus myth. The creation of Pandora was conceived by Zeus to wreak his vengeance upon Prometheus, the champion and benefactor of mankind. A number of gods contributed to the making of the first woman (69-82): Hephaestus formed her out of wet clay; Athena breathed life into her and dressed her; the Charites (Graces) and Peitho (Persuasion) adorned her with jewelry; the Horae (Hours) crowned her with flowers, and Hermes instructed her in all manner of guile and deceit. Thus equipped, Pandora was sent to Prometheus' slow-witted brother, Epimetheus, who received her, though he had been cautioned by his brother against accepting any gift from Zeus. Pandora opened the famous box, containing all sorts of evils, and diseases. They escaped, plaguing men ever since; only Hope was left in the box.

when all the gods bestowed gifts on her, and that is why she is called Pandora. Moses, who was a prophetic rather than a poetic shepherd, tells us that Eve was the first woman and that she girt her loins with leaves rather than her temples with flowers.[3] Pandora, then, never existed. So we have to blush for the fictitious account of the origin of the crown, and no less, as it will soon appear, for the true stories about it.

(4) We know for certain that the inventors or propagators of the custom were figures of doubtful character. Pherecydes[4] relates that Saturn was the first to be crowned. Diodorus tells us that Jupiter was thus honored by the rest of of the gods after his victory over the Titans. To Priapus the same author assigns fillets, and to Ariadne a garland of gold and Indian jewels. This garland was made by Vulcan and given her by Bacchus, and afterwards it became a constellation. Callimachus[5] placed a vine-branch on the head of

---

[3] Cf. Gen. 3.7.
[4] Pherecydes is not the direct source of Tertullian, but Diodorus' *Bibliotheca*, whence, according to the immediately following statement, he also took the stories of the crowning of Jupiter, Priapus, and Ariadne (cf. *Bibl.*, Fragments of Book 6.4). The Ariadne story is recounted by a number of ancient authors (for instance: Aratus, *Phaenomena* 71-73; *Eratosthenis Catasterismorum Reliquiae* nr. 5; Diodorus, *Bibl.* 4.61.5; Ovid, *Fasti* 3.459-516; *Metamorphoses* 8.176-182). Ariadne, forsaken by Theseus on the lonely island of Dia (Naxos), was rescued by Bacchus (Dionysus) and made his bride. Venus and the Hours gave her a wedding crown of gold and Indian gems, wrought by Hephaestus (Vulcan). After her death the crown was placed in the sky, where the gems were turned to stars, forming the constellation of the Northern Crown, still sometimes called 'Ariadne's Crown.'
[5] Again, the Alexandrian poet Callimachus is hardly the direct source of Tertullian; he probably took this information from Claudius Saturninus, a second-century writer, whose *Crowns* he praises (Ch. 7.6-7) as an exhaustive source on the subject of crowns, dealing with 'their origins, causes, varieties and the ceremonies pertaining to them.' Tertullian quotes Claudius thrice more in this treatise (10.9; 12.1; 13.8). Concerning Claudius Saturninus, see W. S. Teuffel, W. Kroll and F. Skutsch, *Geschichte der römischen Literatur*, 6th ed., 3 (Leipzig and Berlin) 85.

Juno. So, too, at Argos, her statue, crowned with a vine-sprig, with a lion's skin placed beneath her feet, exhibits the stepmother exulting over the spoils won from her two step-sons.[6] Hercules is sometimes portrayed with a crown of poplar leaves,[7] again with wild olive leaves[8] or with parsley.[9] (5) You have the tragedy of Cerberus;[10] you have Pindar,[11] and Callimachus as well who tells us that Apollo put on a crown of laurel as a suppliant, after he had killed the serpent at Delphi.[12] For, among the ancients, suppliants always wore crowns.[13] Harpocration argues that Bacchus—Osiris to the Egyptians—crowned himself purposely with ivy because it is

---

6 The two stepsons of Juno (Hera) are Bacchus (Dionysus) and Hercules (Heracles), whom Zeus begot from Semele and Alcmene respectively. Angry because of the love affairs of her husband, Hera did everything in her power to destroy these two sons of Zeus, who had been born out of wedlock. Vine-sprig and lion's skin—'the spoils won from her two stepsons'—are the symbols of Bacchus and Hercules respectively.
7 Cf. Ovid, *Heroides* 9.64.
8 Cf. Pausanias, *Descriptio Graeciae* 5.7.7.
9 Cf. Plutarch, *Quaestiones convivalium* 5.3.3.
10 The text of this passage is corrupted. Tertullian may have had in mind the *Heracles* of Euripides or Seneca's *Hercules Furens*. The main outline of the story is the same in both plays. The opening scene of Euripides' tragedy shows Amphitryon, Heracles' reputed father, Megara, the hero's wife, and his children, taking refuge at the altar of Zeus. While Heracles is absent to undertake the latest and greatest of his labors, namely, to go down to the nether regions and bring Cerberus back with him, a certain Lycus has usurped the royal power of Thebes, and now intends to take advantage of the hero's absence in order to kill his family. As suppliants, Amphitryon, Megara, and the children wear wreaths on their heads. When Heracles appears to rescue his family, he immediately tells them to cast from their heads 'these chaplets of death' (line 562; cf. Seneca, *Hercules Furens* 626-28). He then slays Lycus, but, visited with a dread madness, he also slays his wife and children.
11 Cf., for instance, *Olympian Odes* 3.11ff.; 4.10-12; 11.11-15; 13.24ff.; *Nemean Odes* 1.16-18.
12 Cf. *Aetia*, frg. 88 Pfeiffer (364 Schneider); Aelianus, *Varia Historia* 3.1.
13 The source material on this ancient custom has been collected by J. Köchling, *De coronarum apud antiquos vi atque usu* (Religionsgeschichtliche Versuche und Vorarbeiten 14.2; Giessen 1914) 16-18.

the function of ivy to clear the head after drinking.[14] But also in other passages Bacchus is considered as the originator of the crown—that is, of the laurel crown[15] which he wore on the occasion of his triumphal return from India.[16] Even the man on the street acknowledges this, since he calls the festal days dedicated to him 'The Great Crown.' (6) If you open the books of Leo the Egyptian you will find that Isis was the first who discovered and wore on her head ears of corn, though they rather pertain to the belly.[17] If you want further

---

14 Tertullian refers, perhaps, to the lexicographer Valerius Harpocration of Alexandria. According to Pliny (*Naturalis historia* 24.47.75) ivy not only deranges the mind, but also clears the head. Ovid (*Fasti* 3.767-770) says that ivy was 'most dear' to Bacchus (Dionysus) because, when his stepmother Hera (Juno) sought to destroy her husband's bastard child, 'the nymphs of Nysa screened the cradle with ivy leaves.' In the Attic township of Acharnae the god was worshiped under the title of Ivy Dionysus (Pausanias, *Descriptio Graeciae* 1.31.6).
15 This agrees with a statement in Pliny's *Naturalis historia* (16.4.9) in so far as Bacchus is said to have been the first to set a crown on his head. But, according to Pliny, it was ivy (not laurel) with which the god wreathed himself.
16 Again, according to Pliny (*ibid.* 16.62), it was wreaths of ivy (not laurel) which, 'in imitation of Father Liber' (Bacchus), Alexander's victorious army wore on their return from the Indian campaign. There existed a fairly early saga according to which Dionysus penetrated far into the interior of Asia. Euripides alludes to these feats in his *Bacchae* (13ff.). After the real conquests of Alexander, Dionysus' fabled exploits were extended, and he was represented as having reached India. That the laurel, too, was of some significance in the cult of Dionysus may be seen from the fact that in his temple at Phigalia in Arcadia the lower part of his image was hidden in laurel leaves and ivy (Pausanias, *Descriptio Graeciae* 8.39.6). Laurel and ivy also are the attributes of the god in the 'Homeric' Hymn to Dionysus (line 9).
17 Leo, an Egyptian priest, is also mentioned by St. Augustine, *City of God* 8.27: 'Consider, for example, Isis, the wife of Osiris, the Egyptian goddess . . . While offering a sacrifice to her forebears, she discovered a field of barley and carried some of the ears to the king, her husband, and to his councilor, Mercury [the Egyptian Thoth], and so she has come to be identified with Ceres. Now, anyone who wants to find out how many and monstrous were their wickednesses, as reported by poets and the mystic writings of the Egyptians, can get an

information, look up Claudius Saturninus. On all matters, including this subject, you will find him an excellent commentator. (7) Now, he has a book, entitled *On Crowns,* which treats so completely of their origins, causes, varieties and ceremonies pertaining to them that you will see that there is not one beautiful flower, not one luxuriant leaf, no sod or vine-shoot that has not been consecrated to the head of someone or other.

All this makes it sufficiently clear to us how repugnant this custom of wearing a crown on the head should be to Christians. It was first invented and afterwards dedicated to the honor of those the world calls 'gods.' (8) Now, if the Devil, who was a liar from the beginning even in this matter,[18] produced the phantom of godhead, there is no doubt that he had very wisely also produced those who could be his agents in pretending to divinity. What, then, should be the opinion of men dedicated to the true God, of a thing introduced by the minions of Satan and from the beginning attached to their service and which even then was begun as worship of idols, by idols that were still alive? Not, of course, that the idols really were anything,[19] but because whatever men offer to idols pertains to demons. (9) In fact, if the things that other men offer to idols pertain to demons, how much more what idols offered to themselves while they were still alive! The very demons undoubtedly made provision

---

idea from the letter which Alexander wrote to his mother, Olympia, describing the facts as revealed to him by the priest Leo' (cf. *ibid.* 8.5; 12.11). Leo has remained a somewhat enigmatic figure (cf. W. Otto, *Priester und Tempel im hellenistischen Aegypten* 2 [Leipzig and Berlin 1908] 217 n. 2). However this may be, Leo is hardly the direct source of Tertullian, but Claudius Saturninus (see above, Ch. 7 n. 5), to whose *Crowns* he refers his readers for further information in the following sentence. There he found whatever earlier writers had said on the subject. Tertullian applies the same technique, common among ancient authors, in his *Spectacles.*

18 Cf. John 8.44.
19 Cf. 1 Cor. 10.19.

for themselves by means of those idols whose names they intended to use, before provision had actually been made.

Chapter 8

(1) Now, cling to this explanation, while I examine a question hurled at me, for I already hear the following objection. There are a great many other things invented by those whom the world considers to be gods. Yet, we find these very things in our own present usages, in those of the early faithful, in sacred history, and in the life of Christ Himself, who certainly performed His work as man by no other than the normal agencies of human life. Let us assume that to be so; I have no intention of inquiring any further back into the origin of these things.

(2) Let Mercury be the first who taught the use of letters;[1] I admit they are necessary for both commercial intercourse and our relations to God. And if he also was the inventor of stringed instruments,[2] I will not deny, when I listen to David, that his ingenious invention proved useful to the saints and served God. Let Aesculapius be the pioneer of the art of healing:[3] Isaias mentions that he prescribed some medicine for Ezechias when he was sick,[4] and so was Paul aware that a little wine was good for the stomach.[5] And if Minerva is claimed to have built the first ship,[6] then I recall that Jonas

---
1 Concerning Mercury (Hermes) as inventor of the art of writing, see Cicero, *De natura deorum* 3.22.56; Diodorus, *Bibl.* 1.16; Tertullian, *The Testimony of the Soul* 5.
2 The 'Homeric' Hymn to Hermes (24ff.) recounts how little Hermes (Mercury) left his cradle and walked out of the cave where he lived with his mother. Meeting a tortoise at the entrance, he killed it and converted its shell into the sounding board of the first lyre.
3 Cf. Pindar, *Pythian Odes* 3.
4 Cf. Isa. 38.21.
5 Cf. 1 Tim. 5.23.
6 Homer (*Iliad* 15.411-412) says that the skillful shipbuilder knows well the whole art by the precepts of Athena (Minerva).

and the Apostles traveled by sea. (3) There is even more than this: Christ puts on clothes,[7] and Paul will have a cloak.[8] If you claim that some one of the pagan gods was the inventor of every single piece of furniture or of our ordinary utensils, I will have to admit that Christ reclined on a dining couch,[9] when He presented a basin to wash the feet of His disciples, when He poured water into it from a jug, and when he was girded with a linen cloth[10]—a garment sacred to Osiris.[11] (4) I always give the same answer to this type of question, admitting, indeed, that we use along with others these articles, but stressing the distinction between their rational and irrational use, because the promiscuous employment of them conceals in a deceptive way the corruption of the creature, by which it has been made subject to vanity.

(5) We assert, then, that those things only which meet the necessities of human life by providing plain service, real assistance, and honorable comfort are fit for our own and our ancestors' use as well as for sacred history and for Christ Himself. To that extent they are granted to us by the inspiration of God, who, before anyone else, provided for, and taught and ministered to the enjoyment, I should suppose, of man, His creature. On the other hand, things, I assert, which are out of this class are not fit for our use— and I mean especially those things which, for the same reason, cannot be found either in sacred history or in the life of Christ.

---

7 According to his oppenents, Tertullian implies, Christ (in putting on clothes) used the invention of Minerva, the patroness of the art of weaving.
8 Cf. 2 Tim. 4.13.
9 Cf. Luke 22.14.
10 Cf. John 13.4,5.
11 The garments of Osiris were woven by the goddesses Isis and Nephthys. In Egypt the industry of weaving was brought to great perfection. Linen as fine as silk muslin was woven, and the Egyptians were very proud of their skill in its **manufacture.**

Chapter 9

(1) No crown ever rested upon the head of a patriarch or prophet, levite, priest, or ruler;[1] nor, in the new dispensation, do we read of an Apostle, a preacher of the Gospel or bishop who wore a crown. Not even the Temple of God, I believe, nor the Ark of the Covenant, nor the tabernacle of testimony,[2] nor the altar of sacrifice, nor the [seven-branched] candlestick was ever adorned with a crown. Now, if a crown were worthy of God, these surely would fittingly have been so decorated both in the ceremony of their first dedication and in the jubilation of their restoration. (2) Yet, if all these were figures of ourselves—for we are, indeed, the temples of God,[3] His altars and lights and sacred vessels—then they also foreshadowed this rule: that men of God should not wear the crown. The reality ought to correspond to the image.

If, perhaps, you object that Christ Himself was crowned, I will have a very simple answer for you: 'By all means, you may wear *that* kind of crown.' (3) But, remember, it was not the people that invented this crown of insolent wickedness. It was an idea of the Roman soldiers—a custom of the [heathen] world such as the people of God never permitted either as a sign of public rejoicing or to gratify innate wantonness. They were the people who returned from the Babylonian captivity with timbrels and pipes and psalteries rather than with crowns. And after feasting and drinking, they rose to play,[4] but not with crowns on their heads. (4)

---

1 Tertullian means a leader in the community, who sometimes could also be a member of the Sanhedrin. Cf. John 3.1 (Nicodemus, 'a ruler of the Jews'); Luke 8.41 (Jairus, 'a ruler of the synagogue').
2 Cf. Heb. 9.4; Num. 17.7,10.
3 Cf. 1 Cor. 3.16; 6.19; 2 Cor. 6.16.
4 Cf. Exod. 32.6; 1 Cor. 10.7.

For the account of their rejoicing and the condemnation of their revelry would surely have mentioned the honor or the dishonor of wearing crowns. Hence, Isaias, who said: 'Since they drink wine with timbrels, psalteries and pipes,'[5] surely would have added 'with crowns' if that custom had ever been known in sacred history.

Chapter 10

(1) Hence, when you declare that ornaments of the heathen gods are also found in the service of the true God, so that you may win approval for the wearing of crowns as a part of common usage, you are implicitly basing your argument on this premise: Whatever is not found in sacred history must not be applied to common usage. Now, is there anything more unworthy of God than that which is befitting an idol? And what is so worthy of an idol as that which is fitting for a corpse? (2) For, a crown is placed upon the dead[1] and they hereby become idols in dress and in the worship paid them in their consecration, which practice, to us, is but another sort of idolatry. So, therefore, those who lack sensation ought to use that thing of which they have no perception in the same way in which they would abuse it if they did enjoy power of sensation. For there is no difference between use and abuse when the real use of a thing ceases because natural perception has failed. (3) But we are forbidden by the

---

5 Cf. Isa. 5.12.

1 Crowning of the dead with garlands was a very old custom. Cicero (*De legibus* 2.24.60) quotes a law of the Twelve Tables for this practice. The Christian writers are unanimous in condemning the custom (see, for instance, Minucius Felix, *Octavius* 38.3).

Apostle[2] to abuse anything, who teaches us, rather, to refrain from use. Unless of course, we say that those who have no sensation cannot abuse a thing—how can a man be said to abuse anything, when he has not the power of using it?—so that the whole action comes to nothing. It is a dead thing as regards the idols, but living in so far as it pertains to the demons,[3] to whom this superstition belongs. As David says: 'The idols of the Gentiles are silver and gold. They have eyes and see not; noses, and smell not; hands and feel not.'[4] (4) These are the senses by which we enjoy flowers. Now, if he declares that those who make idols shall become like unto them,[5] then those who make use of anything according to the fashion of idol adornings are themselves like unto them. 'To the clean all things are clean';[6] yes, and to the unclean all things are defiled. Nothing, however, is more defiled than idols.

In all other respects, the substances are pure as being creatures of God and, to that extent, they are fit for common use. Yet it is the application of this use that makes all the difference. (5) For I kill a cock for my benefit, the same as Socrates did for Aesculapius, and, if I find the odor of a place unpleasant, I burn some Arabian incense, but without the same ceremony, the same dress, and the same pomp with which it is done to idols. The Apostle says: 'But if someone says, "This has been sacrificed to idols," touch it not.'[7] Now, if a creature of God is defiled by a mere word, how much more will it be defiled when you have danced around it with

---
2 Cf. 1 Cor. 7.31.
3 Cf. 1 Cor. 10.19,20.
4 Ps. 113.12-15.
5 Cf. Ps. 113.16.
6 Tit. 1.15; cf. Rom. 14.20.
7 1 Cor. 10.28.

the dress, ceremony, and pomp connected with sacrifices to idols. And so the crown is made to be an offering to idols. (6) With this ceremony, dress, and pomp it is offered to idols by their devotees. So closely connected is its use with idols that a thing which is not found in sacred history cannot be admitted to common use.

This is the reason why the Apostle tells us: 'Flee from the worship of idols.'[8] He means idolatry whole and entire. (7) Look closely at a thicket and see how many thorns lie hidden beneath the leaves! Give nothing and take nothing from an idol! If it be against the faith to recline at table in the temple of an idol,[9] what would you call it if one wore the garb of an idol? 'What concord is there between Christ and Belial?'[10] Flee far away from it, then. He commands us to be completely separated from idolatry and have no close dealings with it,[11] because even the earthly serpent sucks men into its jaws at a distance with its breath. (8) St. John goes even further. He says: 'Dear children, guard yourselves from the idols.'[12] Notice that he does not say 'from idolatry' as from a service, but 'from the idols,' that is, from their very image. For it is unfitting that you, an image of the living God,[13] should become the image of an idol and a dead man. And to this extent do we claim for idols the sole ownership of this attire, both because of the origin to which it has been traced and because of its superstitious use. Besides this, the crown is not found in sacred history, and, therefore, is rather

---

8 1 Cor. 10.14.
9 Cf. 1 Cor. 8.10.
10 2 Cor. 6.15.
11 2 Cor. 6.17; cf. Jer. 51.45; Ezech. 20.34,41; Isa. 52.11.
12 1 John 5.21.
13 Cf. Gen. 1.27.

considered as belonging to those with whose early history, festivals, and services it is associated.

(9) Finally, crowns adorn the very doors, victims, and altars of idols; their ministers and priests wear them, also. Claudius[14] lists all the various kinds of crowns worn by the colleges of pagan priests. Now, we have introduced the distinction between things which are altogether different from each other—things, namely, in accordance with reason, and things contrary to it—to meet the assertion of those who on the basis of some random instances defend the indiscriminate use of them on all occasions. (10) To complete this part of our subject, it now remains for us to examine the special grounds for wearing chaplets. For, in showing them to be alien—nay, even opposed—to Christian discipline, we shall also prove that reason does not in the least vindicate the use of this kind of attire, although the wearing of certain [other] articles of dress which our opponents cite by way of example is reasonable.

Chapter 11

(1) Now, to come down to the very heart of this question about the soldier's crown, should we not really first examine the right of a Christian to be in the military service at all? In other words, why discuss the merely accidental detail, when the foundation on which it rests is deserving of censure? Are we to believe it lawful to take an oath of allegiance to a mere human being over and above the oath of fidelity to God? Can we obey another master, having chosen Christ? Can we forsake father, mother, and all our relatives? By

---

14 See above, Ch. 7 nn. 5,17.

divine law we must honor them and our love for them is second only to that which we have toward God.[1] The Gospel also bids us honor our parents,[2] placing none but Christ Himself above them.[3] (2) Is it likely we are permitted to carry a sword when our Lord said that he who takes the sword will perish by the sword?[4] Will the son of peace[5] who is forbidden to engage in a lawsuit[6] espouse the deeds of war? Will a Christian, taught to turn the other cheek when struck unjustly,[7] guard prisoners in chains, and administer torture and capital punishment? (3) Will he rather mount guard for others than for Christ on station days?[8] And what about the Lord's Day? Will he not even then do it for Christ? Will he stand guard before temples, that he has renounced? Will he eat at pagan banquets, which the Apostle forbids?[9] Will he protect by night those very demons whom in the daytime he has put to flight by his exorcisms, leaning on a lance such as pierced the side of Christ [on the cross]?[10] Will he bear, too, a standard that is hostile to Christ, and will he ask the watch-word from his commander-in-chief —he who has already received one from God? Moreover, after death, will he be disturbed by the horn of the trumpeter

---

1 Cf. Exod. 20.12.
2 Matt. 15.4; Mark 7.10; Luke 18.20.
3 Matt. 10.37; Luke 14.26.
4 Cf. Matt. 26.52.
5 The characterization of the Christian as a 'son of peace' is taken from the New Testament, where Christ's teaching is described as 'the gospel of peace' (see, for instance, Eph. 6.15). In his *Spectacles* 16.4, Tertullian calls the Christians 'the priests of peace.'
6 Cf. 1 Cor. 6.7.
7 Cf. Matt. 5.39; Luke 6.29.
8 In military language, *statio* is the post, guard; the Christians called the two weekly fast days (Wednesday and Friday) *stationes*.
9 Cf. 1 Cor. 8.10.
10 Cf. John 19.34.

—he who expects to be aroused by the trumpet of the angel?[11] Will his corpse be cremated according to military custom—when he, a Christian, was not permitted to burn incense in sacrifice, when to him Christ remitted the eternal punishment by fire he had deserved?

(4) Yes, these and many other offenses can be observed in the discharge of military duties—offenses that must be interpreted as acts of desertion. To leave the camp of Light and enlist in the camp of Darkness means going over to the enemy. To be sure, the case is different for those who are converted after they have been bound to military service. St. John admitted soldiers to baptism;[12] then there were the two most faithful centurions: the one whom Christ praised,[13] and the other whom Peter instructed.[14] But, once we have embraced the faith and have been baptized, we either must immediately leave military service (as many have done); or we must resort to all kinds of excuses in order to avoid any action which is also forbidden in civilian life, lest we offend God; or, last of all, for the sake of God we must suffer the fate which a mere citizen-faith was no less ready to accept.

(5) For, military service offers neither exemption from punishment of sins nor relief from martyrdom. The Gospel is one and the same for the Christian at all times whatever his occupation in life. Jesus will deny those who deny Him and confess those who confess Him;[15] He will save the life that has been lost for His Name's sake, but He will destroy the one that has been gained against His Name.[16] With Him

---

11 Cf. 1 Cor. 15.52; 1 Thess. 4.16.
12 Cf. Luke 3.14.
13 Cf. Matt. 8.10; Luke 7.9.
14 Cf. Acts 10.
15 Cf. Matt. 10.32,33; Luke 12.8,9.
16 Cf. Matt. 10.39; Mark 8.35; Luke 9.24.

the faithful citizen is a soldier, just as the faithful soldier is a citizen. (6) The state of faith admits no plea of compulsion. Those are under no compulsion to sin whose sole obligation is not to sin. A Christian may be pressed to the offering of sacrifice and to the straight denial of Christ under threat of torture and punishment. Yet, the law of Christianity does not excuse even that compulsion, since there is a stronger obligation to dread the denial of the faith and to undergo martyrdom than to escape suffering and to perform the sacrificial rite required. (7) Moreover, that kind of argument destroys the very essence of our sacramental oath, since it would loosen the fetters for voluntary sins. For, it will be possible to maintain that inclination is a compulsion, too, since there is, indeed, some sort of compelling force in it. The foregoing principles I wish to have also applied to the other occasions for wearing crowns in some official capacity (it is with reference to such occasions especially that people are wont to plead compulsion), since for this very reason we must either refuse public offices lest we fall into sin, or we must endure martyrdom in order to sever our connection with them.

Chapter 12

(1) I will not waste any more words over the essential point of the question, namely, the unlawfulness of military life itself, but return to the secondary point of the matter. Indeed, if, employing all my efforts, I do away with military service altogether, there will be little point in issuing a challenge on the military crown. Let us assume, then, that military service is permitted up to the point of wearing a crown. Let me say, first, a word about the crown itself. We

know from Claudius[1] that the laurel crown (such as the one in question) is sacred to Apollo as the god of archery[2] and to Bacchus as the god of triumphs.[3] (2) He also tells us that soldiers were often garlanded with myrtle. 'For the myrtle,' he writes, 'belongs to Venus, the mother of the descendants of Aeneas, the mistress also of Mars, who through Ilia and her twins is Roman herself.' But I myself do not believe that Venus shares in this respect the friendly feelings of Mars for Rome, in view of the god's dealing with a concubine.[4] Moreover, when a soldier is crowned with an olive wreath, he commits idolatry to Minerva, who is also a goddess of arms, even though she crowned her head with an olive branch to celebrate her peace with Neptune.[5] In all these relations we see the defiled and all-defiling superstitious character of the military crown. In fact, I think that the very motives for wearing it causes its defilement.

(3) Take the annual public pronouncement of vows.[6] What do you think of it? The first takes place in the general's quarters; the second, in heathen temples. In addition to the places, note the words, also; 'We promise to give to you, then, O Jupiter, an ox with golden horns.' What is the real sense of that pronouncement? Is it not a denial of the faith? Even though the Christian says nothing on that occasion with his mouth, he makes his response by having the crown on his head. The wearing of the laurel crown is likewise enjoined

---

1 See above, Ch. 7 nn. 5,17.
2 In plastic art laurel and bow are Apollo's attributes at a very early time.
3 See above, Ch. 7 n. 16.
4 See above, *Spectacles* 5 n. 10.
5 See *ibid.* 9 n. 2.
6 Tertullian refers to the vows offered for the well-being of the emperor on New Year's Day. Cf. Tacitus *Annales* 4.17; 16.22; Pliny, *Ep.* 10.35 (Kukula).

at the distribution of a largess, though, plainly, you do not attend this ceremony without making a profit.

(4) Idolater! Do you not see that you are selling Christ for a few pieces of gold, just as Judas sold him for silver? It is written: 'You cannot serve God and mammon.'[7] Does this perhaps mean that you can do both things: reach out your hand to mammon and stand on the side of God? And what about 'Render to Caesar the things that are Caesar's and to God the things that are God's'?[8] Does this perhaps mean that you can withhold the man from God and take the denarius from Caesar? Is the laurel of triumph made of leaves, or of corpses? Is it adorned with ribbons, or with tombs? Is it anointed with perfumes, or with the tears of wives and mothers, some of them, perhaps, Christian women, for we know that Christianity has also spread among the barbarians. (5) Has the man who wears a crown as a symbol of glory not actually fought in battle? There is yet another kind of military service—that of the bodyguard in the imperial household. For these men, too, are called 'soldiers of the camp,' and they perform services in connection with the ceremonial observed in the imperial court. But, even then you are still the soldier and servant of another, and if of two masters—God and Caesar—then, certainly, not of Caesar, when you owe yourself to God, who, I am inclined to believe, has a higher claim even in matters in which both have an interest.

---

7 Matt. 6.24; Luke 16.13.
8 Matt. 22.21; Mark 12.17; Luke 20.25.

Chapter 13

(1) For state reasons, the various orders of the citizens also wear laurel crowns, and there are special crowns of gold for the magistrates, as at Athens and Rome. More elaborate even than these are the Etruscan crowns. This is the name given to those crowns that are adorned with gems and oak leaves of gold, sacred to Jupiter; they wear them with togas embroidered with palm leaves when leading the chariots that carry the images of the gods. Then, there are the golden crowns of the provincials; too large for human heads, they rather fit statues.

However, your orders and your magistracies and the very name of the place in which you meet, the church, all are Christ's. For you are His, inscribed in the Book of Life.[1] (2) There is your purple—the Blood of the Lord, there your broad purple stripes—on His cross. There, the axe is already laid to the root of the tree;[2] there is the branch sprung from the root of Jesse.[3] And, pay no attention to the state horses with their crowns. Your Lord, when he wished to enter Jerusalem, as the Scripture tells us, did not even possess an ass of His own.[4] 'Some trust in chariots and some in horses, but we will call upon the name of the Lord our God.'[5] (3) We are cautioned against even dwelling in that Babylon of John's Apocalypse,[6] how much more against its pomp! The rabble, too, wear crowns—now because of some great rejoicing for the successes of the emperors; now on account of

---
1 Cf. Phil. 4.3; Apoc. 17.8.
2 Cf. Matt. 3.10; Luke 3.9.
3 Cf. Isa. 11.1.
4 Cf. Zach. 9.9; Matt. 21.1,2.
5 Ps. 19.8.
6 Cf. Apoc. 18.10.

special municipal festivals. Wantonness, indeed, tries to make its own any occasion of public gladness.

(4) But you are a mere pilgrim in this world[7] and your city is the heavenly Jerusalem. St. Paul tells us: 'But our citizenship is of heaven.'[8] You have your own citizen lists, your own calendar, and you have no part in the joys of this world; in fact, quite the contrary. 'The world will rejoice, but you will be sorrowful.'[9] I rather think the Lord is there saying that they will be happy who mourn,[10] not those who are crowned.

The bridegroom is decked with a crown at marriage, too, and that is the reason why we do not marry pagans, lest they drag us down into idolatry with which their marriage ceremony begins. (5) You have the Law, from the patriarchs themselves, and you have the Apostle, too, bidding us to marry in the Lord.[11]

There is a crowning, also, when a slave is freed, but you have been already redeemed by Christ and that at a great price.[12] How, then, can the world manumit the slave of another? Though the result might seem to be freedom, it really is not, but rather more like slavery. In all worldly things there is but semblance, and nothing is real. For, even then, as ransomed by Christ, you were under no bondage to man; now, though man has given you freedom, you are the slave of Christ.[13] (6) If you really believe the freedom of the world to be real, so much so that you even seal it with a

---

7 Cf. 1 Peter 2.11; Heb. 11.13.
8 Phil. 3.20; cf. Heb. 12.22.
9 John 16.20.
10 Cf. Matt. 5.4.
11 Cf. Gen. 24.3,4; 28.1,2; 1 Cor. 7.39.
12 Cf. 1 Peter 1.18,19; 1 Cor. 6.20.
13 Cf. 1 Cor. 7.22,23.

crown, then you have returned to the slavery of man, imagining it to be freedom; you have lost the liberty of Christ which you imagine to be slavery rather than freedom.

Will there be any need for discussing the games as occasions of the wearing of crowns, when their very names condemn them, being both sacred to the gods and in honor of the dead?[14] All we will need now will be to have Olympian Jupiter, Nemean Hercules, along with that poor Archemorus[15] and the hapless Antinous,[16] crowned in the person of a Christian to make the latter a spectacle disgusting to behold.

(7) I imagine that by now we have covered all the cases in which one might wear a crown, and they are all shown to be totally alien to us as Christians. They are foreign to us, unholy, forbidden, once for all forsworn in our baptismal vow. For they surely are 'the pomps of the Devil and his angels.' What are they but worldly positions and honors, festivals, insincere vows by the people, exhibitions of human servility, empty flatteries, and glory that brings bitterness in its train? And, at the base of them all, what is there but idolatry? For this is at the root of every crown that is placed

---

14 See above, *Spectacles* 6.3, where Tertullian makes the same distinction between 'games in honor of pagan deities and those in honor of dead persons.'
15 Son of Lycurgus of Nemea, who was killed by a dragon, while his nurse Hypsipyle showed a spring to the Seven against Thebes. The Seven gave the boy a magnificent funeral and, on that occasion, celebrated the Nemean Games for the first time. The boy's name was Opheltes, but he was afterwards called Archemorus—'Beginner of Death'—because his was the first of the many lives to be lost in the expedition of the Argive heroes against Thebes.
16 A beautiful youth and favorite of Emperor Hadrian. He died by drowning himself in the Nile in 130. In his memory Hadrian founded the city of Antinoopolis, raised him to the rank of the gods, built temples for his worship, and ordered festivals to be celebrated in his honor.

upon the head of a man. (8) Claudius [17] indeed tells us in his preface that, in the poems of Homer, the very heavens are crowned with stars[18]—crowned, to be sure, by God and for the advantage of man; therefore, man himself, too, should be crowned by God.

Finally, the world places crowns upon brothels, latrines, bakeshops, elementary schools, and the very amphitheater; they crown, too, the place where the clothes are stripped from the slain gladiators, and the very biers of the dead. So, do not determine from a line in Homer about heaven how sacred and holy, how decent and pure, is this article of apparel, but judge it as the whole world does.

(9) But, surely, a Christian will not even defile the door of his house with laurel crowns if he only remembers how many gods the Devil has attached to doors. For, we have Janus for the door itself, Limentinus for the threshold, Forculus and Carna for the partitions and hinges and, among the Greeks, there is Apollo of the Door and other gods of the entrance—devils, all of them.

Chapter 14

(1) You see, then, surely, how unfitting it is for a Christian to put on his head this symbol of idolatry; in fact, I might have said, 'put upon Christ,' since He is the head of a Christian man.[1] His head is as free as Christ Himself, not even submitting to a veil, much less to a band. But even the head that

---

17 See above, Ch. 7 nn. 5, 17.
18 Cf. *Iliad* 18.485.

---

1 Cf. 1 Cor. 11.3.

submits to a veil (I mean woman's), being already provided with this, has no room also for a band. She has the burden of her own lowliness to bear. (2) If the head of a woman should never be seen uncovered because of the angels,[2] much less should she ever wear a crown. It may well be that she also wore a crown when she tempted the sons of God to evil.[3] A crown on the head of woman is merely beauty made seductive, the sign of complete wantonness, the utter denial of modesty and the fanning of the fires of passion. Therefore, a woman will be guided by the advice of the Apostle and avoid a too elaborate adornment, that she may not either be crowned by any skilful arrangement of her hair.[4]

(3) To what kind of a crown, I ask you, did Christ Jesus submit for the salvation of both sexes, He who is the Head of man and the Glory of woman[5] and the Husband of the Church? It was made from thorns and thistles—a symbol of the sins which the soil of the flesh brought forth for us,[6] but which the power of the Cross removed, blunting every sting of death[7] since the head of the Lord bore its pain. And besides the symbol, we are also reminded of the scornful abuse, the degradation, and the vileness of his cruel tormentors. (4) If that is the way the temples of Christ were then defiled and lacerated, why, then, do you now seek to have your head crowned with laurel, myrtle, and olive, or some more exquisite leaf? Perhaps you would choose the hundred-leaved roses plucked from the garden of Midas,[8] or both kinds of

---

2 Cf. 1 Cor. 11.10.
3 Cf. Gen. 6.1,2.
4 Cf. 1 Tim. 2.9.
5 Cf. 1 Cor. 11.3-7.
6 Cf. Gen. 3.18.
7 Cf. 1 Cor. 15.55.
8 Cf. Herodotus 8.138.

lilies, and violets of all sorts, or perhaps you even wish to have jeweled and golden crowns? Of course, only that you might imitate Christ in the crown that He afterwards received! It was after the gall[9] He was given a taste of honey, and He was not hailed as the King of Glory by the angels until he had been proscribed on the cross as 'King of the Jews';[10] being first made by the Father a little less than the angels, He was then crowned with glory and honor.[11] If, then, you owe your head to Him as a debt for these favors, try as best you can to repay Him in the fashion that He offered His head for yours. Or, be not crowned with flowers at all if you cannot bear the thorns, because, with flowers, you cannot be crowned.

Chapter 15

(1) Keep untainted, therefore, for God what is His; He will crown it if so He choose. And, He will; in fact, He invites us to be crowned. To him who conquers He says: 'I will give the crown of life.'[1] Be you, too, faithful unto death; fight, too, the good fight whose crown the Apostle feels so justly confident has been laid up for him.[2] The angel of victory, also, who, riding a white horse, goes forth to conquer, receives a crown, and another is adorned with a rainbow which [in its fair colors] is like a celestial meadow.[3] The elders, too, sit crowned with golden crowns and the Son of

---

9 Cf. Matt. 27.34.
10 Cf. Matt. 27.37; Mark 15.26; Luke 23.38.
11 Cf. Heb. 2.7; Ps. 8.6.

---

1 Apoc 2.10; cf. James 1.12.
2 Cf. 2 Tim. 4.7,8.
3 Cf. Apoc. 6.2; 10.1.

Man Himself, wearing a golden crown, shines forth above the clouds.[4] (2) If such beautiful images are seen in the vision of the seer, what will the realities themselves be? Feast your eyes upon those crowns, savor those odors, and do not demean your brow with a little chaplet or a twisted headband, when your destiny is to wear a diadem. For Christ Jesus has made us to be as kings to God and His Father,[5] so why bother with a flower that is destined to die? Yours is a flower from the root of Jesse, upon which the grace of the divine Spirit has rested in all its fullness, a flower untainted, unfading and everlasting.[6]

(3) Choosing this flower, the good soldier has advanced in rank in the heavenly army. Are you not ashamed, fellow soldiers of Christ, that you will be condemned, not by Christ, but by some soldier of Mithras? At the initiation, deep in a cavern, in the very camp of darkness, a crown is presented to the candidate at the point of a sword, as if in mimicry of martyrdom, and put upon his head; then he is admonished to resist and throw it off and possibly slip it on the shoulder of the god, saying: 'Mithras is my crown.' He is at once acknowledged as a soldier of Mithras if he throws the crown away, saying that in his god he has his crown. (4) And thenceforward he never puts a crown on his head, and he uses that as a sign of identification, if anywhere he be tested as to his oath of initiation. Let us, then, recognize the wiles of the Devil, who imitates some of God's things with no other design than to put us to shame by the faithfulness of his own servants and to condemn us.

---

4 Cf. Apoc. 4.4; 14.14.
5 Cf. Apoc. 1.6.
6 Cf. Isa. 11.1,2.

FLIGHT IN TIME
OF PERSECUTION

Translated by
EDWIN A. QUAIN, S.J., Ph.D.
Fordham University

INTRODUCTION

N AN EARLIER WORK, *The Chaplet* (1.5), Tertullian had touched upon a question which, in those uncertain times, was a matter of grave concern for every fervent Christian: Is the Christian allowed to take refuge in flight under the crucial test of persecution? The promise Tertullian had given on that occasion, namely, to give a detailed answer to this vexing question, he made good by writing a special treatise, *Flight in Time of Persecution*.

The Church never did impose on its members the absolute duty of exposing themselves to martyrdom by boldly waiting for arrest, torture, and death. *The Martyrdom of Polycarp* (Ch. 4), written in 156, contains the explicit statement: 'We do not commend those who give themselves up, since the Gospel does not teach this.' St. Polycarp himself, yielding to the entreaties of friends, quietly left his episcopal city of Smyrna and withdrew to a farm in the neighborhood. Nor did other Christian leaders of unquestionable courage, as, for instance, St. Cyprian, hesitate to retire to a safe place of hiding, when giving themselves up to their persecutors would only have meant uselessly courting death and probably causing greater damage to the Christian community as a whole.

In his Catholic days, Tertullian had found no fault with this attitude. 'In time of persecution,' he wrote in *Ad uxorem* (1.3.4), 'it is better to use the permission granted and "to flee from town to town," than to be apprehended and to deny the faith under torture.' A similar view is implied in his *De patientia* (13.6). As a Montanist, however, Tertullian felt himself compelled to change his opinion in the matter. Did the 'Paraclete' who spoke through the mouth of his Phrygian prophet, Montanus, not make it unmistakably clear that, in persecution, a Christian should never be a coward and seek safety in flight, but be anxious to die a martyr's death (see below, Ch. 9.4)? Hence, consulted by a Catholic Christian, whose name was Fabius, as to whether it was permitted to elude persecution either by going into hiding or by buying off the persecutors, Tertullian categorically condemns both means of escaping danger as equivalent to formal apostasy. Persecution, he argues, is willed by God, the Devil being only the instrument of persecution, not its author. As coming from God, persecution is something intrinsically good. It tests the faith of Christians, separating the chaff from the wheat, and increases religious zeal anl fervor. For those who object to these conclusions by referring to Matt. 23.10, 'When they begin to persecute you, flee from city to city' (see below, Ch. 6.1), Tertullian has a ready answer. The Lord's command, he replies, was only intended for the persons of the Apostles, their times, and the peculiar circumstances of their mission, but does not apply to the present. As to buying one's freedom from persecution by bribing informers, soldiers and judges, such a practice is 'flight' in disguised form, unworthy of God, because it tries to redeem with money a man whom Christ has redeemed with his Blood.

That the treatise belongs to Tertullian's Montanist period is evident from such passages as Ch. 1.1, where the author regrets that the addressee, Fabius, obviously a Catholic Christian, has not yet accepted the 'Paraclete' of the Montanists; Ch. 9.4, where he bolsters his argumentation by quoting two utterances of the 'Paraclete'; Ch. 11.2, where he states that anyone who harkens to the 'Paraclete' 'will hear Him branding the runaways'; Ch. 14.3, where he insists on the necessity of further revelation by the 'Paraclete.' The treatise is usually assigned to the year 212.

The text followed in the present translation is that of J. J. Thierry in *Corpus Christianorum*, Series Latina 2 (Turnholti 1954) 1133-1155.

SELECT BIBLIOGRAPHY

Texts:

- J. J. Thierry, *Corpus Christianorum*, Series Latina 2 (Turnholti 1954) 1133-1155.
- J. J. Thierry, *Tertullianus. De fuga in persectuione*, ed. with [Dutch] introduction, translation, and commentary (Hilversum 1941).
- J. Marra, *Q. Septimii Tertulliani De spectaculis, De fuga in persecutione, De pallio* (Corpus Scriptorum Latinorum Paravianum; Turin 1954).

Secondary Sources:

- E. Jolyon, *La Fuite de la persécution. Ce qu'en a pensé Tertullien et ce qu'en pense l'Eglise* (Lyon 1903).
- H. Leclercq, 'Fuite de la persécution,' *DACL* 5.2 (1923) 2660-2684.
- A. Quacquarelli, 'La persecuzione secondo Tertulliano,' *Gregorianum* 31 (1950) 562-589.

FLIGHT IN TIME OF PERSECUTION

Chapter 1

A SHORT TIME AGO, my brother Fabius,[1] on the occasion of some news or other, you asked me whether flight was justified in time of persecution. On that occasion, I offered some arguments against it—arguments that did justice to the place and the time, and satisfied the earnest requests of certain people—and took the rough draft along with me. Now I intend to take up my pen and to resume my discussion of the topic in fuller detail. For, you see, your request caught my interest and, besides, the conditions of the times made the question a pressing one. For, as bitter persecutions threaten us, with all the more zeal should we pursue a solution to your question, as to how a faithful Christian should conduct himself. It is particularly fitting that I should discuss this matter with you, for, if you are guilty in not accepting the Paraclete, the guide to all truth,[2] deservedly, then, you are guilty even now in other matters also.

---

1 The addressee, otherwise unknown, is obviously a Catholic Christian. For, Tertullian deplores Fabius' obstinacy in not accepting the 'Paraclete' of the Montanists (see the concluding sentence of the paragraph).
2 Cf. John 16.13.

(2) To take up the case you presented in proper order, then, it occurs to me that we should determine the origin of the persecution—whether it comes from God or from the Devil; in that way, we will more easily get an idea of how to face it. The result of any investigation will be the clearer if we know the root of the whole matter. Of course, it is all right to say that nothing happens without God willing it, but, having said that, we must be on our guard lest we give rise to doubts on other questions, and thus be drawn off our course. For instance, someone might immediately conclude: 'Therefore, evil and sin are from God, and no blame is to be attached to the Devil or to ourselves.'

(3) Let us come, then, to the nature of 'persecution'; at the outset, let me say that it never happens without God willing it, and it is fitting—even, at times, necessary—for Him to do so, to the approval or condemnation of His servants. For, what else is the result of a persecution, what finally is its effect, if not the approval or condemnation, when God puts the faith of His children to the test?

(4) In this sense, then, a persecution is a 'judgment,' and the verdict is either approval or condemnation. To be sure, to God alone it belongs to judge, and this is His winnowing fan which even now cleanses the Lord's threshing floor—His Church, winnowing the mixed heap of the faithful and separating the wheat of the martyrs from the chaff of the cowards.[3] This judgment, too, is the ladder of which Jacob dreamed, on which some are ascending on high, while others descend below.[4]

(5) In still another sense, a persecution can be considered as a contest. And who decrees any contest if not the one who

---

3 Cf. Matt. 3.12.
4 Cf. Gen. 28.12.

provides the crown and the prizes? You will find this contest decreed in the Apocalypse where He proclaims the rewards of victory, especially for those who really come through persecution victorious,[5] and in their victorious struggle have fought not merely against flesh and blood, but against the spirits of wickedness.[6] Obviously, then, the superintendent of the games and the one who sets the prize is the one who decides who is the winner of the contest. The essence, then, of a persecution is the glory of God, whether He approves or condemns, raises up or casts down. And whatever concerns the glory of God will certainly flow from the Will of God. But, when is God more sincerely believed than when He is more feared, than in time of persecution?

(6) [When persecution strikes,] the Church is mightily stirred; then the faithful are more careful in their preparations, greater attention is given to fasts and station days, to prayers and humility, to mutual charity and love, to holiness and temperance. Men have time for nothing but fear and hope. Therefore, it is clear that persecution, which works for the improvement of the servants of God, cannot be blamed on the Devil.

Chapter 2

(1) On the other hand, it might seem that persecution stems from the Devil, who commits the evil acts which make up the persecution, if we reason as follows: Evil is not from God but from the Devil, and a persecution is made up of evil actions (for, what could be more evil than to treat the

---
5 Cf. Apoc. 2.7,10,11,17,26-28; 3.5,12,21.
6 Cf. Eph, 6.12.

bishops of the true God and all the followers of truth as if they were the vilest criminals?). Still, we must realize that, as you cannot have a persecution without evil on the part of the Devil, nor a trial of faith without a persecution, the evil that seems required for the trial of faith is not the cause of persecution, but only its instrument. The real cause of the persecution is the act of God's will, choosing that there be a trial of faith; then there follows evil on the part of the Devil as the chosen instrument of persecution which is the proximate cause of the trial of faith. For, in other respects, too, in so far as evil is the rival of justice, to that extent it provides material to give testimony of that of which it is a rival, and so, justice may be said to be perfected in injustice, as strength is perfected in weakness.[1] For the weak things of the world are chosen by God that the strong may be put to shame, and the foolish things of this world to put to shame its wisdom.[2] Thus, even evil may be used that justice may be glorified when evil is put to shame.

(2) However, this instrument in the hands of the Devil does not make him a master, but really a servant; it is the will of the Lord that chooses persecution as a means to the trial of faith, and the Devil is only an instrument to be used so that persecution can take place. Thus, we believe that a persecution happens *through* the Devil, but not *by* him. Satan can have no power over the servants of the living God, unless the Lord permits it, either in order that the Devil may be destroyed by the victory of the faith of the elect in overcoming temptation, or that some men be shown by their defection under fire, to have long since belonged to Satan.

(3) For this we have the example of Job, to whom the

---
1 2 Cor. 12.9.
2 1 Cor. 1.27.

Devil never could have sent a temptation unless he had received the power from God to do so; nor could he have laid a hand on Job's property unless God had said: 'Behold, I give into your hands all things that are his, but on himself, do not lay a hand.' And the Devil never would have done even that unless, when he asked for this power afterwards, God had said: 'I hand him over to you, only, save his life.'[3]

(4) So also, the Devil asked for the power to tempt the Apostles, since he did not have it except with divine permission. Thus, in the Gospel, the Lord said to Peter: 'Behold, Satan has desired to have you, that he may sift you as wheat; but I have prayed for thee, that thy faith may not fail.'[4] That is to say, the Devil could not have so much power as to be able to endanger the faith of Peter. Thus we see that both the threat to our faith as well as its protection are in the power of God, when both are asked of Him—the threat by the Devil and the protection by the Son of God.

(5) And surely, when the Son of God has the protection of our faith in His power, since He asked it of the Father from whom He received all power in heaven and on earth,[5] how could the Devil ever have it in his own power, independently, to pose a threat to our faith? On the other hand, when we say to His Father in the prayer that He has enjoined on us, 'Lead us not into temptation'[6] (and what greater temptation can there be than persecution?), we are effectively admitting that temptation is permitted by Him from whom we are asking help. This is clear from what follows: 'But deliver us from evil.'[7] That is, do not lead us into temptation so

---
3 Job 2.6.
4 Luke 22.31,32.
5 Matt. 28.18.
6 Matt. 6.13.
7 *Ibid.*

that we might fall into the hands of the Devil. For then are we truly snatched from the hands of the Devil, when we are not even exposed to him to be tempted at all.

(6) The Devil and his host would not have had power even over the herd of swine had it not been given them by God;[8] so much the less do they have it over the flock of God. I would go so far as to say that the bristles on the hide of the swine were numbered by God, not less than the hairs on the head of the saints.[9] The Devil has power that might be called his own, only over such as no longer belong to God, the heathen whom He considers once for all as a drop in a bucket,[10] as dust on the threshing floor, as spittle in the mouth —and, as such, totally handed over to the Devil as a quite useless possession.

(7) Otherwise, he may do nothing by his own right, against those who dwell in the house of God, because the cases that are noted in Scripture show us when—that is, for what reasons—he may touch them. The right to tempt a man is granted to the Devil, either for the sake of a trial, as in the texts cited above, whether God or the Devil initiates the plan, or for the purpose of the reprobation of a sinner, who is handed over to the Devil as to an executioner. This was the case with Saul. 'The spirit of the Lord departed from Saul, and an evil spirit from the Lord troubled and stifled him.'[11] Again, it may happen in order to humble a man, as St. Paul tells us that there was given him a thorn, a messenger of Satan, to buffet him,[12] and even this sort of thing is not permitted for the humiliation of holy men through torment of

---

8 Matt. 8.31,32.
9 Matt. 10.30.
10 Cf. Isa. 40.15.
11 1 Kings 16.14.
12 2 Cor. 12.7.

FLIGHT IN TIME OF PERSECUTION   281

the flesh, unless it be done so that their power to resist may be perfected in weakness. The Apostle himself handed Phigellus and Hermogenes over to Satan so that by being chastised they might not blaspheme.[13] And so you see that, far from possessing power in his own right, the Devil can more easily be granted it by the servants of God.

Chapter 3

(1) Now, since it is clear that cases such as these occur in time of persecutions more than at other times (for, it is then that we are approved or condemned, humbled or corrected), it can only be that their general occurrence is permitted or decreed by Him at whose will they happen even partially; in a word, by Him who says: 'I am He who makes peace and creates evil.'[1] And, by 'evil' here is meant 'war,' the antithesis of peace. For persecution is surely the 'war' which destroys our 'peace.' If, indeed, the most striking outcome of persecution is to bring life or death, harm or health, then its author will surely be He who says: 'I will strike and I will heal; I will bring life and I will cause death.'[2] Again, He tells us: 'I will refine them as gold is refined, and I will try them as silver is tried.'[3] For when we are tried in the flame of persecution, then it is that we are tested for the steadfastness of our faith.

(2) These will be the fiery darts of the Devil,[4] by which

---

13 Cf. 2 Tim. 1.15; 1 Tim. 1.20.

1 Isa. 45.7.
2 Deut. 32.39.
3 Zach. 13.9.
4 Cf. Eph. 6.16.

our faith is exposed to the licking flames, yet by the will of God. I do not see how anyone can have doubt of this, unless it take possession of those whose faith is worthless and cold and who with trembling assemble together in the church. I have heard you say: 'Just because we rush madly in crowds to the church, we arouse the curiosity of the pagans, and we fear lest we stir their opposition.' Do you not realize that God is the Lord of all? If He wills it, you will suffer persecution; if He does not, the pagans will not utter a word against you. And that you can believe, if, indeed, you truly believe in that God without whose will not even a worthless sparrow falls to the ground.[5] And surely, we are worth more than a flock of sparrows.[6]

Chapter 4

(1) I suppose we may take it as settled, then, that God is the author of persecution. Now we can go on to your query, and, as a result of this preliminary discussion, conclude that we must not flee in time of persecution. For, if persecution comes from God, we cannot run from it, precisely because God is its cause. And this for two reasons: we may not, and, we cannot. We may not, because what comes from God is good; in fact, anything that God 'sees' is good. Is that not the reason why we are told in Genesis: 'And God saw that it was good'?[1] Not, of course, that He did not know it was good until He saw it; what it really means is that whatever

---
5 Matt. 10.29.
6 Matt. 10.31.

1 Gen. 1.10.

God sees is, for that reason, good. There are, to be sure, many things that happen by God's will, which, incidentally, bring harm to someone. But, the precise reason why a thing is good is that it proceeds from God, because it is divine, because it is rational. For, everything divine is rational, and what is rational and not at the same time good? What good thing is not [to that extent] divine? But, if to man's perception this seems to be the case, surely it is not man's power of perception that predetermines the nature of things, but the other way around. For each and every nature is a definite reality and, because of that fact, it gives to man's perceptive power the norm for perceiving it as it exists. Now, if something that comes from God is good indeed in its natural state (for there is nothing from God that is not good, because it is divine and rational) but seems to be evil to human perception, then, surely, the thing *is* really good and man's senses must be in error. Chastity, truth, and justice are in themselves good things, even though many people find them somewhat distasteful.

(2) Are we to say, then, that the real nature must cede to the sense of perception? Thus, also, persecution is a good thing in itself, since it is a divine and rational decree; to be sure, those who have to undergo it hardly feel it to be pleasant. I am sure you see that, as proceeding from God, even the 'evil' involved in persecution has a reasonable ground, when, by persecution, someone is removed from the path of salvation, just as it is clear that you have a reasonable ground for the 'good,' also, when, by persecution, someone makes progress on the way of salvation—unless, of course, you are willing to admit that a man is damned or saved before the Lord in altogether irrational fashion. Hence,

you cannot say that persecution is an evil; for even in its evil aspect it is a good, while it is dictated by reason.

(3) Therefore, if persecution is an intrinsic good, since it has a natural basis, we must necessarily conclude that we ought not to flee from a good thing, because it would be a sin to refuse what is good and, more so, to shun something that God has seen. As a matter of fact, we cannot really avoid persecution, since it comes from God, and no man can escape what God has willed. Therefore, those who advocate flight either reproach God for perpetrating an evil, if they run from persecution as if from an evil (for no man runs from what is good)—or they consider themselves stronger than God, if they think they can avoid something that God has determined is going to take place.

Chapter 5

(1) But someone may say: 'I only flee in order to save my soul, lest I perish by denying my faith. If God wants me to be a martyr, He can bring me back before the judge, even if I run away.' First answer me this: Are you certain you will succumb, if you stay and face persecution, or are you still uncertain? If you are certain, then you have already denied the faith, because, in presuming you will fall, you have already despaired. Granted that presumption, there is no use in fleeing lest you succumb, since, if you are bound to fall, you have already fallen. If, on the other hand, you are still uncertain [whether or not you will deny the faith under fire], why not presume you could be a confessor, since there is an equal balance of fear of either alternative? In that way you would be saved, without fleeing at all. For,

remember, that is what you had in mind when you planned to flee, lest you run the risk of falling.

(2) Either the choice lies entirely with us, or it is wholly in the power of God. And, if it is ours to decide whether we will be confessors or not, why not assume what is better, namely, that we will bravely face the persecutor? Unless you are willing to confess the faith, you do not want to suffer; and to be unwilling to confess is to deny. If, however, the matter is entirely in the hands of God, why not leave the whole affair to His judgment? Let us recognize His power and might who is equally able to bring us back to the tribunal if we run away, just as He is able to protect us if we do not flee; yes, even living in the midst of the people.

(3) What kind of position are we in if we pretend we are paying honor to God by running away because we admit that He can bring us back, while at the same time we are doing Him a dishonor by despairing of His power to protect us if we stand firm? Would we not be showing more strength and trust in God if we were to say: 'I will do my duty; I will not run away; If God so wills, He will protect me?' This, I think, is our duty, instead—to stay, leaving the matter up to God's will rather than to run away on our own choice. The holy martyr Rutilius time and again fled persecution from place to place, even, so he thought, buying his freedom with money. While enjoying the freedom he had worked so hard to get he was unexpectedly caught, haled before the judge, and worn out with torments (which I suspect were a punishment for his flight!) and, finally, being cast into the fire, he paid to the mercy of God the suffering he had been unwilling to bear.[1] Clearly, God wants us to

---

1 Nothing else is known of this martyr Rutilius. Mention of him is made in the Roman Martyrology for August 2nd.

conclude from that example that we must not flee, since there is no safety in flight if God wills that we should stand.

Chapter 6

(1) 'But,' someone might say, 'in fleeing from city to city, he was merely following the precept [of Christ].' Yes, that is an argument that was adduced by a certain individual, who had himself fled. Others have done the same. They do not want to understand the meaning of the Lord's command, but merely wish to use it as a cloak of their own cowardice. To be sure, the Lord's command might apply to certain persons, times, and circumstances. We read: 'When they begin to persecute you, flee from city to city.'[1] But, I maintain that that text only applied to the persons of the Apostles, and to their times and circumstances; you can see this from the following words, which certainly refer exclusively to the Apostles: 'Do not go in the direction of the Gentiles, nor enter a city of the Samaritans, but rather go to the lost sheep of the house of Israel.'[2]

(2) But to us the way of the Gentiles is also open; in fact, that is where we were found and there will we walk till the end. No city is excepted in our case, but we preach throughout the whole world; no special care for Israel has been laid upon us, except in so far as we are to preach to all nations. And, if we are caught, we will not be haled before the councils of the Jews, nor will we be scourged in their

---
1 Matt. 10.23.
2 Matt. 10.5,6.

synagogues, but we will face the magistrates and courts of Rome.³

(3) So, it would seem that the precise circumstances of the Apostles even required the injunction to flee, since their primary obligation was to preach to the lost sheep of the house of Israel. And, in order that the preaching [of the Gospel] might be fully accomplished in the case of those among whom this task had first to be carried out—that the children of the house might receive bread before the dogs⁴— the Apostles were commanded to flee then for a time. This was not that they might elude danger under the special title of persecution—in fact, He foretold that they would suffer persecutions and He taught them that they must be endured⁵—but in order to help spread the Gospel. For, if they had been killed right at the beginning, the diffusion of the Gospel, too, would have been prevented.

(4) Nor was it His idea that they should secretly flee into some city, but openly proclaim the Gospel everywhere, and, for that very action, expose themselves to persecutions everywhere, until they had fulfilled their apostolate. For He said: 'You will not have gone through the towns of Israel.'⁶ So, the command to flee was restricted to the confines of Judea. But, for us now, there is no restriction to the boundaries of Judea for our preaching, now that the Holy Spirit has been poured out upon all flesh.⁷

(5) Therefore, St. Paul and the Apostles, ever mindful of the Lord's precept, solemnly testified to this before Israel,

---

3 Cf. Matt. 10.17,18.
4 Cf. Matt. 15.26.
5 Cf. Matt. 10.17,18.
6 Matt. 10.23.
7 Cf. Acts 2.17.

which they had now filled with their doctrine: 'It was necessary that the word of God should be brought to you first, but since you have rejected it and have not considered yourselves worthy of eternal life, behold we now turn to the Gentiles.'[8] And, from that time, they turned away from Israel, as they had been taught by those who had gone before them, and they went into the ways of the Gentiles, and they entered into the cities of the Samaritans so that their sound might go forth into all the earth and their words unto the ends of the world.[9]

(6) Now, if the restriction concerning setting foot in the ways of the Gentiles and entering into the cities of the Samaritans has come to an end, why should not the command to flee come also to an end, since it was enunciated at the same time? Accordingly, from that time on, once they had covered Israel, the Apostles turned to the Gentiles; they did not flee from city to city, nor did they hesitate to suffer. In fact, St. Paul who, at a time when the command was still in force, had allowed himself to escape persecution by being let down [in a basket] from a wall,[10] at the end of his apostolate and after the command was in abeyance did precisely the opposite. The disciples were begging him that under no circumstances should he go to Jerusalem, lest he suffer what Agabus had foretold he would suffer, and he refused to accede to their kindly thoughts. 'What do you mean by weeping and troubling my heart? For I would wish not only to suffer bonds, but even to die in Jerusalem for the name of my Lord, Jesus Christ.' And so, they all said: 'The Lord's will be done.'[11] And what was the will of the Lord? Surely not that

---

8 Acts 13.46.
9 Ps. 18.5.
10 Cf. Acts 9.25.
11 Acts 21.10-14.

they should any longer flee from persecution. Otherwise they might surely have mentioned the former command of the Lord to Paul whom they wished to save from that persecution.

(7) Since, therefore, a time limit was set to the command to flee, even in the times of the Apostles, as well as a limit to other precepts given at the same time, it surely would not be right for us to prolong a practice which ceased with our teachers, even' if it had not originally been permitted exclusively to them. If God had wanted it to continue, then the Apostles did wrong in not continuing to flee before persecution to the end of their normal lives.

Chapter 7

(1) Let us examine next whether or not the other commands of the Lord are in accord with a lasting precept of flight from persecution. First of all, if persecution comes from God, how could it be that we would have a command always to avoid it, given by the very one who sends us such trials? If He wanted us to avoid it, He would have done better not to send it at all, lest His will should seem to be thwarted by another will. He wanted us either to face persecution or to flee from it. If we were to flee, how could we suffer? And, if we are destined to suffer, how can we run from it? As you see, there is a basic inconsistency if the same one bids us flee from persecution and at the same time invites us to suffering, which is the very opposite. 'He who will acknowledge me [before men], him will I also acknowledge before my Father.'[1] How can a runaway acknowledge Christ?

---
1 Matt. 10.32.

And, if he is to acknowledge Him, he obviously cannot run away. 'He who is ashamed of Me, him will I be ashamed of before my Father.'² If I avoid suffering, I am ashamed to acknowledge Christ. 'Happy are those who suffer persecution for my name's sake.'³ From that it follows that those who, by fleeing, will avoid suffering according to the divine command will be unhappy! 'He who has persevered to the end will be saved.'⁴

(2) How can you want me to flee and, at the same time, persevere until the end? If such an inconsistency seems hardly in accord with the divine dignity, it should then be clear from all this that there was a specific and temporary reason for the command to flee, as I have shown above. However, someone might offer the explanation that 'the Lord in His goodness took pity on the weakness of some which He foresaw and therefore He suggested a haven of safety in flight.' Do you mean to say that the only way God could have saved some of us whose frailty He recognized would be by offering the mean, unworthy, and slavish chance of flight? In fact, He does not cherish the weak, but always rebuffs them, teaching that persecutors are not to be avoided, but should be boldy faced. Does He not tell us: 'Do not be afraid of those who kill the body, but can do no harm to the soul, but rather be afraid of him who can destroy both soul and body in hell'?⁵ Moreover, what is His answer to cowards? 'He who thinks more of his own life than of Me is not worthy of Me and he who does not take up his cross and follow Me, cannot be My disciple.'⁶ And finally, in the Apocalypse, it is not flight that

---

2 Matt. 10.33; cf: Mark 8.38; Luke 9.26.
3 Cf. Matt. 5.10,11.
4 Matt. 10.22.
5 Matt. 10.28.
6 Cf. Matt. 10.38; Luke 14.26,27.

He offers to the fearful, but a miserable portion among the rest of the damned in the pit of brimstone and fire, which is the second death.[7]

Chapter 8

(1) Christ Himself fled from violence on occasion, but He did it for the same reason for which He had commanded the Apostles do so—namely, until He had fulfilled His mission. When He had done that, He not merely stood firm [to face His persecutors], but He refused to ask of His Father assistance in the form of the angelic hosts, and He even objected when St. Peter reached for his sword.[1] He likewise said that His soul was troubled unto death[2] and His flesh weak. He did this to teach us two lessons: the first—to teach us by the weakness of His body and the timidity of His soul that both of these substances were truly human, lest you should think that the soul and body of Christ were different from ours, as some people have recently suggested;[3] and second—by giving proof of their human weakness, to show us that both of them were unequal to the task without the strength of the Spirit.

---

7 Cf. Apoc. 21.8.

1 Cf. Matt. 26.53,54.
2 Matt. 26.38.
3 Tertullian has in mind the Gnostics (especially Marcion, the latter's chief disciple, Apelles, and Valentinus and his school) whose teachings were based on a radical antithesis between spirit and matter, the latter being regarded inferior to the former and intrinsically evil. Hence, they also found it impossible to think of God becoming man in any real sense, and denied the full humanity of Christ. Though the above-mentioned Gnostics differed widely in their position, they were all Docetists, i.e., they reduced the historic Christ to a phantom Jesus whose suffering was only a 'semblance' (δοκεῖν).

(2) And this is the reason why He says first: 'The Spirit is willing,'[4] so that you might understand that you have the strength of the Spirit as well as the weakness of the flesh, keeping in mind the nature of body and soul. Thus you may learn what it is you have to work with, and which should be subordinate to which—that is, the weak to the strong, and not be doing what you now do, begging off on the score of the weakness of the flesh, while paying no attention to the strength of the Spirit.

(3) He Himself begged of His Father that, if it might be possible, the chalice of suffering might pass from Him.[5] You should offer the same prayer, but also imitate his firmness; pray, to be sure, but be sure you add: 'However, not what I will, but Thy will be done.' How can you pray thus, if you run away? How can you ask that the chalice pass, when you intend to do, not the will of the Father, but your own will?

Chapter 9

(1) Now, it is certain that the Apostles were true to every word of the teaching of God and they omitted not a line of the Gospel. Can you show me any place in which they have reinstated the divine command to flee from city to city? They could never have adduced a precept of flight; that would have been so contrary to their own practice. Were they not writing their letters to the churches from prison, or from islands whither they had gone, not to escape, but were on precisely because they had confessed the faith? St. Paul tells

---
4 Matt. 26.41.
5 Cf. Matt. 26.39.

us that we should support the weak,[1] and he surely does not mean those who have fled. How could you support them if they were not there? By bearing with them? He tells us that we should support them if they have fallen through the weakness of their faith. So, he wants the faint-hearted to be comforted[2] and not encouraged to run away.

(2) When he counsels us not to give place to the evil,[3] he is not telling us to try to escape from it, but he is suggesting that we restrain our anger. When he says that we must make the most of our time because the days are evil,[4] he wishes us to make our earthly pilgrimage profitable not by flight, but by wisdom. Likewise, when he bids us to shine as the children of light,[5] he is not telling us to hide in secret as do the children of darkness. He says we must stand firm—that does not mean to run madly away—and be girt [for battle],[6] and can that mean flight? Does it not rather mean we must boldly profess our faith? He points out our weapons, too, which would hardly be of use to runaways; among them, the shield with which you may turn aside the darts of the Devil.[7] That surely means that you must resist him and take the full force of his attack.

(3) Further, St. John tells us that we must be ready to lay down our lives for our friends;[8] much more, then, for the Lord. How can runaways fulfill that precept? Finally, mindful of what he had heard in his own Apocalypse as to the

---

1 Rom. 15.1.
2 1 Thess. 5.14.
3 Cf. Eph. 4.27.
4 Cf. Eph. 5.16.
5 Cf. Eph. 5.8.
6 Cf. Eph. 6.14.
7 Cf. Eph. 6.16.
8 1 John 3.16.

doom of the fearful,⁹ and speaking from personal knowledge, he warns us that we must cast out fear. 'There is no fear in love; but perfect love casts out fear, because fear brings punishment' (He was, no doubt, thinking of the fire of the pool)' and he who fears is not perfected in love'[10]—that is, love of God.

(4) Yet, who will flee from persecution, if not the man who fears? And, who will fear, if not the one who loves not? If you ask counsel of the Spirit,[11] what will He approve more than that counsel of the Spirit? Indeed, by it almost all are advised to offer themselves for martyrdom, never to flee from it. Hence, I cannot help but quote it, as follows: 'If you are held up to infamy, that is good. He who does not suffer ignominy before men will know it before God. Never be ashamed, because it is your very righteousness that sets you before the public gaze. Why are you ashamed of what is to your glory? You gain power, when you are before the eyes of men.' So also he tells us elsewhere: 'Do not then ask to die on bridal beds, or in miscarriages, or from gentle

---

9 Apoc. 21.8.
10 1 John. 4.18.
11 The 'Spirit' referred to is the 'Paraclete,' speaking through the mouth of Montanus and his associates, Prisca (or Priscilla) and Maximilla. Revelation, the Montanists contended, had reached its full maturity in Montanus and his prophetesses. As a matter of fact, the revelations which the 'Paraclete' gave through them were considered a direct continuation of the prophetic mission of Christ and the Apostles. Their utterances, the result of a new and last outpouring of the Spirit, were supposed to complete the Gospels by filling up the gaps which had been left therein. The following sentences contain two utterances of the 'Paraclete,' the second of which is paraphrased by Tertullian in *De anima* 55.5, as follows: 'If you lay down your life for God as the "Paraclete" recommends, then it will not be of some gentle fever in a soft bed, but in the torture of martyrdom.' Other *effata* of the Phrygian prophets are found in Tertullian's *De pudicitia* 21; *De exhortatione castitatis* 10; *De resurrectione carnis* 11.

fevers; rather, seek to die a martyr that He may be glorified who suffered for you.'

Chapter 10

(1) Some will refuse to consider the divine commands in this matter and will turn instead to the worldly wisdom supposed to be contained in the Greek proverb: 'He who turns and runs away lives to fight another day.'[1] And runs away again in the next battle? When is he going to win, if he runs away defeated? He surely acts as a fine soldier of his Leader, Christ, who, having been so fully armed by the Apostle,[2] takes to his heels at the first sound of the trumpet of persecution! I will give you a worldly answer to that one: 'Is it such a terrible thing to die?'

(2) He is going to die some way, anyhow, whether in victory or in defeat, and, even if he dies denying his faith, he will at least have faced and fought the tormentor. Personally, I would rather be an object of pity than of shame. Far nobler is the soldier who is lost in battle than he who goes off completely free by running. O Christian, are you afraid of man?—you whom the angels should fear as their judge;[3] you who should be feared by the demons, since you have received power over the devils, too;[4] you who should be feared by the whole world, since the world will be judged by you, too.[5]

---
1 This Greek proverb is quoted by the second-century writer Aulus Gellius in his *Noctes Atticae* 17.21.
2 Cf. Eph. 6.13-17.
3 Cf. 1 Cor. 6.3.
4 Cf. Matt. 10.8; Mark 16.17.
5 Cf. 1 Cor. 6.2.

You have put on Christ, you have been baptized into Christ,⁶ yet you flee before the Devil! You certainly make little of Christ who is in you when, as a fugitive, you hand yourself back to the Devil!

(3) In trying to run away from the Lord you show up the fickleness of all who plan flight. A certain headstrong Prophet also had run away from the Lord, crossing the sea from Joppa to Tarsus,⁷ as if he could escape from God, but God found him, not on land or on sea, but in the belly of a beast, where for three days he could not die,⁸ or even in that way escape from the eyes of God. Is that man not better off who, though he fears the enemy of God, does not flee from, but despises, him, trusting in the protection of God, or, if you will, has an even greater fear of God, having stood the longer in His eyes and says: 'He is the Lord, He is mighty, all things are His, and wherever I shall be I am in His hands; let Him do what He will, I shall not run away, and if He wishes me to die, let Him destroy me, as long as I faithfully serve Him. Much would I rather bring odium on Him, by dying according to His Will, than to live by my own cowardice.'

Chapter 11

(1) Thus should every servant of God both think and act, even if he is in a lower station of life, that he might rise higher, if, perchance, by bearing the storm of persecution he may raise himself somewhat. But, when those in authority—

---
6 Cf. Gal. 3.27.
7 Cf. Jonas 1.3.
8 Cf. Jonas 2.1.

I mean deacons, priests, and bishops—take flight, how is the mere layman to understand the sense in which it was said: 'Flee from city to city'? When the leaders run away, who of the common crowd can hope to persuade anyone to stand firm in battle? Without a doubt, the good shepherd lays down his life for his sheep,[1] as Moses said, at a time when Christ, the Lord, had not yet come, but was prefigured in Moses: 'If you will destroy this people, then destroy me also along with it.'[2]

(2) Besides, Christ Himself has confirmed this prefigurement of Himself when He said that he is a wicked shepherd who flees when he sees the wolf and leaves the flock to be devoured.[3] Such a shepherd will be banished from the farm, his separation pay will be kept from him as compensation for the damage; in fact, he will have to pay back something from his former wages, to indemnify the losses of his master. 'For to him who has shall be given and from him who does not have even that which he seems to have shall be taken away.'[4] Thus Zacharias threatens: 'Arise, O sword, against the shepherds, and pluck ye out the sheep and I will turn my hand against the shepherds.'[5] And against them Ezechiel and Jeremias thunder with similar recriminations, in that they have not merely battened upon their sheep and fattened themselves, but they have themselves dispersed the flock and, without a leader to guide them, left them the prey to all the beasts of the field.[6] For, this is what happens when the Church is deserted by the clergy in time of persecution.

---
1 Cf. John 10.11.
2 Cf. Exod. 32.32.
3 Cf. John 10.12.
4 Luke 8.18.
5 Zach. 13.7.
6 Cf. Ezech. 34.2ff.; Jer. 23.1ff.

And, if anyone recognizes the Spirit, he will hear Him branding the runaways.

(3) But, if it is not fitting that the leaders of the flock should flee when the wolves descend upon the sheep—if indeed, it is forbidden—for He who called such a one a wicked shepherd, certainly condemned him, and whatever has been condemned is certainly thereafter unlawful—then those who have been given charge over the Church cannot flee in time of persecution. If however, the flock were obliged to flee, then the shepherd would not be obliged to stand his ground. In that case, there would be no reason for him to stay 'to protect his flock,' since, as a matter of fact, they would have no need of protection, as a result of their liberty, of course, to flee.

Chapter 12

(1) That, I think, should be a sufficient answer to the question that you raised, my brother, and you have my decision and encouragement. But, the man who raises the question as to flight in time of persecution must go on to ask the next one, namely, if we cannot flee, then may we buy our freedom when persecution comes? I will also have a few suggestions for you on this point, declaring that we can no more buy our freedom than we can run away when persecution strikes. And the key to my answer lies in the payment: just as flight is getting your freedom without money, so buying your freedom is a 'money-flight.' This, surely, is the counsel of fear. Because you fear, you pay, and when you pay, you flee. As regards your feet, you have stood still; as regards the money you paid, you have run away. By

this very fact that your money permitted you to stay, you have run away.

(2) Oh how unworthy is it of God and His will that you try to redeem with mere money a man who has been ransomed by the Blood of Christ! God spared not His own Son for you,[1] letting Him become a curse for us; for 'cursed is he who hangs on a tree';[2] as a sheep He was led to the sacrifice, as a lamb to the shearer, and He did not open His mouth,[3] but bared His back to the scourge and His cheeks to those who would smite Him; He did not turn away from those who would spit on Him[4] and among the wicked He was reputed,[5] and was delivered up to death, even unto the death of the cross.[6] And all this that He might redeem us from our sins. The sun was darkened on the day of our redemption;[7] hell lost its right to us and we were enrolled for heaven. The eternal gates were lifted up that the King of Glory, the Lord of Might, might enter in,[8] and man, born of the earth, destined for hell, was purchased for heaven.

(3) What kind of man is he who struggles against Christ, in fact, misprizes the goods that were bought at so high a price, namely, the precious blood of the Immaculate Lamb?[9] Far better that he run away than to become so mean, that a man should not prize himself for as much as Christ was willing to pay for him. Christ indeed ransomed man from the angels who rule over the world, from the powers and spirits

---

1 Rom. 8.32.
2 Gal. 3:13.
3 Cf. Isa. 53.7.
4 Cf. Isa. 50.6.
5 Cf. Isa. 53.12.
6 Phil. 2.8.
7 Cf. Matt. 27.45.
8 Cf. Ps. 23.7.
9 Cf. 1 Peter 1.19.

of wickedness, from the darkness of this world,[10] from eternal judgment, from eternal death. And you bargain for him with an informer, or some soldier, or some petty thief of a ruler, passing money from up your sleeves, as they say, as if he were stolen goods, whom Christ redeemed before the whole world and, in fact, freed from slavery! Can you price this free man, and buy him for any sum less (as we have said) than what he cost Christ—His own Blood? Why do you haggle with a man as to the price of a man in whom Christ dwells?

(4) That is precisely what Simon [Magus] was trying to do when he offered the Apostles money for the Spirit of Christ.[11] Anyone who, by buying his freedom, has tried to buy the Spirit of Christ, will also hear: 'Thy money go to destruction with thee, because thou hast thought that the grace of God could be purchased at a price.'[12] We can have nothing but contempt for such a denier. What does the extortioner say? 'Give me money!' You pay him so that he may not betray you, because all he sells you is what he is going to give you for the money you hand over to him. When you pay, you do it so that you will not be turned in to the authorities; not being turned in, you wish not to be betrayed. Therefore, by wishing not to be handed over, at the same time you do not want to be betrayed; by that unwillingness of yours you have denied that you are what you have been unwilling to have made public. 'Yes,' you say, 'in not wanting to be betrayed I confess to be what I do not want to have made public, that is, that I am a Christian.'

(5) Can you boast that you have shown yourself a brave and constant witness to Christ? By buying Christ, you have

---

10 Cf. Eph. 6.12.
11 Cf. Acts 8.18.
12 Acts 8.20.

not shown it! Oh yes, perhaps you have admitted you are a Christian to some individual, but, in refusing to do so before many, you have denied Him. The very fact that a man is still free indicates that he has fallen while getting out of persecution's way. He has fallen because his desire has been to escape. The refusal of martyrdom is denial. A Christian is freed by money, and for this end he has his wealth, that he may not suffer, but he is rich by offending God; Christ became rich for him, but by His Blood. 'Blessed are the poor,' He tells us, 'for theirs is the kingdom of heaven';[13] their only stored-up wealth is their soul.

(6) If we cannot serve both God and mammon,[14] can we be redeemed by mammon and by God? And who is the greater servant of mammon than he who is freed by money? Finally, what example do you use to justify your redeeming yourself by money? When did the Apostles, dealing with the matter, ever gain their freedom from the troubles of persecution with money? They certainly had enough money from the prices of the lands that were laid at their feet,[15] and there were plenty of wealthy men and women among Christians who would gladly have ministered to their comfort. Did Onesiphorus or Aquila or Stephanas ever finance them in time of persecution?[16] When Felix the governor hoped to get some money from the disciples for Paul, and even took the matter up privately with Paul himself,[17] he got not one coin either from Paul or from the faithful. Those disciples who wept because Paul was determined to go to Jerusalem and

---

13 Matt. 5.3.
14 Cf. Matt. 6.24.
15 Cf. Acts 4.34,35.
16 Cf. 2 Tim. 1.16; Rom. 16.3,4; 1 Cor. 16.15-18.
17 Cf. Acts 24.26.

would not protect himself againt the torments that had been foretold for him there finally said: 'The Lord's will be done.'[18] And, what was that will? No doubt it was that he should suffer for the name of the Lord, and not that he should be bought off.

(7) Just as Christ laid down His life for us, so should we do the same for Him, and not only for Him, but for our brethren, for His sake. It is the teaching of St. John not that we should pay for our brethren, but that we should die for them.[19] It makes no difference whether we are forbidden to buy *off* a Christian, or to *buy* one.

(8) And so, this is the will of God: Look at the situation of the kingdoms and empires as arranged by God, in whose hand the heart of the king lies.[20] Every day they plan for future income, from the registration of property, taxes in kind, gifts and taxes payable in money; but never up to this time has there been procured any such income by bringing the Christians under some sales tax for the person and the sect, when that could be a tremendous source of income because of our vast numbers, known to all. We are bought with blood, we are paid for in blood, we owe no money for our head, because Christ is our Head.[21] It is not fitting that Christ should cost us money. How could martyrdoms bring glory to God if by tribute we should pay for the liberty of our sect? And so, the man who bargains to have his freedom at a price goes counter to the divine dispensation.

(9) Since, therefore, Caesar has made no law that makes us a tributary sect—in fact, such a law is impossible—with

---

18 Cf. Acts 21.12-14.
19 Cf. 1 John 3.16.
20 Cf. Prov. 21.1.
21 Cf. Eph. 5.23.

Antichrist lowering over us,[22] demanding the blood of Christians and not their money, how can anyone quote the text to me: 'Render to Caesar the things that are Caesar's'?[23] A soldier, be he informer or personal enemy, extorts money from me by threats, exacting nothing on Caesar's behalf—in fact, doing quite the opposite—when for a bribe he lets me go, Christian that I am, and guilty by human law. Of a different kind is the *denarius* that I owe to Caesar, a thing that he has a right to, about which the question then was raised, it being a coin of tribute due from people subject to tribute and not from free men.

(10) And how shall I render to God the things that are God's?[24] Surely by paying him that coin which bears His image and name—that is to say, a Christian man. But, what do I owe to God as a *denarius* is owed to Caesar, except the blood of His Son, shed for me? If, indeed, what I owe to God is a man and my own blood, and if I am now being asked to pay my debts, am I not cheating God if I refuse to pay? The law of tribute due to Caesar I have observed to the letter, but what I owe to God I refuse to pay!

---

22 Cf. 1 John 2.18.
23 Matt. 22.21.
24 Cf. Matt. 22.21.

Chapter 13

(1) For the sake of charity I will give to everyone who asks, but not under duress. Christ said: 'To the one who asks,'[1] but the man who uses intimidation does not ask. The man who threatens harm if you do not pay is not 'asking' for money, he is extorting it. It is not alms he looks for who comes not to be pitied, but to be feared. I will give out of pity, but not out of fear, and when the man who receives honors God and renders me a blessing. But I will not give when the receiver thinks that he is doing me a favor and, looking at his loot, says 'blood money.' Should I be angry at an enemy? But enmity has other titles: Christ did not speak of a betrayer or persecutor or extortionist. Oh, how much more shall I heap coals of fire upon his head[2] when I refuse to buy myself off! Christ said also: 'To the man who would take your tunic, grant your cloak also.'[3] But that refers to the one who wants to steal my property, not my faith. I will grant my cloak to the one who asks, if he does not threaten with betrayal; if he threatens, I will take back my tunic, too.

(2) Even now, all the precepts of the Lord have reasons and rules of their own; He did not make them infinite in extent or applicable to all cases. To be sure, He tells us to give to the one who asks. But, He gave us no infallible sign of the one who 'asks.' Otherwise, if you take His command generally, you would be giving not only wine to a man with a fever, but also poison or a sword to one who wanted to die. 'Make friends for yourselves with the mammon [of iniquity].'[4]

---

1 Cf. Luke 6.30.
2 Cf. Rom. 12.20.
3 Matt. 5.40.
4 Luke 16.9.

You can find out what that means by reading the preceding parable. It was told to the Jewish people, who, after having managed badly the business of the Lord that had been entrusted to them, ought to have provided for themselves out of the men of mammon—which we were then—friends rather than enemies, and to have delivered us from the dues of sins by which we were separated from God. If they bestowed this boon upon us, according to the design of the Lord, when grace began to depart from them, they might turn to our faith and be received into the eternal tabernacles. Now, you can adopt any interpretation you like of that parable and saying, as long as you do not believe that those who would extort money from us will become friends of ours through mammon and then receive us into the eternal tabernacles!

(3) When a man is afraid he will try any kind of a subterfuge. As if God would permit us to flee and, at the same time, bid us to buy our freedom from persecution! Finally, it is of no importance if one or other man is freed that way. Whole churches put themselves under bond *en masse*. I do not know if it is a case more for sorrow than shame, when you have Christians added to the tax lists of privileged soldiers and spies, along with hucksters, money-changers, bath-thieves, gamblers, and panderers! Did the Apostles establish the episcopacy in this fashion with such foresight, so that they might enjoy their rule in safety on the pretence of providing similar freedom to their flocks? I am sure that must be the kind of peace that Christ demanded when He returned to His Father[5]—to be bought from the soldiers by gifts like those you have at the Saturnalia![6]

---
5 Cf. John 14.27,28.
6 The presentation of gifts was one of the characteristic features of the popular festival of the Saturnalia in December.

Chapter 14

(1) You may ask me: 'How, then, shall we gather together? How shall we celebrate the divine mysteries?' To be sure, just as the Apostles also did, protected by faith, not by money. If this faith can remove a mountain,[1] it can much more remove a soldier. Let your protection be wisdom, not a bribe. And, even if you buy off the interference of the soldiers, will you then at once have security, also, from the people? All you need for your protection is to have both faith and wisdom. If you fail to use them, you may lose even the freedom you have bought for yourself; if you do use them, you will have no need of ransom. Finally, if you cannot gather together by day, you have the night, the light of Christ illuminating its darkness.[2] Can you not come together by different ways in small groups, if for you three are enough for a gathering of the faithful?[3] It is better that sometimes you do not see the vast crowds of your brethren than that you submit to the payment of ransom.

(2) Keep pure for Christ His virgin bride;[4] let no one make money out of her. These words may seem to you, my brother, to be harsh and unbearable, but remember that God said: 'He who accepts it, let him accept.'[5] That is to say: 'He who does not accept it, let him go his way.' The man who is afraid to suffer cannot belong to Him who suffered for us. But, the one who does not fear suffering, he will be perfect in love—that is, in the love of God; for, 'perfect love casts out

---
1 Cf. 1 Cor. 13.2.
2 Cf. Eph. 5.14.
3 Cf. Matt. 18.20.
4 Cf. Eph. 5.27.
5 Matt. 19.12.

fear.'⁶ And so, 'many are called but few are chosen.'⁷ It is not asked who is ready to follow the wide road, but who the narrow path.⁸

(3) And, therefore, the Paraclete is needed, the guide to all truth,⁹ the source of all endurance. Those who have received Him will never care to flee from persecution or basely to buy their freedom, for they will have Him who will be at our side, ready to speak for us when we are questioned[10] as well as to comfort us in suffering.

---
6 Cf. 1 John 4.18.
7 Matt. 22.14.
8 Cf. Matt. 7.13,14.
9 Cf. John 16.13.
10 Cf. Matt. 10.19,20.

INDEX

INDEX

Aaron, 203
Abraham, 133, 166, 204
Acharnae, 247 n.
Adam, 179, 200, 201
Aeacus, 106 n.
Aelianus, 246 n.
Aeneas, 26 n., 259
Aesculapius, 249, 253
Agabus, 288
Agobard, Bishop of Lyons, 44
agones, 40, 42, 57 n., 77 n., 89, 90 n.
Alcmene, 246 n.
Alexander the Great, 247 n., 248 n.
'Alleluia,' used at end of prayers, 185
Ambrose, St., 99 n.
Ammianus Marcellinus, 68 n.
amphitheater, cruelty of, 90-91
Amphitryon, 246 n.

amusements. *See* spectacles
Ancus Martius, 62
Antichrist, 303
Antinous, favorite of Hadrian, 263
Antoninus Pius, Emperor, 64 n.
Apelles, heretic, 291 n.
Apollo, 63, 75 n., 77, 246, 259, 264
Apuleius, 80 n.
Aquila, 301
Aratus, 245 n.
Archemorus, 263
Ariadne, 245
Aristogiton, tyrannicide, 27 n.
Artemis Orthia, festival of, 27 n.
Ascensio Isaiae, 218 n.
Atellan farces, 87
Athena, 71 n., 244 n., 249 n.
Augustine, St., 67 n., 80 n., 83 n., 85 n., 247 n.

Augustus, Emperor, 27 n., 40, 55 n., 68 n., 105 n.
Aulus Gellius, 26 n., 295 n.

Babylon, 261; king of, 216
Babylonians, 118, 122
Bacchus, 74, 245, 246, 247, 259
Bainton, R. H., 229
baptism, 57; by immersion, 56, 236
Bardenhewer, O., 16, 45
Baus, K:, 229
Beatus Rhenanus, 15
Belial, 120, 254
Bieber, M., 45, 54 n.
Bindley, T. H., 16
Blumenthal, A. von, 61 n.
Book of Henoch, 112, 119 n., 143 n.; its genuineness defended, 121, 122; rejected by the Jews, 122
Borleffs, J. G. Ph., 192
Boulanger, A., 44, 45
Büchner, J., 44, 45

Caesar, C. Julius, 105 n.
Cain, 166, 201
Callimachus, 245, 246
Calpurnius, poet, 55 n.
Campus Martius, 60 n.
Cannae, 63 n.
Capitol, 61 n., 63 n., 65 n., 69, 81
Caracalla, M. Aurelius Antoninus, Emperor, 225, 231 n.
Carlson, M. L., 192

Carna, Roman deity, 264
Carpus, 171
Carthage, 14, 26
Castor, 67, 70, 78 n.
catechumens, addressed in *Prayer*, 153, 154, 158 n.; in *Spectacles*, 47 n., in *To the Martyrs*, 17; recipients of *Patience*, 192
cathedra, 55
Cato the Younger, 88 n.
Cerberus, 246
Cerealia, 75 n.
Ceres, 63, 75 n.; identified with Isis, 247 n.
Chambers, E. K., 45
Charites (Graces), 244 n.
charity, related to patience, 215
Chase, R. M., 45
Chinese, 118
Christians, accused of cannibalism, 90 n.; of incest, 135 n.; apostacy of, 19 n.; called priests, 85; called priests of peace, 85 n.; called sons of peace, 256; called the third race, 86 n.; detachment of, 48; eagerness for martyrdom of, 48 n.; as image of God, 303; in military service, 255, 257; incorporated in God, 161; in public affairs, 258
Church, the, as 'Mother,' 14, 17, 160

Cicero, 25 n., 26 n., 239 n., 249 n., 252 n.
Circe, 66
circus, description of, 66-68; etymology of, 66 n.
Circus Maximus, 40, 61, 65 n., 66 n.
Claudius, Emperor, 80 n.
Clement of Alexandria, 37, 53 n.
Cleopatra, 27
Clodius Albinus, 13, 29 n.
Consualia, 59 n., 60, 62 n., 72 n.
Consus, Roman deity, 60, 61, 66 n., 68, 71 n.
Cortellezzi, G., 116
cosmetics, 119, 135, 136, 149
Cross, Sign of the, 237
crowns, associated with idolatry, 90 n.; Etruscan, 261; occasions for wearing, 259-263; placed upon corpses, 252; pomps of the Devil, 263; to be avoided by women, 265; used in Mithras cult, 267
Cybele, 63 n., 68 n., 74 n.
Cyprian, St., 39, 115, 155, 156, 173 n., 183 n., 271

David, 249, 253
Dekkers, E., 15, 16, 44, 45
de Labriolle, P., 46
Delphi, 246
Demeter, 75 n.
demonism, 51 n.
Demoteles, 68 n.

de Plinval, G., 230
Devil, 69, 182, 220, 264, 293, 296; assails Job, 218, 279; corrupter of nature, 112, 113; and crowns, 263; dominion over things of world, 84; fall of, 85; as God's rival, 50 n., 52, 126, 127, 136, 199, 221, 243; identified with Erichthonius, 71; inspires deceit, 96, 97; inspires wrestling, 90; a liar, 248; persecutor, 272, 276-282; power dependent on God, 199-201, 278-280; present in prison, 18; renounced at baptism, 56, 98, 236, 263; as source of impatience, 191; and the spectacles, 57, 97, 99-102; as tempter, 166; of Christ, 167, 196; wiles of, 267; and women, 118, 125
devils, 295
diamastigosis, 27
Diana, 81
Dido, 25, 26 n.
Diehl, E., 80 n.
Diercks, G. F., 156
Digesta, 95 n., 239 n.
Dio Chrysostom, 34
Diodorus, historian, 245, 249 n.
Diogenes Laertius, 25 n.
Dionysia, 59 n., 75
Dionysius of Halicarnassus, 65 n.
Dionysus, 59 n., 75 n.
Docetists, 291 n.

Dölger, F. J., 156
Domitian, Emperor, 232 n.

Ecurria, 59 n., 60
Egypt, 56
Elias, 96, 104 n., 220
Empedocles of Acragas, 25
Epicureans, 102 n.
Epimetheus, 244 n.
Erichthonius, demon-monster, 71
Esdras, 122
Ethiopia, 56
Etna, Mt., 25
Etruscans, origin of, 58 n.
Eucharist, received in morning, 237
Euripides, 246 n., 247 n.
Eusebius, historian, 17 n.
Eve, 112, 117, 118, 177, 179, 200, 201, 245
Ezechias, 249

Fabius, Christian addressee of *Flight in Persecution*, 272-274
fasting, prolonged, 216 n.
Felicitas, St., 233 n.
Felix, Roman governor, 301
flight, in persecution, enjoined upon Apostles, 286, 287; of leaders reproved, 296-298
Flora, Roman deity, 63
Floralia, 88 n.
Florus, 27 n.
Forculus, Roman deity, 264

Fowler, W. W., 45
Franchi de' Cavalieri, P., 229
Friedländer, L., 45

Gallienus, Emperor, 232 n.
games, Capitoline, 61, 62 n.; deities honored in, 60-63; gladiatorial, introduction of, 78 n.; funereal origin of, 78, 79; in provinces, 65, 66; sacred and funereal, 64; Tarpeian, 61; *see also Ludi*
Geta, Emperor, 225, 231 n.
gladiatorial combats, advertisements for, 80; awnings provided for, 80 n.; called *munera*, 78; expenses of, 80 n.; origin of, in Etruria, 78 n., 79; sponsored by magistrates, 79, 80 n.
gladiators, 91 n.; popularity rewarded, 94, 95 n.; reluctance punished, 93 n.; schools for, 79 n.; socially and legally debased, 95
Glover, T. R., 44, 45
Gnostics, 291 n.
God, author of persecution, 282; blasphemed at the spectacles, 101; as Creator, 50; exemplar of patience, 195; as Father, 159, 160; forbids murder, 51; generosity of, 164, 165; goodness of His creatures, 49; indulgence of, 165, 166; misuse

of His creatures, 51, 52; omnipresent, 158; wills men's salvation, 162; witness of men's sins, 92
Good Friday, 155
Great Mother, the, 63, 68, 74 n.

Habacuc, 186 n.
Hadrian, Emperor, 64 n., 263 n.
hair, arranging of, 138; dyeing of, 137, 140; use of wigs, 138-139
Haller, W., 156
Hannibal, 63 n.
Harmodius, tyrannicide, 27 n.
Harpocration, Valerius, of Alexandria, 246, 247 n.
Harvey, W. W., 36
Hasdrubal, wife of, 26
Heliodorus, 22 n.
Hephaestus, 71 n., 244 n., 245 n.
Hera, 246 n., 247 n.
Heraclitus, philosopher, 25
Hercules, 77, 78 n., 246, 263
Hermapion, 68 n.
Hermas, Shepherd of, 171
Hermateles, 39, 68
Hermes, 244 n., 249 n.
Hermogenes, 281
Herodotus, 58 n., 154, 173 n., 265 n.
Hesiod, 244
Hofmann, J. B., 58 n.
Homer, 249 n., 264
Horace, 26 n., 27 n.

Horae (Hours), 244 n., 245 n.
Hosius, C., 46
hymns, Christian, 104 n.
Hypsipyle, 263 n.

Idolatry, 36, 40, 41, 51, 53, 56, 57, 64, 66, 72, 76, 79, 81-83, 127, 169, 195, 226, 227, 248, 252, 254, 259, 262-264
Ilia (Rhea Silvia), 60 n., 259
Impatience, born of the Devil, 200; cause of Israel's sin, 202, 203; opposed to faith, 199; prime source of sin, 201, 202
incest, charge of, against Christians, 135 n.
India, 247
Irenaeus, St., 36
Isidore of Seville, St., 44
Isis, 96, 247, 250 n.
Israel, 160, 170, 179, 184, 202, 286, 288
Israelites, 55
Isthmian Games, 77

Jairus, 251 n.
Janus, 264
Jerome, St., 22 n.
Jerusalem, 288, 301
Jewelry, denounced, 143, 144; imitation, 28; undermines virtue, 148; varieties of, 128
Joannes Clemens Anglus, 44
Job, 186 n., 218, 219, 278, 279
John the Baptist, St., 158, 257

John the Evangelist, St., 183, 254, 261, 293
John Chrysostom, St., 37, 104 n.
Jolyon, E., 273
Jonas, 173, 249
Joseph of Arimathea, 54 n.
Joseph of Egypt, 168
Juba, King of Mauretania, 39
Juda, 146
Judas, 106, 260
Judea, 287
Judgment, Last, 105, 106
Juno, 71, 246
Jupiter, 66, 67, 69, 77, 105, 245, 259, 261, 263; Capitolinus, 62 n.; Feretrius, 61, 62 n.; Latiaris, 63
Juturna, 70 n.
Juvenal, 33

Kaderschafka, R., 192
Kellner, K. A. H., 16, 44, 45
kiss of peace, 153, 155, 173, 174, 184
Koch, H., 116
Köchling, J., 230, 246 n.
Köhne, J., 46
Kore, 75 n.
Kroll, W., 245 n.
Kroyman, A., 111 n., 116, 192, 220 n., 229
Krüger, G., 46

Lactantius, 88 n., 91 n., 94 n.
Lamech, 166

Lares, 61
Lawler, L. B., 116
Leaena, 27 n.
Leclercq, H., 273
Leda, 67 n.
Leo the Egyptian, 247, 248 n.
Lepidus, M. Aemilius, 64 n.
Libanius, 34
Liber, 59, 63 n., 74, 75, 96, 247 n.
Libera (Kore), 63 n., 75 n.
Liberalia, 59, 74, 75 n.
Lieftinck, G. I., 46
Limentinus, Roman deity, 264
liturgy, 'Alleluia' added at end of prayer, 185; fasting, 237; kiss of peace, 173; kneeling, 237; observance of Sunday, 237; station days, 174, 175; Tertullian's contribution to history of, 155
Livy, 25 n., 58 n., 60 n., 62-64 nn., 74 n.
Loeschke, G., 156
Löfstedt, E., 46
logos, 157 n.
Lucian of Samosata, 25 n., 78 n.
Lucretia, 24
Ludi, enumeration of, 57 n.; institution of, 63 n.; occasion of, 64 n.; origin of, in Etruria, 57, 58
Ludi circenses, colors of factions, 72; skill displayed in, 70
Ludi scaenici, 72-75

Lupercalia, 59 n.
Luperci, college of priests, 59
Lycurgus of Nemea, 263 n.
Lydians, 57, 58
Lyons, 13, 17 n., 29 n.

Macrobius, 67 n.
magic, fertility rites, 59 n.; power of incantation, 51 n.; rites at races, 84 n.
Malchus, 197
Man, as image of God, 254
Marcion, heretic, 291 n.
Mark Antony, 27 n.
Marquardt, J., 46, 55 n.
Marra, J., 45, 116, 229, 273
Mars, 60, 61, 73 n., 77, 81, 259
Martial, 95 n.
martrydom, a second baptism, 217
martyrs, tortures inflicted on, 24
Mass, Preface of, 155, 161 n.; Sanctus of, 155, 161 n.; use of the Lord's Prayer at, 155
Mathusala, 121
Maximilla, 10, 228, 294 n.
Megara, 246 n.
Mercury, 70, 73 n., 75 n., 78 n., 247 n., 249
Mesnartius, Martinus, 44
Messia, Roman deity, 67
Midas, 265
Milesians, 118
military service, unlawful for Christians, 258

Millennium, 104, 105, 163
mime, buffoonery of, 96 n.; description of, 87 n.; participation of courtesans in, 88 n.
Minerva, 71, 73 n., 75 n., 77, 249, 250 n., 259
Minos, 106
Minucius Felix, 90 n., 252 n.
Mithras, 267
Moffat, J., 156
Montanism, 7, 9, 226, 228; doctrines of, 10
Montanus, 10, 103 n., 226, 228, 233 n., 272, 294 n.
Moon, as deity, 71
Morgan, J., 46
Moses, 160, 203, 245, 297
Mucius (C. Mucius Scaevola), 24, 25 n.
Muncey, R. W., 156
Murcia, 69
Murcian Goals, 68, 69 n.
Muses, 75, 77

natural law, 242
Nemean Games, 263 n.
Nephthys, 250 n.
Neptune, 60, 63, 67, 70, 71 n., 73 n., 77, 259
Nero, Emperor, 68 n.
Nicodemus, 251 n.
Noe, 121
none (the ninth hour), 183
Nonius, 59 n.
Northern Crown, 245 n.

Novatian, 39
Numa, 61

obelisk, Egyptian, 68
Octavian, 27 n.
Onesiphorus, 301
Opheltes, 263 n.
original sin, 117
Osiris, 246, 247 n., 250
Otto, A., 99 n.
Otto, W., 248 n.
Ovid, 62 n., 145 n., 245-247 nn.

Pamelius, Jacobus, 44
Pandora, 244, 245
pankration, 89 n.
pantomime, 87
Paraclete, 10, 233 n., 272, 273, 275, 294 n., 307
Passion of SS. Perpetua and Felicitas, 14, 18 n., 94 n., 97 n.
patience, alleviates grief of death, 209; begets obedience, 199; esteemed by pagan philosophers, 194; exemplified by God, 195; by Christ, 195-197; fulfillment of the Law, 191; inseparable companion of Holy Spirit, 220; practised by the heathens, 221; prerequisite for any virtuous act, 194; produces joy, 208
Paul, St., 171, 176, 183, 226, 238, 249, 250, 262, 280, 287-289, 292, 301

Pausanias, 27 n., 246 n., 247 n.
Peitho (Persuasion), 244 n.
pentathlon, 89 n.
Pentecost, 182
Peregrinus Proteus, philosopher, 25
Perpetua, St., 18 n., 233 n.
persecution, likened to a contest, 267, 277; to a judgment, 276; need to pray in time of, 292; origin of, 276; test of faith, 281
Peter, St., 175, 183, 257, 279, 291
Pherecydes, 245
Philocalus, 63 n.
philosophers, pagan, 106
Phrygia, 17 n.
Phrygians, 118
Phigellus, 281
Pilate, 170
pilleus, 94 n., 198 n.
Pindar, 246, 249 n.
Piso, L. Calpurnius, 39, 61
Pliny the Elder, 27 n., 63 n., 67 n., 68 n., 247 n.
Pliny the Younger, 259 n.
Plumpe, J., 17 n.
Plutarch, 90 n., 246 n.
Polycarp, St., 237 n., 271
pompa, 65, 73 n.
Pompeii, 79 n., 80 n., 95 n.
Pompey the Great, 74
Pollux, 67, 70, 78 n.
Poseidon, 71 n.
Porsenna, Etruscan king, 25 n.

318

prayer, for all men, 161; armor of a Christian, 187; Christian, contrasted with pagan sacrifice, 185, 186; demeanor required for, 153; disposition for, 153; elements of, 158; offered by all creation, 187; offices of, 159; posture for, 170, 182; power of, 186, 187; practices not recommended, 169-173; requisite conditions for, 168; in secret, 158; time and place for, 153, 182-184; vitiated by anger, 169
Priapus, 245 n.
Prisca (Priscilla), 10, 228, 294 n.
prison, life in, compared to the world, 19-21
Prometheus, 244 n.
Propertius, 62 n.
Prophets, 21, 167, 217
Pseudo-Cyprian, 96 n.
pugilists, disfigurement of, 97

Quacquarelli, A., 273
Quasten, J., 7 n., 16, 46, 116, 156
Quirinus, 61, 71, 72 n.; flamen of, 61

Rameses, King, 68 n.
Rebecca, 181, 238
Regulus, M. Atilius, 26
Reifferscheid, A., 44, 45, 156
Resurrection, of Christ, 209; commemorated on Sunday, 182
Rhadamanthus, 106
Rhea Silvia (Ilia), 60 n.
Robigalia, 62 n.
Robigo, Roman deity, 61, 62 n.
Romulus, 60, 61, 62 n., 71, 72 n.
Rush, A. C., 18 n., 209 n., 237 n.
Rutilius, martyr, 285
Ryan, E. A., 230

Sabbath, 182
Sabine girls, rape of, 60
sacramentum, 22 n.
sacrifice, human, at funerals, 79
Salii, college of priests, 59 n.
Salvian, 73 n.
Sanhedrin, 251 n.
Sara, 133
Satan, 69; as God's rival, 50 n., 52, 199
Saturn, 96, 245
Saturnalia, 305
Saturninus, Claudius, 245 n., 248, 255, 259, 264
Saul, 280
Schäfer, O., 156
Schanz, M., 46
Schlegel, G. D., 16
Scipio (P. Cornelius Scipio Aemilianus Africanus minor), 26
Scipio (P. Cornelius Scipio Nasica), 74 n.
Scripture, Holy: Quotations from or references to:

319

Acts, 183 n., 218 n., 232 n., 257 n., 287 n., 288 n., 300-302 nn.
Apocalypse, 85 n., 105 n., 146 n., 149 n., 161 n., 163 n., 212 n., 261 n., 266 n., 267 n., 277 n., 290, 291 n., 293, 294 n.
1 Corinthians, 20 n., 23 n., 81 n., 88 n., 89 n., 107 n., 120 n., 129 n., 132 n., 138 n., 141 n., 144 n., 145 n., 175 n., 176 n., 178-180 nn., 194 n., 215 n., 237-240 nn., 242 n., 248 n., 251 n., 253 n., 254 n., 256 n., 257 n., 262 n., 264 n,, 265 n., 278 n., 295 n., 301 n., 306 n.
2 Corinthians, 100 n., 120 n., 129 n., 138 n., 210 n., 251 n., 254 n., 278 n., 280 n.
Daniel, 171 n., 184, 186 n., 217 n., 238 n., 239 n.
Deuteronomy, 97 n., 207 n., 211 n., 281 n.
Ephesians, 18 n., 20 n., 83 n., 85 n., 88 n., 129 n., 149 n., 169 n., 214 n., 233 n., 256 n., 277 n., 293 n., 295 n., 300 n., 302 n., 306 n.
Exodus, 51 n., 53 n., 148 n., 149 n., 160 n., 203 n., 204 n., 232 n., 251 n., 256 n., 297 n.
Ezechiel, 20 n., 165 n., 254 n., 297
Galatians, 207 n., 296 n., 299 n.

Genesis, 51 n., 89 n., 117 n., 119-121 nn., 125 n., 133 n., 147 n., 166 n., 168 n., 177, 179 n., 181 n., 184 n., 200 n., 203 n., 204 n., 238 n., 245 n., 254 n., 262 n., 265 n., 276 n., 282 n.
Hebrews, 184 n., 233 n., 237 n., 251 n., 262 n., 266 n.
Isaias, 143 n., 160 n., 161 n., 170, 185 n., 194 n., 196 n. 249, 252, 254 n., 261 n., 267 n., 280 n., 281 n., 299 n.
James, 134 n., 266 n.
Jeremias, 149 n., 254 n., 297
Job, 186 n., 218, 219, 278, 279 n.
John, 102 n., 106 n., 107 n., 122 n., 158 n., 159 n., 160 n., 162 n., 164 n., 185 n., 196 n., 233 n., 240 n., 248 n., 251 n., 256 n., 262 n., 274 n., 297 n., 305 n., 307 n.
1 John, 23 n., 82 n., 254 n., 293 n., 294 n., 302 n., 303 n., 307 n.
Jonas, 296 n.
Josue, 148 n.
Jude, 122
1 Kings, 147 n., 280 n.
3 Kings, 21 n., 220 n.
4 Kings, 96 n.
Leviticus, 132 n.
Luke, 21 n., 54 n., 85 n., 96 n., 97 n., 99 n., 106 n., 147 n., 157 n., 162 n., 164-168 nn., 172 n.,

184 n., 196 n., 197 n., 206 n., 213 n., 214 n., 231 n., 240 n., 250 n., 251 n., 256 n., 257 n., 260 n., 261 n., 266 n., 279 n., 290 n., 297 n., 304 n.
Mark, 18 n., 21 n., 24 n., 88 n., 106 n., 147 n., 157 n., 164 n., 207 n., 237 n., 256 n., 257 n., 260 n., 266 n., 290 n., 295 n.
Matthew, 18 n., 20 n., 21 n., 24 n., 51 n., 82 n., 86 n., 88 n., 96 n., 97 n., 99 n., 100 n., 106 n., 120 n., 130-134 nn., 137 n., 138 n., 142 n., 147 n., 149 n., 157 n., 159 n., 164-166 nn., 168 n., 184 n., 195-197 nn., 204 n., 206-208 nn., 211 n., 213 n., 214 n., 217 n., 231 n., 233 n., 237 n., 256 n., 257 n., 260-262 nn., 266 n., 272, 276 n., 279 n., 280 n., 282 n., 286 n., 287 n., 289-292 nn., 295 n., 299 n., 301 n., 303 n., 304 n., 306 n., 307 n.
Numbers, 251 n.
1 Peter, 134 n., 175 n., 237 n., 262 n., 299 n.
2 Peter, 21 n.
Philippians, 102 n., 134 n., 145 n., 147 n.., 209 n., 240 n., 261 n., 262 n., 299 n.
Proverbs, 163 n., 212 n., 302 n.
Psalms, 37, 53 n., 84 n., 101 n., 253 n., 261 n., 288 n., 299 n.
Romans, 86 n., 103 n., 134 n., 210 n., 242 n., 243 n., 253 n., 293 n., 299 n., 301 n., 304 n.
1 Thessalonians, 20 n., 130 n., 209 n., 257 n., 293 n.
1 Timothy, 23 n., 175 n., 176 n., 182 n., 205 n., 249 n., 265 n., 281 n.
2 Timothy, 122 n., 171 n., 250 n., 266 n., 281 n., 301 n.
Titus, 82 n., 253 n.
Wisdom, 20 n.
Zacharias, 261 n., 281 n., 297 n.

Segetia, Roman deity, 67 n.
Seia, Roman deity, 67
Semele, 246 n.
Seneca, philosopher, 34, 94 n., 246 n.
Severus, L. Septimius, Emperor, 13, 29 n., 225, 231-233 nn.
Serapis, 69
Servius, 79 n.
signaculum, 56 n.
sext (the sixth hour), 183
Simon Magus, 300
Simovic, B., 156
Sinnius Capito, 38
Sixtus V, Pope, 68 n.
Skutsch, F., 245 n.
Smyrna, 271
Socrates, 253
Soveri, H. F., 46
Spartans, endurance of, 27
spectacles, animosity displayed, 86 n.; application of Psalm

1.1 to, 37, 53-55; attitude of Christian writers toward, 34; of pagan writers, 33, 34; Christians deny faith by attending, 98; crudities of, 34; displeasing to God, 96, 97; effect on passions, 83, 84; excitement of spectators at, 84, 85, 93 n.; heathens' defense of, 48; idolatrous character of, 36; incompatible with Christian living, 98, 99; inconsistency of spectators at gladiatorial combats, 93, 94; kinds of, 33, 49 n.; origin of, 57-64; outline of treatise on, 57; *pompa*, 65; preceded by betting, 84; status of performers in, 95; *see* also games and *Ludi*.
spina, 67 n., 68 n.
station days, 153, 155, 174, 175, 182, 256
Stephen, St., 218
Stephanas, 301
Stesichorus, 39, 70
Suetonius, 38-40, 61 n., 62, 68 n., 77 n., 80 n., 86 n., 105 n.
suicide, instances of, 24-27
Suidas, 38
Sun, as deity, 66, 71
Susanna, 238

Tacitus, 66 n., 259 n.
Tarpeian Rock, 61, 62 n.
Tarquinius, Sextus, 25 n.

Tarquinius Superbus, 25 n.
terce (the third hour), 183
Tertullian, attitude toward confessors, 14, 15; toward crowns, 90 n., 225-267; toward demons, 100; toward dramatic texts, 88 n.; toward persecution, 272; toward pleasure, 103; toward spectacles, 35; belief in power of magic, 51 n.; belittles his knowledge of pagan literature, 244; contributes to knowledge of development of liturgy, 155; estimate of the world, 19-21; expectation of the millennium, 104, 105; familiarity with ancient authors, 39, 40; with Greek, 43, 243; intransigence, 36, 37; lack of moderation, 38; predisposed to Montanism, 103 n.; rigorism, 17 n., 19 n., 228; style, 47 n., 49 n., 53 n., 55 n., 154; works: *Ad martyras*, 13-15, 17-29, 129 n., 184 n.; *Ad nationes*, 13, 26-28 nn.; *Ad uxorem*, 272; *Adversus Hermogenem*, 68 n., 157 n.; *Apologeticum*, 13, 20 n., 25-27 nn., 35, 48 n., 90 n., 101 n., 102 n., 106 n., 157 n., 187 n., 227; *De anima*, 294 n.; *De baptismo*, 183 n.; *De carne Christi*, 157 n.; *De corona*, 35, 85 n., 225-229; *De cultu fe-*

minarum, 35, 111-115, 175 n.; *De exhortatione castitatis,* 216 n., 294 n.; *De fuga in persecutione,* 271-273; *De idololatria,* 100 n., 228; *De ieiunio,* 17 n., 183 n., 216 n.; *De oratione,* 129 n., 153-156; *De paenitentia,* 165 n.; *De patientia,* 191, 192; 216 n., 272; *De pudicitia,* 35, 294 n.; *De resurrectione carnis,* 294 n.; *De spectaculis,* 33-44, 47-107, 127 n., 145 n., 236 n., 243 n.; *De testimonio animae,* 249 n.; *De virginibus velandis,* 176 n., 181 n.; *Scorpiace,* 35, 86 n.
testudo, 22 n.
Teuffel, W. S., 245 n.
Thamar, 146
theater, a shrine of Venus, 73; censors' opposition to, 73; description of, 54 n.; first, of stone, 74; licentiousness of, 87, 88; of Timgad, 54 n.; seats for women at, 55 n.
Thelwall, S., 16, 45
Theseus, 245 n.
Thierry, J. J., 273
Tiberius, Emperor, 86 n.
Timaeus, historian, 39, 57, 58 n.
Trajan, Emperor, 64 n.
tribune, military, 232 n.
Trochilus, 71

Tullus Hostilius, 62
Tutilina, Roman deity, 67 n.
Tutulina, Roman deity, 67
Tyrians, 118
Tyrrhenus, 58

Vacandard, E., 230
Valentinus, heretic, 291 n.
Valerius Maximus, 25 n., 26 n., 88 n.
vanity, 28, 119, 145; male, 140
Varro, M. Terentius, 38-40, 59 n., 61 n., 68 n., 69 n., 79 n.
Velabrum, 65 n.
Venus, 69 n., 73-75, 245 n., 259
Vestal Virgins, 61
Vienne, 17 n.
Virgil, 26 n., 39, 59 n., 62 n., 71 n.
virgins, consecrated to God, 180; should veil heads, 176-181
Vitruvius, 54 n.
Vulcan, 71, 245

Walde, A., 58 n.
Waszink, J. H., 46
Wissowa, G., 44, 45, 156
women, and Devil, 118, 125; fortitude of, 24
wrestling, the Devil's trade, 90

Zacharias, 297
Zeus, 244 n., 246 n.

www.ingramcontent.com/pod-product-compliance
Lightning Source LLC
Chambersburg PA
CBHW032028290426
44110CB00012B/709